P9-EGN-383

Due
2/1

Wally's World

Also by Marsha Boulton

Letters from the Country IV
Letters from the Country Omnibus
Just a Minute Omnibus
Just a Minute More
Letters from Across the Country
Just Another Minute
More Letters from the Country
Letters from the Country
Just a Minute

Life with

Wally the

Wonder

Dog

Wally's World

MARSHA BOULTON

Thomas Dunne Books
St. Martin's Press ✼ New York

THOMAS DUNNE BOOKS.
An imprint of St. Martin's Press.

WALLY'S WORLD. Copyright © 2006, 2008 by Marsha Boulton. All rights reserved.
Printed in the United States of America. For information, address
St. Martin's Press, 175 Fifth Avenue, New York, N.Y. 10010.

www.thomasdunnebooks.com
www.stmartins.com

Grateful acknowledgment is given for permission to reprint the following:
"The Snow Man," copyright 1923 and renewed 1951 by Wallace Stevens, from
The Collected Poems of Wallace Stevens. Used by permission of
Alfred A. Knopf, a division of Random House, Inc.

"Stop All the Clocks," copyright 1940 and renewed 1968 by W. H. Auden,
from *Collected Poems by W. H. Auden*. Used by permission of
Random House, Inc.

"The Cosmo Story" by Robert Bollong, Sr. Used by permission of the Estate of
Robert Bollong, Sr.

ISBN-13: 978-0-312-37959-9
ISBN-10: 0-312-37959-5

Original edition published in Canada in slightly different form by
McArthur & Company

10   9   8   7   6   5   4   3   2

Contents

Contents

Acknowledgments

Having written a book that is grounded by a dog, it seems appropriate to acknowledge the role that dogs played in the publication of the book. Specifically, I owe a debt of gratitude to Winston and Floyd, two bull terriers who have inspired and informed the life of Jeffrey Capshew, the vice president of sales for the Macmillan Publishing Group.

I first met Jeff through an online Internet bull terrier list where he occasionally offered information about dog-laced literary offerings such as Jonathan Carroll's uniquely fantastical *The Land of Laughs* and Diane Jessup's redemptive *The Dog Who Spoke with Gods*. So when I thought I had a book, I boldly contacted him for advice. A terrier personality in his own right, Jeff insisted that the book would find a home within the labyrinth of publishers at Macmillan. Enter Thomas Dunne, whose imprint at St. Martin's Press has a dachshund as a colophon, modeled after Tom's beloved doxy, Sparky. Dog lovers bond across breed lines. *Wally's World* found a fitting publisher.

Many thanks to Lorrie Grace McCann for herding the book through the editing process with the silky self-confidence and steady intelligence of a bearded collie and the good-natured sensitivity of a Spinone Italiano.

Wally's World has been a gift of words to me. It flowed from the core of my being in a way that no other book has. I went to bed with the last line I had written in my head and I woke up with the next line already forming. My partner and best friend, Stephen Williams, saw the catharsis as it occurred and did everything he could to help me enjoy the process, from the mundane formatting of the manuscript to making his own lunch. Stephen also helped me find my agent, Christy Fletcher, of Fletcher & Parry LLC, who believed in the book before I even finished writing it and guided it around the world with infectious enthusiasm.

Thanks also to the many friends who read along as the book was written, offering their insights and barking at the gaffes. Marlene Markle, Shari Mann, Victoria Corse, and John Kincaid are among those who tended my prose with the steadfast devotion of bloodhounds and sharp eyes of Brussels griffons. My cancer-survivor sisterhood stood by me as a pack—true as foxhounds and as protective as komondors.

It takes the courage of a Karelian bear dog to stand up to challenges facing our companion animals today—everything from the scourge of dog fighting to the euthanizing of innocents simply because of their appearance. I salute those who care, who write letters, sign petitions, and put some figurative bite into following their convictions. The no-kill animal shelter movement is growing thanks to the efforts of caring workers and volunteers who seek creative, compassionate solutions and reach out to their communities. Thanks are not enough for those who rescue, adopt, and foster animals in need. They give back more than we can hope for.

I have owned all kinds of dogs, but there's one I've always wanted and never had. I wonder if he still exists? There used to be a white, English Bull Terrier. He was stocky, but quick. His muzzle was pointed and his eyes triangular, so his expression was that of cynical laughter. He was friendly and not quarrelsome but forced into a fight he was very good at it. He had a fine, decent sense of himself and was never craven. He was a thoughtful, inward dog, and yet he had enormous curiosity. He was heavy of bone and shoulder. He had a fine arch to his neck. His ears were sometimes cropped, but his tail never. He was a good dog for a walk. An excellent dog to sleep beside a man's bed. He showed a delicacy of sentiment. I have always wanted one of him.

—JOHN STEINBECK, from "Random Thoughts on Random Dogs,"
Saturday Review, October 8, 1955

Wally's World

1

There Were Always Dogs

t takes about sixty-three days to make a litter of puppies, but sixty-three years later the people who loved those puppies remember the dogs they became.

I know I remember Lady, the fawn-colored boxer who came to live at the Boulton bungalow on Sprucedale Circle when I was just three years old. People say, "How can you possibly remember something that far back?" But I can, and it is not something that comes from looking at old pictures. I remember my pink crib and my spring-loaded rocking horse and the texture of the gray rug on which I took my first step. So I could never forget a free spirit like Lady. Those were the days before I learned to think and plot, so there was nothing to interfere with me talking to Lady, which I did on a regular basis.

The gray brick house on Sprucedale backed onto a ravine that fell sharply at the edge of the backyard picket fence into a ravine woodlot. Lady was forever running off into the mystical forest and returning to tell me of her adventures. She met other dogs, and she chased rabbits and smelled all sorts of stinky stuff.

Her muzzle was soft as velvet, and her button eyes sparkled. A hellion on paws, Lady loved nothing more than crashing through the screen door and escaping to the hills and gullies of the ravine while my beleaguered mother stood screaming in her apron.

My mother had served as an air force secretary to a brigadier general during World War II, but she was taxed to tend me, let alone a renegade boxer. I was adopted when I was two weeks old, after as much planning as the invasion of Normandy—none of it terribly practical. No one remembered to get a baby carriage.

It was the 1950s, and a physicist named Murray Gell-Mann demonstrated that certain subatomic particles have a property he called "strangeness." Strangeness, a fundamental component of human life— I think I knew that instinctively while watching my mother standing on the back stoop hollering after Lady.

In those days it seemed anything could happen. Arthur Miller's *The Crucible,* about the witch hunts in Salem, Massachusetts, in 1692, played off U.S. Senator Joseph McCarthy's probing for Communists embedded in Hollywood and the government. Nineteen assorted townsfolk and two dogs were executed on Gallows Hill, a barren slope near Salem Village. Thousands of lives were ruined before investigative reporter Edward R. Murrow publicly eviscerated the drunk and sweaty McCarthy.

Strangeness led to big things, like James Watson and Francis Crick showing that the DNA molecule was a double helix, a genetic "code" unique to each person—and each dog. Things like the DNA double helix made big brains tremble with excitement, while others proclaimed the beginning of the end for baseball when an umpire, Bill Klein, was voted into the Hall of Fame. J. D. Salinger captured adolescent angst in *The Catcher in the Rye,* while a "noise" called rock and roll first made the pop charts with "Crazy Man, Crazy" by Bill Haley and the Comets. Malcolm Little became Malcolm "X." The war that followed the war-to-end-all-wars was over, and possibilities were endless.

In the 1950s, adoptive parents could choose the baby they were going to get—color of hair and eyes, that sort of thing. There was no question that white people would get a white baby. That was just the way things were. As soon as I was old enough to understand, I knew I was a "chosen one." My father, a dentist, told me that one day he and his wife went to the Baby Store. They rolled a shopping cart up and down the aisles full of babies. He saw a handsome boy and was getting ready to put him in the cart, but his wife insisted on looking at the girls. Harrumph. He went along with her. They found a lovely baby girl with red hair and cheeks as pink as peaches. Then they found a sweetheart with long black hair and red lips. They could not make up their minds which to choose and were about to play eenie, meenie, minie, moe when they heard a dreadful shriek from the end of the aisle. They went to see what it was and found the homeliest baby girl anyone had ever seen. She had no hair, beady blue eyes, and when she opened her mouth she sounded like a sick parrot.

"Your mother said, 'If we don't take her, nobody will,'" my father trumpeted with a flourish.

My mother, the only one I have ever known, was the youngest of six, rock-scrabble, Irish-French children. As "the baby" she had scant experience with babies herself, but women of that era were expected to know how to raise a family intuitively, just as they were expected to know that their hat should be as wide as the widest part of their face. Family and friends gave advice, but the truth of my mother's terror rests in the diaries she kept during my first six months as a Boulton, which often featured entries such as "Fed her."

I knew that I really came from Aunt Jean Gray's home for unwed mothers. We visited Aunt Jean Gray a couple of times when I was little. She was a big-bosomed woman who kept her long gray hair carefully scrolled on top of her head. We had tea and cucumber sandwiches in her lavender-scented living room. Then a "nurse" wheeled in a baby carriage and we took home a new sister or brother for me.

I never knew where Lady came from. She just bounded through the door with my father one day, and we had a dog. Dogs could talk in my storybooks. It did not surprise me that Lady had stories to tell, just like her namesake, the honey-colored spaniel in the Disney film *Lady and the Tramp*. My Lady did not have dulcet tones; she was more a street-wise jokester. Through her eyes, smell, and touch, I charged along the edge of muddy riverbanks, feeling the dappled sun filtering through the trees while crisp autumn leaves crackled in the breeze. When we played fetch-a-stick in the backyard, it did not matter that my casts were only a few feet. To Lady and to me, they were massive tosses, flung from mountaintops and retrieved by a winged canine that galloped across a kingdom to return it to her mighty mistress.

I do not know if Lady understood the stories I made up as adventures for us, but I know that she was my friend, and I thought we talked all the time.

"Will you please stop that barking," my mother used to say—to both of us.

One day Lady reached the end of the ravine and discovered traffic. I never saw her again, but to this day I remember that rambunctious, frisky dog with the waggly stump of a tail. She has a place in my heart forever.

Other dogs followed Lady. The family grew. We moved to a bigger suburban house, which mirrored the house across the street, up the street, and down the street. There was no ravine behind the house on Penworth Avenue. Instead, the yard opened onto a parklike, green space with one majestic elm tree in the middle. Just beyond was the school where I would be variously delighted, bored, humiliated, and entertained for the next eight years.

My first puppy came to live with us on Penworth. He was a squirmy little mutt that I picked out of a box full of brown puppies at a local gas station. By this time I had learned how to think and plot, and spent a

considerable amount of time manipulating my parents and ensuring that my siblings knew I was the first of the chosen. When I was registering for kindergarten, my father took me to the school. I was definitely "daddy's girl" and preyed mercilessly on his emotions to get whatever I wanted.

"Is this your father?" the school registrar asked, tongue in cheek.

"This is Dr. Boulton," I informed her.

"So you must be Marsha," she said.

"Well, my name is Marsha Boulton but my daddy calls me Frou-Frou Pants," I replied, referring to the nickname I had earned by wearing a particularly grotesque pair of shorts covered with frills.

After registration, Father and I went for ice cream, something that was forbidden in our tooth-conscious house. It was just one of the secrets we kept between us.

I was one of "those" kids—the precocious kind who liked to sing and dance on tables. My mother's diaries are filled with entries like: "In the bank with Dad—so quiet—so M. starts to sing at top of voice and everyone turns." Such behavior delighted my shy, conservative father, and I pandered to him, sparking entries such as: "Carries all sorts of things. Carries Daddy's beer to him one-handed now." And I was game for a joke: "While Mom went out for butter at lunch, Daddy taught Marsha: 'What's Mommy? Nuts?'" My best trick was memorizing books and pretending to "read" them for guests: "When I say, 'Marsha your book is upside down' she turns it around right away.'"

I called my puppy Bingo, and he came with his own incessant clapping song, a little ditty that came from who knows where, much like the dog.

There was a farmer had a dog,
And Bingo was his name—Oh.
B-I-N-G-O!

B-I-N-G-O!
B-I-N-G-O!
And Bingo was his name—Oh!

These lyrics are repeated and repeated with one letter of the name replaced by a clap with each chanting. Little kids love it. Parents soon learn to hate it. At least, my parents did.

What started out as a shoe box–size puppy soon grew into an ungainly creature with the legs of a greyhound, the body of a Labrador, and the head of a German shepherd. I fancied him as a sort of pony, since I was also thoroughly enamored of horses.

Bingo was a crackerjack of a dog—big and kind of dopey. He never seemed to figure out that he had grown larger than a shoe box and was constantly knocking things over.

As usual, the burden of care fell to my mother, whose priorities gravitated to babes in arms. Bingo did not care. There were plenty of other houses, garages, and backyards for him to investigate. It was when I started following him that Bingo's travels became a concern.

In those days, there was a government agency that followed up rigorously on the placement and care of adopted children. Since we gradually grew into a three-child family, a child services social worker visited a couple of times a year, especially when children younger than two were in the house.

These visits caused terror in my mother's heart. An exact date and time were not usually stipulated, just that "Mrs. White" or "Mrs. Smith" would be in our area such and such a week and would be dropping by. At the beginning of that week, my mother had the Dutch cleaning lady come in and do a scrub-down of the house, so that it smelled of Bon Ami and Johnson's Wax. The dolls I never played with were cushioned against the plethora of pillows in my bedroom, where the pink wallpaper featured black line drawings of ballerinas frolicking in tutus.

Everything had to be spruced up. I went to the hairdresser to have my bangs trimmed to midforehead and the rest of my skimpy, blond locks clipped evenly to ear length. The salon smelled strange and was filled with plastic aprons and baskets of hair rollers. My mother got a "cut and perm," emerging from a row of hair dryers as sheared and curled as a standard poodle. I was horrified. The mother I knew had thick, jet-black hair that swayed around her shoulders in luscious waves. She looked like a beguiling Snow White, and I thought of her that way—brightly innocent, even when dealing with peckish or scandalous dwarfs like me. Now she had become as tightly kinked and bobbed as all of the other women on our street.

A baby brother with brown hair and amazingly long eyelashes occupied my freshly modernized mother, so I retreated into play with Bingo-dog. Having taught him to roll over, shake a paw, and bark when I raised one finger, I decided we should take our show on the road, literally. Next thing you knew, I was knocking on the neighbors' doors, asking if they would pay a nickel to see a dog show. This came to an abrupt conclusion when Jimmy Soliskie's mother called my mother and asked her to retrieve her barking daughter.

Mother was beside herself. If word got out to Children's Services that I was rolling around with the dog on the doorsteps of strangers there could be serious consequences. It was left to my father to convey the importance of being a "good girl" when our case-file worker came calling. Manners were important in our house. Things like excusing oneself from the table or saying "pardon me" when something was missed in conversation came naturally with enough repetition. Now I was to understand that barking was unacceptable behavior.

Bingo was banished to the basement when the lady in the blue suit showed up to inspect my baby brother and "assess" my progress. After much cooing over the carefully swaddled and impeccably clean infant, we sat down for tea at the dining room table. All week long my father had been on alert to leave his dental office and come home as soon as the inquisitor appeared. I imagined him hunched over a patient in the middle of a filling, receiving the call, pounding filling compound into a hapless tooth, and bolting the office, leaving a rather surprised patient. Sure enough, my father's Pontiac was soon in the driveway.

The assessment went well, although I know my parents considered it invasive. They liked nothing better than to go out with their children and have people comment on how much we looked like them. I found that amusing, but it pleased them endlessly. After an hour or so of polite conversation, I was allowed to sing and clap the Bingo song, and the poor dog was heard barking from the basement. This sparked the interest of our visitor, who wondered how such a large-sounding dog fit into a household with such young children. My mother's lips began to quiver.

"He does tricks," I said. My father gave me a look that growled.

Released from the basement, Bingo came bounding up the steps as though chased by the monster I knew lived under the basement steps. He wanted to sniff and lick this new person. In his enthusiasm, he managed to shift the tablecloth, sending my mother sprawling to catch a glass of water before it tipped into our guest's lap. Father stood back primly, avoiding dog slobber, while Bingo made his best effort to become a lapdog.

I ended up showing off Bingo's tricks, without a single bark out of me. As I always suspected, the Children's Services lady was quite pleased to see children placed in the home of a "professional," who had an enthusiastic wife and middle-class everything. We waved her off for another six months.

Then disaster struck. It happened because of a newfangled thing called television, which had dominated the family living room for a couple of years. I liked television well enough. Watching Roy Rogers gallop around beating the bad guys on his golden horse, Trigger, was a favorite pastime. I even had a special cowgirl outfit to wear while I watched the show. This was not unusual in the early days of television. We had a neighbor who said "excuse me" to quiz-show host Groucho Marx every time she left the television room—something that a Marx brother would have appreciated. I made Bingo watch Rin Tin Tin and Lassie on TV, but none of their smarts rubbed off on him, and he usually ended up sleeping with some part of his warm brown body draped over me.

The problem was that I had become obsessed with the story of Peter Pan. I had a picture book of J. M. Barrie's famous children's story that had been pored over so frequently it was in tatters. I loved Never-Never Land—that place where dreams that do come true are born and all you need to fly is "trust and a little pixie dust." When a live version of the stage play aired on television, nothing could have kept me away from the set. It was magic to see Peter flying with the Darling children. I longed to be just like him—riding the wind's back and following the second star on the right "straight on til morning."

One fine summer day, I decided to practice flying while my friend Gregory looked on and Bingo bounced around the backyard. We had a metal swing set, and I climbed up on the horizontal bar that served as a brace, one I used to hang upside down from while making monkey sounds. This time I stood on the bar, facing the elm in the open field. It was a hot day, and I imagined that flying into the shady boughs of the great tree would be a satisfactory first flight. I balanced carefully, all the while chanting, "I believe in fairies, I believe in fairies." Then I reached into the pocket of my shorts and pulled out a pinch of sweet-smelling powder pilfered from my mother's toiletries. I smeared the makeshift pixie dust on my face.

My arms were raised, and I could feel lightness in my diaphragm. As I launched toward the tree, arms flapping, Gregory and Bingo ran by me and I looked down. Mistake. It seemed to me that I fell a great distance. Landing hard on the baked ground, I heard a horrible crunching sound.

Bingo was on me in an instant, washing my ears while I tried to figure out what had gone wrong. Gregory ran from the yard screaming. When my frantic mother arrived, I was standing with my right arm dangling at an impossible angle. It scared me. It did not work.

Thank goodness my father had insisted on making his new Pontiac a station wagon. He whisked me into it and drove full tilt to the hospital, managing to pick up a police escort along the way. It was exciting, but my mother kept crying. I remembered Peter Pan telling Captain Hook, "I am youth. I am joy. I am a little bird that has broken out of the egg." The operative word was *broken*, and I heard it said a lot that day.

Mother sang to me while I lay on the hospital gurney in the hall. "You are my sunshine, my only sunshine." She left me alone only once, when she and my father had to sign papers allowing the doctors to amputate if there was nothing else to be done. I had fallen with my full weight on the arm, bending it backward, causing a messy break and severing many nerves.

Then, in one of those happy coincidences that have permeated my life, a young surgeon suggested trying a daring procedure involving some new materials to reconnect damaged nerves and veins. They operated for hours, and I came out of surgery with a huge cast covering my right arm. It folded across my chest, with my hand resting over my heart.

A lot of fuss was made over me in the days that followed. A steady stream of toys and tears flowed freely, especially when I was able to wiggle my fingers. After a week of close observation and an endless number of doctors dropping by to see my moving digits, I was sent home with severe mobility restrictions. Anything that jarred the cast or caused the arm to shift could negate what was being viewed as either medical genius or a miracle.

Bingo was gone. My parents told me he had gone to live on a farm. The only farms I knew of belonged to my uncles, but Bingo had not gone to their farms. He had gone somewhere strange, and I would never see him again. There was nothing I could do. I felt the helpless pain of a child, and I could not see how sending my best friend away could possibly be "for the best."

The arm healed gradually throughout that dog-less summer of sitting still. My mother, her friends, and our neighbors read to me constantly. I memorized so many books that even I thought I could read.

The cast was itchy and smelly. When removal day came, I was taken into the bowels of the hospital to a room that looked more like my father's tool table than a place of healing. The gray-white cast covered with the signatures of everyone I had met over the months of wear went under the electric saw while my father held me steady and I turned my head into my mother's soft stomach.

Liberated, the arm stayed in position, frozen, as it had been in the cast. My gnomish godmother, known as Auntie Doris, gave me a sling with a picture of a basset hound, which became my favorite fashion accessory. Months of rehabilitation followed, using sandbags to gradually straighten the arm. It hurt, and I had a long, angry, red scar at the joint. The only promise at the end of all that dreary exercise was getting another dog.

Fourteen years later, when I was leaving the family home to discover the world, I found Bingo's puppy collar in one of my ancient treasure boxes. It still bore the scent of leather and dog. It sometimes seems to me that I grew up from dog to dog rather than year to year. Between kindergarten and the end of high school, three dachshunds and a Labrador retriever framed my life.

Princess, Duchess, and Winston—the dachshunds—were lovable red-brown characters, whose nails clicked sharply on the green linoleum in the old stone country house we moved into. They followed one another in sequence as back problems inevitably ended their time with us. My sister once allowed Princess to jump out of a car window. I am not sure that she was ever forgiven.

Those bright-eyed little dogs would dance on their hind legs to please and dig holes deeper than their body length. They had an acre of land to protect and clear of vermin, and they were dedicated souls. The mere prospect of a mouse hiding under a neatly raked pile of autumn leaves was enough incitement for those pointy-nosed, deep-chested torpedoes on paws to scatter leaves to the wind. As their muzzles grew gray and their focus faded, each one of them showed us the heart of a lion.

Charm, the black Lab, was to the water born from puppyhood. There was a river behind the farm field and woodlot that backed our house. I would ride to the river on Playboy, a bay Morgan horse my parents bought me when I was twelve. Charm followed, and together we swam through a deep, fast-flowing stretch of water with me clinging to the sturdy horse by the mane and Charm happily at our side. Then we fell, exhausted, on the riverbank, Playboy to graze quietly while Charm sought sticks for me to throw until my arm hurt.

The dogs went everywhere with us. Sometimes my father closed his practice for six weeks during the summer. Hitching up a foldout camper to the station wagon, we headed off in whatever direction seemed most agreeable. Charm swam in both oceans, and the dachshunds visited deserts, climbed the footpaths of the Rocky Mountains, and worried armadillos. Their sound and smell and the textures of their coats are favorite memories of a privileged childhood in which function largely won out over dysfunction.

Education, career, and the simple necessity of finding a place in the world where I could responsibly have my own dog distanced me from them for almost a decade. Then I moved to the farm, and a whole world of animal possibilities was opened. There would be dogs and cats, and sheep and horses, cows and chickens and ducks and unusual goats that faint.

Throughout the adventure, there would also be a man, Stephen Williams. Together, we would find Wally the Wonder Dog, who shaped our life and saved it, too, in the way that only a dog can do.

2

We Move to the Farm

I t was the year Ronald Reagan was elected president of the United States and Canadian ambassador Ken Taylor rescued six American diplomats held hostage in Iran.

I met Stephen Williams on the white line in the road in front of a restaurant that was celebrating its opening on May 1, 1980. As the People section editor at *Maclean's*, Canada's answer to *Time* magazine, I received many invitations, and life in my midtwenties was consumed by the pursuit of celebrities and gossip. My choice that fateful spring day was to either go home and defrost something for myself or allow a restaurant to feed me for free. I hailed a cab from work, and Stephen opened the door when it pulled up at the neon-lit café. He was tall, dark, handsome—and rakishly groomed, wearing sunglasses and a smile.

"My, aren't you beautiful," he said. We have been a couple ever since.

He made me laugh with the classic pickup line, "Hey, baby, wanna go for a ride in my new Pontiac?" I had not known anyone since my father who had a new Pontiac. The car in question turned out to be a souped-up, black Trans Am with gold trim and a firebird decal on the hood, just like the one Burt Reynolds drove in the *Smokey and the Bandit* films. From the beginning, I knew our life together would not be boring.

At the time, Stephen was a freelance writer, one of the young lions of the literary scene. While I wrote glib squibs, his prose was more thought provoking, ranging from profiles of the poet Leonard Cohen to an in-depth examination of a gruesome pedophile homicide. I hauled him off to film festivals and embassy parties, and he introduced me to the denizens of the artistic and writerly community.

Our households soon melded. I left my one-bedroom spinster's apartment and moved with my white cat, Johnny, into Stephen's book-cluttered, two-story digs, which came with two young children and an Irish nanny. He was in the throes of a messy, long-distance divorce, his wife having run off with a West Coast sports promoter. Most of the men I had met up to this point in my life could barely feed themselves, let alone raise a family. I was impressed.

Children and relationships had never preoccupied me, but now they did. Eleven-year-old Andrew was wary of a new woman in the house he had once shared with his mother, but he did tell his father he thought I was pretty. Four-year-old Adrienne commanded attention, the reading of books, and the brushing of her long chestnut hair. Nanny Betty, a twenty-two-year-old Dubliner, had her own set schedule and feared I would take her job. In the meantime, I had a full dance card of interviews to conduct, public relations people to respond to, and movie premieres to attend. Stephen and I began looking for a large house to buy. I was wildly in love and had no caution.

Shortly after our commitment, and right out of the blue, the children's estranged mother showed up from California and snatched them while we were out with a real estate agent. This sent the redheaded nanny off to find a Guinness at the nearest Irish pub. We came home to a scrawled note pinned to the door. Stephen was distraught. The police came and went, unable to interfere in what they considered "a domestic incident." Clothing and toys were gone. All of the artwork in the house had been stripped. Johnny Cat ran away.

The next day, we were at the lawyer's office. It took five days, a court order, and thousands of dollars to have the children returned. Although the soon-to-be ex-wife had been absent from the household for years, it was clear that my status as the "other woman" was unwelcome. In the heat of divorce passion and propaganda, I learned there is no reason. The process was damaging to already fragile children. The nanny was definitely taking to drink. Still, all I had to do was squeeze Stephen's hand to know that for some reason I was in the right place. The cat came back.

About this time, the concept of a slower pace of life came to mind. Stephen was granted custody of the children, and their mother returned to her new life in California. Settling took some time. Neighborhood tomcats took to beating up Johnny. Nanny Betty found a boyfriend. Notices were being sent from the children's school about everything from head lice to "the seven signs of pot smoking." There had to be a better way to live.

We bought the hundred-acre farm that summer. It was the largest impulse purchase I have ever made and, quite possibly, the wisest. We walked through the house, gazed at the land, and signed on the dotted line. That was it. I never even turned on a tap to make sure there was water.

Set well back from the road and forest, the two-story, Victorian farmhouse perched on a gentle hill. More than a century before, its yellow bricks had been fired at some pioneer brickyard down the road. A circle drive at the end of the lane was comforted by a huge maple tree that had seen generations of owners come and go. Something about the house spoke to me. It had four bedrooms, hardly any closets, and a big front porch. The kitchen was huge, with lots of light and windows overlooking what I knew would become my gardens.

Gradually, over the next year, we began moving to the farm. Every weekend, the Trans Am was loaded and stacked with useful items. We got to know a few neighbors and experienced a rural winter. The formal parlor, where Sunday guests once visited and where the former inhabitants would have had their corpses laid out for visitation before burial, was transformed into a family Ping-Pong room. We skied as a family and tobogganed and fell down in the snow a lot.

Convincing ourselves that it would be possible to live in the country and work on writing projects that were generated in the city was easier than I thought it would be. There existed such a thing as a facsimile machine to facilitate communications. We felt as though we were on the cutting edge of technology.

Stephen had ideas for books he wanted to write. I had dreams about combining farming and journalism, maybe writing a column. The more country-raised children we met, the better I felt about removing Andrew and Adrienne from the city. These youngsters had structure in their lives and chores that they did without question. They had responsibilities, such as raising their own 4H calf. Without malls to linger in, their complexions reflected the time they spent outdoors doing things other than "hanging." The schools were small, and the teachers both personable and involved. I gave up my thoughts about homeschooling.

It was the kind of childhood environment I would have chosen for myself. And my secret heart delighted in the notion that we could have a horse and a dog, and any other animals we wanted. In a way, I was revisiting my own childhood place of deepest happiness, and I wanted to share that with the people who had become the most important in my life.

The first dog came to the farm during an Indian summer night in

October. We heard him baying at the moon in a nearby pasture. In answer to our whistles and calling, an amiable black-and-tan coonhound came to the porch, wagging a solid upright tail with floppy ears hanging in great folds at the side of his oval forehead. He was a big dog with a deep chest and a nose that poked at you. No collar provided a clue as to where he belonged. We fed him hamburger and milk on the front porch and put out a blanket for him to lie on. In the morning, a low-slung, female mongrel that looked a bit like a collie with a wiry brown coat had joined him. She was a skittish young thing in contrast to the coonhound's majesty.

The neighbors did not recognize our descriptions of either dog, and none of them offered a haven to the strays. We could not take them home with us, so we set out blankets and a bag of dog kibble on the porch and hoped that they would find their way back to their owners. The children had already named them. Andrew called the hound "Og" and Adrienne called the shy bitch "Flora." We posted FOUND DOGS notices in the supermarket and the post office but heard nothing.

Og and Flora greeted us for several more weekends, wagging happily and waiting for another bag of food. Two dogs as different as chalk and cheese, but they had bonded. We threw sticks for them and rubbed them behind the ears. On a woodlot walk, the prepossessing Og surveyed the forest as his own domain. If we did not have a stick to throw, he simply pulled one off a tree. Flora jogged worshipfully after him.

Then one weekend, Og and Flora were nowhere to be found. Blankets had moved and food had been eaten, but the dogs were gone. We called and whistled and waited. We asked the neighbors and were no more the wiser. The children were confused. The dogs loved them. Adrienne opened her bedroom window at night and barked to try to call them in. Perhaps their owner had found them. Perhaps they were visiting another farm that weekend. It was hard to understand why they would leave us.

Every weekend, we searched for the odd couple, but "His Majesty" Og and his shadow, Flora, were gone. Only years later, in a confidential moment between farmers, would I learn that they had been buried two farms away—shot for chasing sheep and goats. The country solution is a bullet and a burial, including the collar, if there is one. The farmer might know that the dog is a pet of a neighbor's child. The farmer might even know the dog personally and like it. However, when a dog strays and threatens livestock, there is no one-time warning and no quarter given, just quiet, efficient disposal.

Even if I had known of such attitudes and behavior in advance, I would have moved to the farm. I loved the acres of wildflowers that turned out to be weeds and the idea that they were my responsibility made me giddy. My library expanded with titles like: *Raising Sheep the Modern Way* and *Chickens in Your Backyard* taking space beside contemporary novels and classics. Along with subscriptions to industry magazines such as *Variety* and *Billboard*, which I used to keep in touch with entertainment news, the mail carrier was now carrying copies of the *Mother Earth News* and *Rural Delivery*. I signed up for government newsletters concerning farmers, and I was inundated with large envelopes containing single pages of information.

None of my friends would ever have pictured me on a farm. My feet fit naturally into the highest of high heels, which were my trademark. I enjoyed making fashion statements, and the magazine assisted me by providing a clothing allowance. In fact, I always had a set of evening clothes stashed at the office in case I got a last-minute call to attend something.

All of those shoes and glitzy clothes ended up in storage when I decided to become a shepherd. I tendered my resignation at the magazine amid looks of disbelief. There were women who could not believe I would walk away from a job that paid for my clothes. Still others could not believe I would take on the responsibilities of another woman's children and then give up having a nanny. I felt no obligation to explain. I was too busy finding us a puppy.

We decided we wanted a big dog to fill the hole left by Og and Flora. We wanted a dog that was friendly and smart enough to learn tricks, but also imposing enough so that strangers might not trespass. We looked through dog magazines, bought some dog books, and we looked at dogs in the street. We waffled from Weimaraners to wolfhounds.

One day Andrew's class went on a school outing and he saw a bullmastiff, who he said was the size of a Shetland pony and a friendly sort of fellow. We decided to take a closer look at these dogs whose origins were described as 60 percent mastiff and 40 percent bulldog. They were bred in England at the end of the nineteenth century as "gamekeepers' dogs." It seems that poachers were trouble on the estates of the aristocracy, and since the penalty for poaching was death, gamekeepers found themselves confronting armed and dangerous thieves with everything to lose unless they killed the gamekeeper. The solution was found in the bullmastiff, a swift and obedient dog capable of felling a poacher and holding him to ground, without mauling or biting. I fancied a big, solid dog squashing a deer hunter. We found a breeder and obtained an interview.

I say we "obtained an interview" because I had to pull out every stop I knew to convince the breeder that we were truly committed to the breed and capable of providing a dog with amenities even a popular rock band could not have written into a contract. Certainly there were many more requirements than the simple "to love, honor, and cherish," involving everything from types of collars to neutering. When we finally got into the car to make the two-hour trip for the "breeder interview," I realized I had dressed and coached the children as carefully as my mother used to do with me when the Child Services lady was coming for inspection.

It was a lovely kennel/home in a wooded lot, with none of the barking and doggy smells associated with pet stores where freshly weaned puppies cry pitifully and vie for any sign of affection. In fact, we barely saw a single dog. They were off in a building separate from the house, which had long outdoor dog runs where a few could be seen lazing about. In the breeder's living room, I was given a clipboard with questions we were to answer aloud.

I claimed to be of Irish-English heritage like my adoptive parents, although I had been told my true background was Norwegian. I thought the breeder sniffed a falsehood. It was obvious that the dark-haired, dark-eyed children were not mine. Their body type was totally different, and they bore no trace of my high cheekbones or fair skin. We confessed to being a family once-divided, and clouds crossed the breeder's face. The inquiry continued, with many of the questions reminding me of a banker's when applying for a mortgage—place of work, years there, annual income. Would we commit to training the dog? Would there be someone home with the dog at all times? If we went away, would the dog accompany us or be kenneled? Which kennel? Was there an enclosed yard for the dog? Describe the fencing. Did we have a dog crate? Did we know how to use a dog crate? Name of veterinarian? Own or rent?

Somehow we passed. When the breeder said that she thought she had the right puppy for our family, the children jumped and cheered, and quickly sat down. We filled out paperwork and wrote a rather large check for the breeder's husband while she went to fetch the puppy from the whelping room.

He was the color of sand on a Mediterranean beach. A black mask framed his blunt muzzle, outlining his eyes in a diamond shape, making him appear to be on the verge of asking an intelligent question. He dashed around the living room, zipping across the giggling children to hide behind an armchair. The breeder picked him up, and he flopped across her lap like a stuffed toy, with loose skin in rolls at his shoulder and hips waiting for him to grow into it.

The next question from the breeder came as a total surprise. What would we name the puppy? She always registered her dogs with names associated with musical genres. This litter was "country music singers." Naturally, the puppy became "Hank Williams." We each held him, marveling at his wide, wet nostrils, huge puppy paws, and furrowed brow. Puppy breath does not vary from breed to breed. I closed my eyes and inhaled. Baby Hank could have been baby Bingo. If it could be bottled, puppy breath could probably stop all wars.

We picked up Hank Williams two weeks later. His new home would be the farm, where we moved as soon as the school term ended in June 1981.

3

Passing Southern Winds

Sometime between the day I planted my first cucumber seed and the day the first ewe set foot in a pasture, Stephen strayed from the farm. A lucrative job offer in the advertising business lured him away from the bucolic. While I traded my high heels for Wellington boots, he chased the Madison Avenue dragon, traveling all over the world on behalf of high-tech clients. The children alternated nights of having Hank sleep on their beds, and I discovered that long-distance romance is just that.

My decision to raise sheep was a matter of simple logic and logistics. By all accounts, sheep were gentle creatures, creatures of habit that actually did "follow like sheep." They only have teeth on their lower jaw, so they could not bite me terribly hard.

Having livestock meant building something to house them, as well as fences to contain them. If we had all of that in place, we might as well add a horse. I rationalized everything to come up with the answers I wanted. Lady, the American saddlebred palomino of my dreams, was the culmination of such a rationale. I recovered the old English saddle and bridle of my childhood from my parents' garage, where they maintained an archive of all-things Marsha.

We started with thirteen Hampshire ewes, one of which came with two lambs, promptly named Fred and Flicka. They arrived as the final gate was hung on the fences. All of those government newsletters on agriculture paid off. Although I had fewer sheep than many of the teenage members of the local 4H Sheep Club, I successfully applied for a government rebate of 50 percent of the fencing costs. I was beginning to figure out this farming business. I contracted to grow pickle cucumbers because I read an advertisement saying you could make up to $2,000 per acre. Not to be greedy, I had two acres plowed.

The children helped me plant cucumber seeds while the loose-limbed puppy bounded from row to row, challenging us for games of chase. I got an old, turquoise Ford pickup truck, and we would all load into the front seat and crawl along the unfamiliar country roads, singing country-and-western songs that played on the tinny radio. That summer, our favorite was Don Williams singing "Good Ole Boys Like Me," a lazy kind of song that talks about southern wind passing through live oak trees and runs the literary gamut from Uncle Remus to Thomas Wolfe. We all chimed in at the line: "And those Williams boys, they still mean a lot to me—Hank and Tennessee."

It was a dusty, hot, sharecropper summer. The children left to visit their mother as soon as the cucumbers grew to pickle-picking size. It was just Hank and me and the two-acre field. Once, while I was busy trying to fill a burlap sack with gherkin-size cucumbers, Hank got hold of a full sack that I had leaned against a fence. He tugged on the bottom of the bag and spilled the precious contents across the crusted ground before I even noticed. Running toward me through the vines, he held the bag aloft and was delighted with himself. For a moment, I considered dumping my half-filled bag of cukes and running around with the bag myself, if I could ever approach feeling the devilish joy that Hank had writ large on himself. I thought better of it, however, since the neighbors were already taken aback by the notion of a woman picking pickles in a bikini.

Hank and I had the month of August together and pretty much to ourselves. We drove bags of cucumbers to the pickle depot in the turquoise truck with the windows down. We walked among the sheep, and he trotted along when I played Roy Rogers, riding the horse along the new fence lines. He was growing into his skin, and we were both sucking up every delicious moment of this new adventure. The only money to be made in growing pickle cucumbers is in the tiny gherkins. After costs, I earned $23.16 in pickle money for that back-breaking summer, but I also earned the respect of my farming neighbors because I kept at it and did not lose money. I had a tan that was so richly bronze I was begging for skin cancer and a dusty puppy that liked nothing better than to lie on his back with his legs splayed like a spatch-cocked chicken on the barbecue.

The cucumber folly ended as the school year began and the sheep entered the breeding phase. Farm life was one beginning after another, everything from building a barn to hatching chicks. On weekends, Stephen came home to find out what money pit I had thrown us into this time.

One of the first things we installed in the old farmhouse was an air-tight woodstove. It sits in the kitchen, which is the heart of the house. In winter, the house holds the heat, and two floors can be warmed through the night by the woodstove. When the wind howls furiously and the hydro is knocked out, the old woodstove is a comfort beyond description. I have even cooked lamb chops and made chicken soup on top of the woodstove. It provides a wonderful sense of self-sufficiency.

That first year, we had no idea how much wood we would need to get us through the winter. One thing we did know was that there was wood all around us. About twenty acres were planted in evergreen trees, white pine, and spruce, that stood about four feet tall and have subsequently grown into substantial, three-story-high trees. Another twenty-five acres were mixed forest, maple, birch, poplar, elm, wild apple, and cherry trees jumbled with evergreens and the odd oak or beech. Walking into the depths of the forest was a hard slog, but once in its midst, the splendor of silence followed by the rustle of a breeze, the calling of birds, and the creak of branches made it a holy place.

The pioneers were "hewers of wood and drawers of water." So we decided we should "hew" some wood, first by culling dead elms in a scrubby part of the forest near the road. Stephen bought the most imposing chain saw he could find, and we set off to harvest the winter heating fuel, starting with a smallish elm in a clear area. The children and I stood back and shouted "timber!" as the tree thudded to the ground. Stephen chopped its long trunk into firewood, and we stacked it loosely to dry. There was far less than I had anticipated such a tree would yield. So we moved to a bigger one.

Hank was with us, sniffing things we could not smell and digging open groundhog holes. The forest was like an amusement park to him, with squirrels leaping from tree branch to tree branch and rabbits hopping to their hidey-holes. We had seen the bark-stripping signs of porcupines and hoped he would not find one.

The chain saw was quiet as the big leafless elm tipped toward the afternoon sun perched low in the sky. Stephen stepped backward. The tree teetered and leaned, beginning its descent. The rabbit caught Hank's eye. Everything after that I see in slow motion. There was the flash of the rabbit's white tail and Hank's eyes gleaming in their black diamond frames, his dark ears alert. He was after it in a flash. The tree in free fall. The dog running. Then the impossible collision of the two.

We ran, stumbling over the uneven forest floor, tripping and wailing. Hank was pinned under the massive elm trunk that lay across his lower back. Unimaginable as it may seem, he wagged his tail when we reached him. Who knows where superhuman strength comes from? Stephen lifted the tree and I pulled the young dog free. The children were silent and pale. Hank yelped in fear and pain and confusion.

I can cry about it now. Not then. My mind was racing far too fast for tears. Stephen is a big man—linebacker size—but anything to do with pain renders him shaken and sickly. He cut his finger assembling the Ping-Pong table and passed out at the sight of his own blood. I checked, and Hank was not bleeding. He wobbled and finally stood up. It was astounding that his back had not been broken. Stephen carried him to the truck, where we wrapped him in a blanket and headed back to the house to regroup.

As the dog was in danger of falling into shock, so were the children. They sat with Hank and petted him gently. His tail thumped, but his eyes oozed pain. A local veterinarian agreed to meet us at his office. Of course, it was a Sunday.

Hank was stabilized on fluids and given pain medication. He needed more sophisticated testing equipment than the local vet had at hand. We were given a referral to a clinic that would see Hank first thing in the morning. The drowsy patient returned home to children who could not spare him enough gentle hugs.

We blamed ourselves, silently. The emotion was too thick for recrimination. Stephen had to fly off for a business meeting the next day. He buried his face next to Hank's before leaving. The children asked to take the morning off school to go to the veterinary clinic with their dog. We agreed. I remembered the times I had sat at the vet's office, waiting to learn whether or not a dachshund could be repaired. My mother's red eyes always told the answer, but it meant something to be there, to have a last pat and feel that bond of love one last time.

Veterinarians and their assistants can be such a special breed of human. Hank was handled gently. When prodded, he cried out reluctantly. He had X-rays and blood tests and anything else that was needed. We stood around the examining table and took a special minute while Hank's sturdy tail thumped fiercely.

Our dear boy did not make it. His kidneys had been crushed and other organs compromised. When I was told, I thought "dialysis" and "transplant," but the damage was too extensive. Although he must have been in terrible pain, Hank never complained or raised a lip to his caregivers. We could not let him suffer. While the first blizzard of an early winter cast snowdrifts across the lane, we remembered him and wondered if a soft southern wind would ever pass our way again.

Such an accident could not be staged or repeated ever again, but Stephen never cut another stick of firewood, and we never walked in that part of the forest. Writing a letter to his breeder took weeks. I never heard back.

We mourned Hank, and we waited until the children started to ask for another dog. On Andrew's early spring birthday, Hank was followed by a solid red bullmastiff puppy. I found the dog in the worst possible way, through a newspaper advertisement that turned out to involve a young man who was not a legitimate breeder. He had a litter that had been born in his basement apartment. We could have the biggest male. The seller said they were "good dogs." He wanted cash. No questions asked. Stephen had been away on business so much. He wanted to get his son a special birthday present. Pickup was set for the eve of Andrew's birthday. Even then, the timing almost failed when a flight out of Atlanta was rerouted through Dallas and delayed. Stephen took a limousine straight from the airport to the basement apartment and brought the puppy home in the lap of luxury.

He was a roly-poly fellow, as stout as Hank had been lanky. The limousine pulled in the lane around 3:00 A.M., but there was no keeping the children asleep, not when they heard barking coming from the kitchen. That night the puppy slept in his open crate next to the bed of a happy boy.

This puppy bulldozed his way everywhere. He was solid as a rock, and his tail was always beating on something. We named him Mingus after the jazz bass player Charles Mingus. A joy of a puppy, he loved nothing better than to try to squeeze his way behind the refrigerator, where he liked to hide his stuffed yellow duck. At twelve weeks he was powerful enough to actually shift the refrigerator. Mingus became a large dog.

I know now how difficult it must have been for the children's mother to think of them living in what must have seemed an idyllic rural setting with puppies and lambs and a golden horse that a strange blond woman was teaching them to ride. Adrienne had gymnastics classes, and Andrew played hockey. They rode the bus to school each day and raced up the lane to be slobbered on by Mingus. On weekends, when their father was home, they favored us with pantomime shows and improvised entertainments. For their mother, it must have been a scenario that was hard to be excluded from.

"Marsha must cry a lot," is what Adrienne told me her mother said after one of their weekly telephone conversations. I suppose it was preferable for her to imagine my life as a torment of some sort.

Often, in the days after such phone calls, the children would act out in unpredictable ways. They would demand new this or new that and ask odd questions like: "Why don't we have a washing machine?" and "Are you going to have a baby?"

Having been raised by people who were not my "real" parents, I knew what was going on in their squirrelly heads. Just as children are manipulated, they will countermanipulate, and if there is an alternative to the person who insists you have your homework done by the time you go to bed, the alternative is much preferable. The myth of the evil stepmother is easy to play off, and I was played.

That summer when the children went to California for their vacation with their mother, they never returned. It was July 1983, and the summer Olympics were being held in Los Angeles the following year. Their mother's sports-promoter partner had a job assisting at the Women's Field Hockey venue. There was the promise of being involved in the buildup to the Olympics, as well as tickets to various events.

To children who had been living on a farm it was exciting and glamorous. Andrew was a teenager, and there is no doubt that the girls in California are more comely and likely to reveal flesh than our Mennonite neighbors' daughters. I remembered how withdrawn and needy the normally outgoing and affectionate Adrienne had been before they left. Secrets never sat well with her. Andrew had been riding the horse into frothy sweats and roughhousing with Mingus every evening. He had a camp-out party with friends just days before they flew off. It had all been prepared and orchestrated, and the legal papers were served a few days later, demanding custodies.

The immediate reaction when such a shocking thing happens is to resolve to fight to the death. To me, my parents, and our friends, this arbitrary kidnapping made no sense. Custody had been decided years earlier, but apparently custody is a fluid concept, not a fixed result. Most certainly, the allegations contained in the affidavits coaxed from young Andrew were vicious and hurtful. The notion that any mother could endorse such false witness gives one pause. Sadly, that is the name of the game that often accompanies the acrimony of divorce and custody battles.

Stephen's mother, a chronic bearer of bad tidings, wallowed in every weary accusation of derelict child care and abuse. Once, when she called to chastise me with the usual admonishments about my inadequacies, she capped it by saying, "And did you know that Andrew has told everyone that you slept with him?"

The absurdity of the statement—and the will that existed to believe it—was too much for me. "Dorothy," I said calmly, "if I had slept with Andrew he would never have left."

We presented our case to the same family court judge who had awarded custody three years earlier. While he had some sympathy for our position, he explained that a grant of custody was not absolute. Teenagers that appear to be as intelligent and well mannered as Andrew are permitted to demand a review of their custodial circumstances and can dramatically influence the outcome. Jurisdictional issues aside, there was little the judge could do. Perhaps the solution would be to separate brother and sister? We refused to entertain the possibility and decided to let the children go.

Amid the pathos, only one thing was clear. We were keeping the dog.

4

All Good Dogs

For a few intense years, parenting had defined what I did with my days. Suddenly that was over, and cleaning up the mess was all that was left to be done. Stephen and I had talks in those days that led me to conclude that it really might all be "for the best," provided that the children were cared for and loved. I had undergone surgery for fertility issues and it had failed. Unwilling to have a child named after a Petri dish, and unwilling to invest my heart in another woman's child again, it was time for new beginnings.

If Stephen was my rock, Mingus was my healer. He grew to be massive enough to truly take the breath away from any poacher. I threw myself into the business of farming. Expanding the flock with purebred Suffolk sheep, my fields were dotted with black-headed ewes. Lady had a foal that was her spitting image. We named her Karma. Stephen sold my free-range chickens to the health-conscious account executives at the advertising agency in the big city.

Dogs just seemed to come to the farm. A hairstylist Stephen knew had to part with a seven-year-old Akita named Stella in order to care for an ailing friend. Akitas are big dogs, with dense, double coats and long tails that curl tightly over their backs balancing their triangular heads and ears. Stella was a fine example. With her thick pink tongue dragging out of the side of her face and a broad grin on her black lips, she looked like a dog version of a teddy bear. Stella had grown up on the twenty-eighth floor of an apartment building, but even when she had room to roam, she preferred the view from the porch. A sweet dog, she was thick as fog and never did master the art of going upstairs.

Then came Sheltie, a Shetland sheepdog whose terribly unoriginal name came from her wealthy owners, the Black family. Sheltie had been purchased at a pet store on a whim, and she was not necessarily her master's choice. She liked to urinate in men's shoes; the larger the shoes the better. The yappiest dog I have ever met, she drove visitors crazy and would only be quiet for me. If Sheltie wanted something, she took it, even from the imposing Mingus. It was not unusual to find the tri-color, mini-Lassie lying on top of Mingus's dog bed with every dog toy in the house stuffed under her long frilly coat. An exceptional goose herder, Sheltie is the only dog who ever did a lick of work on the farm.

After a while in a three-dog household, Mingus wearied of too many females taking up his space. He took to strolling over to visit the neighbor's little dog. Like a goat, he could get through any fence. I would run across fields, shouting for him to stop, and he would ignore me with an insouciance only a dog can convey. Exasperated, I resorted to watching his backside enter the neighbor's field and got in the truck to fetch him.

Not only was Mingus a large dog, but he was also heavy. If I loaded him into the cab of the truck, he tended to sprawl across both seats or the floor. Either way shifting gears was impossible. Invariably, I ended up putting him into the box of the pickup truck, a process akin to lifting a stoned teenager into an upper bunk. Positioning his front paws first, I hoisted his rump and relied on forward thrust. The neighbors found this amusing and always waved as we left, knowing Mingus would be back to sample the chicken bones they liked to give him as treats. Even though I exhorted them to stop, like Mingus, they ignored me. I could not bear to chain any dog, and it would have taken an eight-foot-high glass fence drenched with vegetable oil to contain Mingus. Electric fencing was just a bee sting to him.

One day, I got the call I dreaded. The neighbors had gone to town with their dog, and when they got back Mingus was in the ditch at the end of their lane. They said something about a cement truck. I went to him and found a shallow breath in his broken body. His tail thumped when I raised his great head and spoke to him. He gave a long sigh, and the light went out of his loving eyes.

It took a backhoe to dig a burial hole big enough for Mingus. It is not marked, but I know the spot on the knoll across from the house. Stephen knows where Mingus rests, too. He had not raised a dog to adulthood since the last Labrador of his childhood. Together, Mingus and Stephen were like two big guys playing. Mingus went to Stephen's slow-pitch baseball games with the local "townies." Occasionally, the big red dog broke ranks to fetch a ball that was in play in the outfield. He became a mascot for the beer-drinking Boys of Summer, sometimes joining them at the pub patio after a game. If you gave him the V for victory sign, Mingus would let out a howl. If you held up a cookie, he would beg like a grizzly in a circus act.

A wake was held for Mingus at the hotel, where all things are eventually celebrated, revealed, mourned, and decided. The boys from the team lifted a few to the memory of Mingus, and they sang chorus after chorus of the Bob Dylan folk song "The Mighty Quinn," adapted to suit their purpose: "You'll not see nothing like the mighty Ming."

It has always seemed to me an odd song in the Dylan canon of the

1970s, but it has a simple, rousing joy. It is about expecting that something good is going to happen. Mingus always did.

Stella succumbed to cancer shortly after Mingus left us. She never seemed to be an old dog, although she was. Her Japanese dog smile was forever young. Stella saw things at the farm that she had never seen in the city. Her favorite thing of all was newborn lambs in the barn. Although she was spayed and never had puppies herself, the sight of the lambs wobbling on soft hooves brought out the maternal wolf in her. Sheep that would charge any other dog that got into the pen allowed furry Stella to lie silent beside them while they labored to deliver. If she was favored—if she was allowed—Stella's greatest pleasure was to lick a newborn lamb while the ewe attended another. There was a night in the lambing pens when quadruplets were born, and Stella was an invaluable aide to me and the ewe. If I brought an orphan lamb into the house to warm it beside the woodstove, Stella hovered nearby. There was no guile in her.

With Mingus and Stella resting side by side on the knoll with Hank and all of the lambs that did not make it, I decided to get a puppy for myself. I wanted a dog I could pamper and one that would not overwhelm Sheltie. Instead of making a sensible assessment of various breeds and their purpose and temperaments, I became a victim of dog fashion.

Diva was a pure black Chinese shar-pei—black right down to her tongue. She was sold to me as a show-quality, breeding prospect for a ghastly sum, which was a measure of the overpopularity of "wrinkle dogs" in the 1980s, when they were still a relatively rare breed. I signed a formal-looking contract obliging me to show the dog, breed the dog, and relinquish the best puppy back to the breeder. All I wanted was the little black puppy that tumbled out of the litter pack and ran into my arms.

Stephen was occupied with worldly things, and Diva became my dog to raise and train. Although she had plenty of spare puppy skin and a brow full of furrows, the pricey puppy never did sport the rolls of wrinkles so coveted in the world of shar-peis. I took Diva to a couple of all-shar-pei specialty dog shows when she was a puppy, and it was apparent from the reaction of other exhibitors that I had been sold a lemon.

"Oh look, it's a Hong Kong shar-pei," they sniffed. I could only presume that the dogs they were walking had MADE IN CHINA stamped somewhere under a generous fold of fur.

Diva was so sparsely wrinkled that people mistook her for a worried-looking Staffordshire bull terrier or a refined pit bull. Her breeder proved to be a crackpot, and I never did get registration papers for her. I tore up the "contracts."

What Diva did prove to be was a goddess. Every aspect of her had a quirky elegance. As a limber puppy, leading me on a chase through a thigh-high barley field, she bounced through the greenery, teasing me with a glimpse of her face. With her head popping up here and then there, she looked like Steven Spielberg's endearing space alien, E.T.

While other dogs took great interest in the smells and artifacts of the barnyard, Diva trod delicately through it, avoiding anything that could soil her catlike paws. She was solid, sculpted muscle between her coiled tail and her shell-shaped ears. It was impossible to look into that dog's almond eyes without feeling that she was an equal.

Diva and Sheltie made an ideal pair, racing around the yard, catching petunias in their collars. Having a frisky companion gave Sheltie a new lease on life—at high speeds.

It was not only the dogs who were running in the fast lane. Stephen was busy with his own boutique advertising and communications agency, operating out of a huge, chic office/apartment in the city, which was located on the twenty-first floor of a privately owned hotel. Times were buoyant. His cell phone became an extension of his ear. The brilliance of it was that I could choose to leave the farm for days at a time and enjoy the advantages of city life while hired farm helpers took care of the chores and maintained the farm. It was like having a secret life. I had one wardrobe in the city and a distinctly different set of clothes for the country.

Everything about the city place was designer perfect—butterscotch, black, and red lacquer walls set off startling artwork and Oriental screens. Everything about the farm was a work in progress and a labor of love. Stephen's urban designer came out to the farm to see what there was to be done. There was plenty. I felt woefully inadequate, having devoted my energies to improving the land rather than worrying about window treatments. When the barn was being built and additions made to it, I clung to the advice of a wise farmer who told me to make it a space where I wanted to be and then the sheep would be well cared for. So the barn had a little picture gallery and a place where I could pull up a bale of straw and have a cup of tea. In the house, I painted walls basic white and created comfortable places to read books and write.

My farm helpers were handy at building sheep feeders, and now they were called upon to measure cabinetry and prepare the kitchen counter for a granite countertop. A husband-and-wife team, Jim and Cheryl, constantly baited each other while they worked, with Jim usually taking the worst of it. They could not imagine why anyone would paint a kitchen cornflower blue, but they did it. When two long chunks of granite fit perfectly in place around a new double sink they were astounded by the accuracy of their own measurements.

The remodeled kitchen was a blend of old and new. With its turned legs and three extra leaves, our old oak table could expand to seat twelve. New appliances abutted original wainscoting that I had painstakingly stripped of layers of putrid paint colors. In the corner there was a hutch for china—a whimsical piece in vibrant shades of orange, green, and yellow that was made about 150 years ago by a Ukrainian who had pioneered the West. Overhead, the lighting was all halogen. One room down, nine to go.

When I was in the city, I felt like a country girl all dressed up. Everyone I met wanted to know what it was like to be a shepherd. In the country, I was viewed as a city person who used too many big words and asked too many questions. Stephen needed me at his side both socially and professionally, but the duality of our living circumstances put a strain on the relationship. To top it off, Stephen bought a twenty-eight-foot cabin cruiser, which he intended to outfit for salmon fishing. I would need yet another wardrobe.

I was happiest at the farm with the dogs and the animals. Diva and Sheltie were both independent minded, and they needed structure, much as children do. If I had to be in the city, I at least wanted to bring Diva, but that meant Sheltie had to trust another human to look after her. When Cheryl and Jim came over to paint a barn or build a shed, she either ran and hid or barked at them constantly in the most irritating manner. I decided the only way to make things work out would be to have Sheltie bond with Cheryl.

A basically shy person who hid her self-consciousness behind incessant henpecking, it took some cajoling to talk Cheryl into handling Sheltie in a dog obedience class, while I worked with Diva. Classes were one evening weekly, in the Horse Palace arena at the nearby fairgrounds. We enrolled and set off on a learning curve.

Our instructor was a sinewy British woman who raised Rhodesian ridgebacks that appeared to outweigh her. As soon as I heard her accent, I thought of dog trainer Barbara Woodhouse, who believed there were no bad dogs, just inexperienced owners. Woodhouse could make an elephant sit when she gave her imperious "sit" command, always ending with a hard *t*. Dogs' ears always perked when she bellowed "walkies!" Like Woodhouse, our instructor addressed us by our dogs' names. I was "Mrs. Diva-dog" and Cheryl was "Mrs. Sheltie." I never did learn the names of the other humans in the class, but I knew what breed of dog they had.

There are many schools of obedience training. Some favor almost military-style domination of the dog, and some use treats to cajole the desired behavior. Our instructor used praise as a reward and insisted that it was our responsibility to ensure that the dog enjoyed training sessions in class and at home.

Diva was a natural. From the moment the instructor gave the command "left foot forward and all dogs heel," she was perfection. Sheltie, however, was spooked and did not like being anywhere near these other dogs, most especially not a chow chow who insisted on sniffing her. When Cheryl draped her leash as instructed and marched forward, Sheltie dug in her heels and refused to heel. Cheryl was mortified.

The instructor took over the leash. Kneeling in the cedar-scented wood shavings that lined the arena floor, she talked sweetly to Sheltie, telling her what a good dog she was. Then she stood beside the dog and said in her cheery voice, "Here we go girl, and heel." Off trotted Sheltie right at her side, looking up to make sure she was doing the right thing. When they stopped, Sheltie got more praise. The instructor returned leash and dog to Cheryl, with the instruction "and heel." Off they went, showing every sign of becoming a team.

Over the next six weeks, Mrs. Diva-dog and Mrs. Sheltie vied openly to see whose dog could be the top dog in the class. This culminated in the pie-plate incident in the fifth week. By this time our dogs had learned to sit and stay when we left them. The pie-plate test required all dogs and owners to form a big circle. There were ten of us in the group, with the biggest dog a Newfoundland and the smallest a Yorkshire terrier. The instructor spread nine aluminum pie plates in the center of the circle. We were to walk our dogs until the instructor said "stay and fetch." Then it was up to us to instruct our dogs to stay while we raced to the center of the ring to get a pie plate. Failure of a dog to stay resulted in disqualification, as did failure of a human to fetch a pie plate.

Cheryl and I had spent many hours with the dogs practicing long stays. We could leave them both on the front lawn and walk around the house without having them move. Praise worked wonders on Sheltie. When they were practicing walking in a figure eight, if Sheltie made a neat turn Cheryl heaped praise on her. Diva would give me a look, as if to say, "We can do better." There was a competitive thing going on, and it came to a head over the pie plates.

When the pie-plate game got down to four dog/handler teams battling over three pie plates, Cheryl's face glazed over. As soon as the "fetch" instruction was called, she did not even have to say a word. Sheltie stayed stock still. Buxom and thick in the hips, Cheryl bullied her way to grab a plate before the rest of us knew what was happening. She whooped. It continued in that maniacal way until only the two of us were left.

While the others looked on with amusement, we took the final turns of the ring around a lone pie plate. The instructor barely got out "fff" when Cheryl was off. I was coming from the opposite side and thought it best not to get in her way. She launched herself at the pie plate with the same forceful intent one sees when World Cup goalkeepers are defending a striker's ball. In the final slide across the arena floor Cheryl grasped the pie plate. She also discovered the reason the cedar shavings are layered up in the Horse Palace. Stained and weary, Cheryl had her victory. Sheltie praised her.

The bonding complete, I had no problem leaving Sheltie in good hands at the farm while Diva and I slipped into the city for a few days or spent a week on the boat stalking salmon.

Stephen had never taken to Diva the way that I had, largely because he was not around her. She fit in with the elegant office/apartment decor and enjoyed her "walkies" on the street and in the urban parkettes where grass was at a premium. However, on the boat, Stephen developed a tremendous respect for her. Diva could stay on the water for eight hours without begging for land. She had a cast iron bladder and—as Stephen could finally see—an enchanted soul.

Traveling did not suit Sheltie. She was happy to stay at the farm and rule her roost. Then one Christmas morning, she had a fit. Staggering, she fell to one side, with her legs paddling and teeth chattering. Although her eyes were open, there was no sign of Sheltie in them. It scared the biscuits out of me, although it only lasted a couple of minutes. All of the tests the vet performed came back normal, which is not unusual in dogs that have what is called idiopathic epilepsy. After that, Sheltie could go for months and months without an incident, but then—all of a sudden—an attack would strike her hard. There was nothing to do except comfort her and make sure she did not hurt herself.

We are convinced epilepsy finally took Sheltie. Like an ancient Inuit, she wandered out into a snowstorm, never to return. We never did find her body. It was so like her not to want to be a bother. That silky narrow head was always filled with quirky thoughts.

Only then did I notice that Diva was slowing down with age. She had never been without the company of one of her own kind. She needed another dog to prod her into play.

Stephen had never quite gotten over the loss of his beer-drinking buddy Mingus, or young Hank. He could not listen to the Jerry Jeff Walker song "Mr. Bojangles" without tearing up at the part about Bojangles dancing at southern minstrel shows, always traveling with his dog until the dog "up and died" after fifteen years. "After twenty years he still grieved."

Wearied of advertising, Stephen had returned to the farm, where we were both living as writers. I had written and syndicated two columns that grew into a series of award-winning books. Stephen's first book had been published, and it became a best seller. Almost twenty years had passed, and our lives were unfolding as we imagined they might.

It was time for us to have a puppy.

5

We Find Wally

Hank felled by a tree. Mingus terminated by a cement truck. All dogs come to an end, but those senseless accidents left Stephen heartsick. If we were getting another dog, he insisted that it be indestructible. Sturdy was the best I thought we could do. Then I had a dream, one that I have relived and retold many times, and there is nothing Freudian about it.

The dream is set in the lane of the farm. It is a long lane flanked by a cedar-rail fence, pine trees, and lilac bushes. There is a Zen quality to the lane that never fails to provide a calm when walking it. At dusk in the winter, white-tailed deer use it as a crossing, on their way to the forest where they yard up. In spring, we let loose the turtles we rescue from the roadways into a swampy wetland near the end of lane. In summer, we watch wild apples grow and ripen above the black-eyed Susans and bluebells and Queen Anne's lace that fringe the lane with a flourish. Autumn brings the slash of red sumac and the gilding of the tamarack trees. The lane is not paved, and a strip of dandelions and mixed weeds winds between the rough gravel where tires tread.

The dream takes place in the spring. I am standing in my office on the second story of the farmhouse, overlooking a small pasture with a couple of gnarled apple trees and, beyond that, the lane. Stephen is walking down the lane. I catch glimpses of him filtered through the purple haze of a lilac bush. He is not alone. I need to know who he is with.

Then I am standing at the top of the lane, looking for Stephen. I see him, and he has something beside him. I focus. It is a rhinoceros, not a full-blown African version that would fill the lane, rather a miniature version, about knee-high and moving with surprising grace considering its leather plating. Stephen tosses a soccer ball to the small beast, and it rises to head it with its horn. There is such beauty in the moment, and little rhino is the essence of "sturdy." It was a sign. The leaping rhino stuck with me.

A few days later I was coaxed into watching a season finale hockey game on television. The highlight of these quintessential Canadian games is a between-periods commentary session called Coach's Corner featuring bombastic hockey guru and former Boston Bruins coach Don Cherry. Noted for his taste in wildly patterned suit jackets and unrestrained opinions, Mr. Cherry has only to say, "Listen up, kids," and generations of hockey fans hang on his every word. Aside from his personal charisma, Don Cherry has always been associated with a constant companion—a white bull terrier named Blue.

While the Coach's Corner theme music played, images of Blue crouching, barking, and running filled the screen. The muscular dog had the eyes of a rhinoceros and a Roman nose that could carry a horn. The appearance was unique. I had found our dog.

It was not just looks and dreams that attracted me to the bull terrier. I remembered Bodger from the Sheila Burnford novel, *The Incredible Journey*, in which two family dogs and a Siamese cat go through extreme travails to be reunited with their family. The book is a children's classic that translated well into film. A person could not be human whose throat did not catch with emotion when aged Bodger the bull terrier emerged from the woods and dragged himself across a meadow toward the Hunter family in the 1963 Disney film.

I had also done some homework researching bull terriers years earlier, but I had filed it in a recess of my memory reserved for unpleasantries. It concerned a black blotch on the whole notion that country life is idyllic and the rural community is kinder and gentler than that of urban cribs.

A few concessions away from my farm, a report of two dogs running at large was reported to the township office. The "dog catcher," as he was known before the term "animal control officer" was coined, visited the owner and told him to keep the dogs from straying and get them licenses within a week. This was a new dog catcher, one who came to the job with little experience and no training. He did, however, know about the dog licensing requirement, and when he discovered that the owner in question had not complied with his arbitrary, seven-day deadline, he decided to wield the power vested in him.

In the company of the road superintendent, the dog catcher attended the property. The owner was at work, and the two dogs were chained in the yard. The large German shepherd, Max, and the easily excited bull terrier, Dylan, began barking at the strangers. The dog catcher decided to take it upon himself to teach the owner a lesson. He later said that he intended to impound the dogs, but without any training he was unable to wrangle the tethered dogs into his pickup truck. Flummoxed, he went back to the truck, where the road superintendent stood watching. Drawing out his .22 caliber rifle, the dog catcher shot Max and Dylan dead.

There was a trial. Despite his protestations about not having any training, the dog catcher was convicted of unlawfully killing two dogs. The penalty was a slap on the wrist. There were probably grounds for a civil lawsuit against both the dog catcher and the township. Instead, the owner chose to move away. In the slim file of newspaper clippings that

I kept on the case, I found some dog magazine articles I had clipped about bull terriers. They were described as jaunty characters, keen and intelligent. Originally bred in England for fighting and baiting bulls, they had evolved into a gentleman's companion animal, referred to as the "white cavalier." I thought of Dylan, stilled in the yard of his own home, and resolved that I would have one of him.

Bull terriers have been called "the smallmouth bass of the dog world," and that was a good enough recommendation for Stephen. We would have a Budweiser dog, like Spuds MacKenzie, the infamous "party animal" who brightened so many television commercials in the late 1980s. Like General George S. Patton's scrappy World War II bull terrier, Willie, our dog would go everywhere with us. Our dog would be smart and friendly, like Patsy Ann, the stone-deaf, dockside bull terrier who was designated as the Official Greeter of Juneau, Alaska, in 1934. Rex, humorist James Thurber's battered bull terrier, would fetch a piano if one was tossed—and so would ours. In the tradition of romantic novelist and poet Sir Walter Scott's cherished bull terrier, Camp, ours would be "possessed of a great turn for gaiety and drollery." As with everything, once a decision had been made, Stephen wanted it to become a reality immediately.

It can be difficult to find a responsible breeder of bull terriers who is willing to part with a puppy. Many have waiting lists, and if you are after a particular gender in a specific color, you may have to wait for years. Like the experience of acquiring Hank, the bullmastiff, bull terrier breeder interviews can be more like the Spanish Inquisition than polite inquiry. I simply stumbled on a breeder who had a listing in a dog magazine, and she just happened to have a litter. Her kennel was an hour away, and she had five puppies that were four weeks old. The females were spoken for, but we could take a look and talk about the dogs. We went to see them that afternoon.

At the front door of a low-slung bungalow, we were greeted by a red-and-white dog that nosed our knees. Having never seen a bull terrier in the flesh, I slipped to the floor, getting up close and personal with the stocky bitch, who I learned was the grandmother of the puppies. She crawled all over me with enthusiasm. After that, moving into the family room, where the puppies were, was difficult and I nearly tripped over "Granny" a couple of times.

"That's what they are like," said the breeder. "Always under your feet. They just want to be with you all the time."

The puppies were in a large box lined with paper. Daisy, their mint white mother, lay at one end of the box where the puppies swarmed her nipples. They fixed themselves to those swollen pink faucets of life and sucked greedily, pulling for all they were worth. If one slipped off, another took over. Puppies crowded on one another in a jumble of white and brown, all paws paddling. They had no manners whatsoever and their grunting made the temper of the dining experience all the more medieval and lusty.

When they were finished, or rather when their mother decided they were finished, the breeder took Daisy to an enclosed patio, where she could lay in the sun without having nipple-nipping monkeys scaling her. We finally had a chance to look at the puppies. Eating had exhausted them. Like newly hatched chicks, the tubby pups tottered around the pen until they came to a stop, eyelids drooping, and then they tipped over fast asleep, sometimes rolling on their backs before lying perfectly still.

We observed the entire process in silent reverie. When the breeder returned, she began a light banter, describing the puppies' routine and the stage they were at. Shortly they would be weaned because their teeth were becoming too sharp to continue nursing with such vigor. It would be a month before they could leave. Hearing us, the puppies squirmed awake, yawning and twisting.

All three of the females were white with different touches of color to their faces—one had a black eye patch, one had ears trimmed in red, and the smallest looked to have a brown eyebrow etched over her left eye. The males were colored. One was dark brown, almost black, with bold white trim. Then there was a squat fellow wearing a brindle coat striped with orange. A white blaze that started in the ruff around his neck extended to his muzzle and up between his eyes, where it stopped in two devilish points at the top of his head. His black nose was framed in a ragged heart, and a perfect black dot centered his chin.

The brindle puppy lifted himself toward our voices. He stood his ground firmly on four white paws. Hauling back on his haunches, he gave a flirtatious yip. Four siblings jumped him, and the pen turned into a writhing pile of rounded tummies, waving paws, and gnawing jaws. The breeder encouraged us to interact with the puppies. Our hands in the pen turned them away from one another to focus on these new toys. Stephen beckoned the tiger-striped boy and he ran over as fast as a puppy can run, taking a header into the wall and performing a back flip. They were all wonderful puppies, but this was "the one."

Taking turns holding the puppy helped the breeder interview to pass painlessly. His sire was English, and his dam came from a long line of Canadian and American champions. Politely, we leafed through many pictures of his relatives posing with various trophies and dog show judges who tended to look like trees. All the while, we were noting little things, like the short dash of white on the right side of the puppy's back and the pink skin with Dalmatian-type polka dots that showed through the fine, white hair on his belly. By the time our boy went back into the pen, we had committed our lives and our checkbook to him.

I rode home with the scent of the puppy lingering. He was emblazoned in memory. Sturdy. He looked quite sturdy.

6

The Homecoming

We spent the following four weeks getting ready for the dog. The breeder provided us with lots of information, including an article by someone with the improbable name of Winkie Mackay-Smith, who suggested that young bull terriers are "almost indistinguishable from a three-year-old child in a dog suit."

I was to discover that Winkie was on to something.

We installed childproof gates that were supposed to keep the puppy in the kitchen area while we were housebreaking him. The kitchen cabinets were checked to insure that they closed tightly and could not be popped open by an inquiring puppy nose. There were already chew marks from previous puppies on a couple of wooden captain's chairs. I could live with a few more.

We bought a big plastic dog crate to be his den and lined it with a cushion decorated with dog bones. Diva assumed it was hers and promptly settled in. This could get tricky. Her own original crate, a much smaller model, was now in service in the chicken pen, where it had become a place of comfort to lay eggs. It was not about to return to the house. We got Diva a matching crate with a different cushion. The kitchen was beginning to look like a kennel.

Buying things for a new puppy is like shopping for a baby. We found an impossibly small collar decorated with paw prints and a slim long leash to match. New brushes, new nail clippers, and new bowls for all dogs were ordered. Diva never bothered with toys, largely because Sheltie would steal and hide them. Now she discovered the joy of bouncing and rolling things as I stocked a wicker basket with hard rubber Kong toys. I could not resist adding a rubber alligator and a blue teddy bear that squeaked when squeezed.

Naming the puppy was the subject of much debate. "Tyson" was in the running for a while, but former heavyweight boxing champion Mike Tyson's ear-biting incident involving Evander Holyfield was far too fresh in memory. We decided to avoid tough-guy names, since breeds with the word *bull* in them were already getting enough of a bad rap. Our puppy was no gangster, and he would not be wearing a studded collar more befitting a Roman dog of war.

We thought about "Snoopy," but we did not want our dog to be confused with a beagle, even though it was said that cartoonist Charles Schulz modeled Charlie Brown's dog on a white bull terrier puppy owned by his gardener and a black-and-white mutt he had as a child. If you look at Snoopy, it really does make sense that he is not much of a beagle. He is pure white with black ears that flop, like a bull terrier pup's. Snoopy's round muzzle, which arcs under small black eyes, is hardly the straight and square-cut version found on a beagle. In fact, a Roman nose on a beagle is considered a conformation fault. Good grief, Schulz even allowed Snoopy to decry his hound origins in a December 1960 strip in which Snoopy declared: "I ain't no stupid beagle." However, the mythology of Snoopy as a beagle became enshrined, both in the comic strip and in the public consciousness.

Our dog needed a name that was friendly and confident, as well as a name that would have a special meaning to us. As a young man, Stephen was a student of poetry and had his first poem published when he was eighteen in an American journal. He soon discovered that tall, dark-haired poets with tortured pentameters attracted girls, girls, girls but failed to earn a living. Still, his extensive collection of poetry reflected his continuing interest. Could we name the puppy "Eliot," after T.S.? No, that did not sound like the kind of name a farm dog would have. I liked "Whitman," but it struck me as a name better suited to an Airedale or a schnauzer. "Longfellow" was definitely dachshund material. "Byron" had bluster. "Ginsberg" was too long. "Larkin" and "Lowell" did not sound like names for a dog. Stephen knew Leonard Cohen and had written about him, so "Lenny" was stricken from the list. I remembered lines from one of Stephen's favorite poems, "The Snow Man," by Wallace Stevens.

> One must have a mind of winter
> To regard the frost and the boughs
> Of the pine-trees crusted with snow.

Stevens was an enigma, a man who led two distinctly different lives—one as a Pulitzer Prize–winning poet and another as an accomplished corporate insurance lawyer and vice chairman of the Hartford Accident and Indemnity Company. There was a story Stephen liked to tell about the disparate crowd that gathered for Stevens's funeral in 1955. Many were from the business community, but others were writers and poets. At a lull in the service, one of the men in a suit, overhearing a comment from his Bohemian seatmate, blurted out in surprise, "Wally, a poet? You're kidding."

Wallace Stevens once observed that "the purpose of poetry is to contribute to man's happiness." I expect the same thing could be said about dogs. On his registration papers, our dog would be named after the poet, with his breeder's kennel name followed by "Wallace Stevens." Lovingly, we called him Wally.

The momentous day came to pick up the puppy. We took Diva with us, this being a "family" event. I had a blanket, a pillow, toys, treats, and even ice cubes, in case the puppy was thirsty on the road.

The Wally we had last seen could have fit into a baseball cap. In a month he had grown to top-hat size. The puppy pen looked much smaller now, and eager puppies pressed against its sides, barking a greeting. They were a mass of motion, trouncing one another, pulling on ears and tails. We called "Wally," and his brindle shoulders turned our way, all the while maintaining pressure on the white sister he seemed intent on suffocating Sumo-wrestler style. At four weeks, Wally fit into the palm of Stephen's large hand like a Beanie Baby; but holding him now demanded a two-handed effort. We slipped on his collar, and he began to look like the actual precursor of a dog.

The breeder was fussy, and I understood her reluctance to part with any one of the gems in the pen. We sat on the sofa and received our final instructions. Wally was to have goat's milk every day, and yogurt mixed with baby food or dog kibble. He liked bananas.

We knew the breeder had concerns about our bringing the puppy into a household where another dog had held sway for such a long time. All that changed when she met Diva and I put her through some of her obedience paces. Diva sniffed the puppy at her paws. Wally licked her face. When he made a move to see if Diva was packing any milk in her slim underbelly, he was promptly corrected. They would work things out. We left the breeder's with a jug of goat's milk, a jar of chicken-and-rice baby food, and instructions to call with any questions.

During the ride home, I held Wally, cradling him on my shoulder until he had cleaned my ears thoroughly. He tried looking out the window, but the specter of an unfamiliar landscape passing so quickly made his head bobble. On the floor, at my feet, he nestled in the cushion and fell asleep for about five minutes before jerking awake suddenly when we came to a stop sign. Then he climbed my leg, scaling his way to my lap. I breathed in his puppy breath, and Wally started to hiccup. Hic, pause, Hic, pause. He was in no distress, but I was.

"What's the matter? What's he doing?" asked Stephen as he pulled over to the side of the road.

Then came the inevitable accusation. "What have you done to him?"

I was wondering the same thing myself. Stephen reached for the puppy, whose hind leg was twitching in perfect spasm with each hiccup. I tried giving Wally an ice cube to chew, and his head tilted sideways in that way dogs have when asking, "Are you nuts?" He spit the ice cube down the front of Stephen's shirt, and I was glad we were out of traffic, because Wally was not the only creature squirming in the front seat.

We put Wally back on the floor cushion and hoped he would fall asleep and forget about hiccupping, but he found the squeaky teddy bear toy and proceeded to chew on it, with hiccups providing a backbeat to the high-pitched squawks coming from the bear. When that stopped, when there was only the sound of puppy hiccups, I grabbed the bear and discovered that Wally had disemboweled it and was in the process of savoring its voice box before swallowing it. I grabbed the puppy and jammed my fingers in his mouth to retrieve the thumb-tip-size squeeze box that Wally had decommissioned.

We had only had the puppy for half an hour, and he had developed a hiccup tic, committed to a lifetime of property damage, and tried to kill himself. The rest of the trip home was uneventful. Hard to imagine, but a puppy can snore and hiccup at the same time.

As soon as Wally was placed on his own front lawn, the hiccupping stopped. Perhaps he was intimidated by the Foghorn Leghorn of a rooster who strutted up to inspect this new brown patch in the grass and let out a crow that could crack an egg. Wally went down on his haunches and looked up in awe. Then he levitated about a foot off the ground like a cartoon Tasmanian devil. He did a few twirls and took off at full speed—racing around the yard, shaving his turns closely around the legs of lawn chairs and decorative flowerpots. Falling in front of the imperious rooster, he rolled on his back, punching his paws at the sky.

Inside the house, Wally had to poke his nose into every nook and cranny of the kitchen. It was a good thing I had virtually sterilized the kitchen floor, since everything his nose investigated was also checked for edibility.

The mind of a bull terrier works in simple ways and has certain rules, the primary one being: "If it isn't fun, it isn't worth doing." Going in his crate and lying down was not fun for Wally. Going in his crate and bouncing off the walls in circles until his cushion looked like a French twist was fun. Once he finished dominating his crate, he moved on to rearrange Diva's. Simple.

World domination was a concept that appealed to Wally from an early age. In his world, if a toy went under a chair, the solution was to move the chair, forcibly, with his whole body if necessary. It did not matter who was sitting in the chair.

He was respectful of certain things, such as his food. When his bowl was placed on the floor he approached it almost shyly, like a nervous suitor, stepping forward on the balls of his feet. The first taste was tentative—a lover's kiss. After that, he took no prisoners. Wally did not just eat his food; he wore it on his nose and on his paws. Like a Dickensian orphan, "food, glorious food" became his all-consuming rallying cry.

Other puppies I have had cried at night for the first few days after leaving their pack. When I closed the door of Wally's crate, there was not a whimper, not even a sigh. It was as though he had been shot out of a cannon into a new dimension and had no past to pine for.

Wally was glad to be home.

7

House Rules

do not know how people with jobs manage raising puppies. Not that writing is not a job—it simply allows the dog to be with you in the comfort of a home that is also an office.

Housebreaking is the first order of the day with a new puppy. When I was growing up there was a cruel school of thought that recommended mistakes be punished by rubbing a pup's nose in "it," or hitting its nose with a rolled-up newspaper and yelling. No one would think of doing that to a baby, so it never made sense to me to do it to a puppy. My brother, my sister, and all of the babies I have been around were toilet trained through praise and good timing. The same premise would apply to Wally.

Puppies learn from their mothers that they are not to soil their den, but anywhere outside of that sacred ground is fair game. The trick is to be there when the puppy needs release and to praise the desired behavior so effusively that the puppy thinks it has reinvented the bone. It is a natural bonding experience in which the owner observes the puppy acutely for that whine or wiggle or sniffing around that signals an impending elimination event. It is also easier said than done.

For the first week, I was up with Wally every few hours during the night, checking to see if he had business to attend to. Shepherds are used to keeping these sorts of hours because during lambing season the ewes have to be monitored in case they need the helping hand of a midwife. I did not mind. It was early autumn, the time when the harvest moon hangs in the sky like a pendulous pumpkin, and a fine time for walking the dewy night grass with a puppy. Usually, the sound of my feet on the steps woke Wally before I could open his crate. When he got out, no matter how close to bursting, he would first dash to his toy box and grab his squeaky rubber alligator to carry outside. I felt fortunate to live in the country, where I did not have to worry about disturbing sleeping neighbors while my puppy piddled and made his alligator squeak.

Like all puppies, if Wally's eyes were open, he was up to something. During the day, he was underfoot. If he fell asleep for any length of time, we watched for the moment he awoke so that he could be taken outside. Whoever was closest said "outies," plucking Wally up and scooting him across the front porch so he could touch a little green. He was surprisingly modest about moving his bowels in front of us and preferred that we at least turn away. Who knows why some dogs develop such privacy concerns? Diva certainly had none. I still recall with horror the sunny day she chose to make a walloping deposit perilously close to the edge of a friend's swimming pool while an entire terrace of luncheon guests looked on.

At least Wally provided us with a signal when we were to avert our eyes. Prior to a bowel movement, his anus puckers and pushes before anything happens. We took to calling this portent of things to come "Winky Bum." Once observed, Wally sniffs, circles, and gets down to business, allowing one plenty of time to ready the disposal bag.

Wake, eliminate, eat, eliminate, play, sleep, became a regular Wally pattern. Soon I was able to sleep from the eleven o'clock news to the wake-up six o'clock news. The crate door could stay open all night without any accidents indoors, but we were not in the clear yet.

Somewhat like a hound, bull terriers explore the world with their snout, not so much for scent as for poking and knocking things about. If said snout happens to come upon something that might fit into a bull terrier's mouth, chances are it will be sampled and swallowed. Puppies are particularly prone to Hoovering up anything they come across, but I know of bull terriers well into middle age who have eaten everything from rocks to baseballs, resulting in costly, life-saving surgery. Some dogs become serial abusers, enduring repeated surgeries. As a result, such stem-to-stern incisions are referred to as "zippers."

When Wally was allowed into the family room or into an office space he was scrupulously monitored. I wanted to reserve the word *no* for serious behavioral issues such as food theft and cat assault, so when the inquisitive puppy tried to gnaw a book on a low shelf in the library or pull on a doorstop, I used a loud and irritated "uh-oh" to draw his attention to the misdemeanor. Cords and plugs were "uh-oh, danger." Wally came to learn that if he heard those words and stopped what he was doing, he would get a wonderful round of praise and play from the human who gave the command.

Still, there was no stopping him sneaking things past even the most watchful eye. I had a plastic bottle in the barn that was fitted with a red rubber "nipple." I used it to feed milk formula to orphan lambs. Wally must have jumped four feet in the air to rip it off of the bottle while my back was turned. Luckily, it showed up in his stool. That was the beginning of my long career as "The Oracle of What Comes Out."

Surprising and embarrassing things pass through dogs. I have a friend who recounted—in excruciating detail—the grief he suffered when a missing formal dress sock presented its toe dangling from the end of his Irish setter's alimentary canal. The dog began fretting, and the owner resolved to gently remove the sock, which was made out of a nylon material that had considerable stretch to it. Only after he had retrieved and bagged the sock did he realize that his ministration had been within view of every busybody in the neighborhood. The same poor setter was also prone to ingesting his mistress's panties and proved adept at unhinging all manner of laundry hamper. Resigned, the woman took to buying cheap, flimsy undergarments that she hoped would slide through said setter without incident. When the dog finally required surgery to resolve its gastronomic misadventures, a brassiere and a pair of panty hose were found amid assorted socks and underwear.

String, yarn, rubber bands, and dental floss are easy for dogs to swallow. All it takes is one wrong twist or turn in the intestinal system and a dog can be in real trouble. Zinc, which is found in everything from pennies to police badges, can also trigger dreadful things like hemolytic anemia, in which the red blood cells are destroyed. Ask any vet and you will hear horrific and icky stories of items retrieved from dog guts. Dentures, hearing aids, diamond rings, condoms, and television remote controls have clogged canine intestines. A survey of employee excuses for tardiness once revealed that blaming the dog was second only to blaming children. Most excuses were lame fabrications, but when an employee said they were late because the dog ate their car keys, all too often it was true.

Nothing can be left lying around for dogs to inhale. A friend's daughter ran screaming into her house when the family Bouvier excreted the head of a Barbie doll. Another friend recovered a missing watch, still ticking. I prefer to believe that the rumor about the prosthetic eyeball is an urban myth.

Diva set a good example for Wally to follow. Anywhere she went, he had to go. The older dog tolerated puppy roughhousing, but she put Wally in his place when he went too far. His favorite thing was to slide underneath her belly and use her as a tent while chewing on her forelegs.

Actually, Wally chewed on anything he could get his mouth around but could not swallow. He applied his sharp puppy teeth with the fury of a starved piranha. More than one garden hose became a sprinkler, and the tire on the wheelbarrow was constantly flat. He nosed open closets and found a couple of my historic high heels to whittle into toothpicks. A pair of my reading glasses left on a coffee table came to his attention. He was mouthing them lightly when I saw him. Just as I cried out "drop it," his jaw closed slowly, carving a perfect puppy-tooth hole in the prescription lens. His face was a study in innocence.

Wally's destruction was nowhere near as extensive as tales I have heard about bull terriers who are truly dedicated engineers of mayhem. There are bull terrier owners who regularly lose screen doors because the dogs simply fly through them. Some dogs like jumping on beds and doing bank shots off the headboard. Vehicles are often prime targets. I know people who have had every seat belt in an eight-seat van rendered to ribbons. Empty child car seats have been decimated, and maps shredded. Grown men cry when Porsche gearshift knobs are found chewed and disengaged from their intended purpose. Any stuffed figure with a bobbing head left in the back window is a goner.

Wally also liked to chew me. If I had been a puppy, I would have chewed him right back to let him know how it feels. Instead, I let him know that it hurt with a loud "ouch," carefully extricating my finger, wrist, or ankle and replacing it with a hard rubber chew toy. I fed him his gooey mashed food from my fingertips so that he learned that taking things gently had its rewards. My reward came when he sprawled contentedly over my shoulder and burped in my ear.

I used every technique and every trick I could think of to make Wally's adjustment to our household an easy one. If he made a mistake, I took a rolled-up newspaper and whacked myself upside the head, chanting, "I wasn't watching Wally. I wasn't watching Wally." He required more effort than other puppies and dogs because there was an intensity about him that is indigenous to terriers and seems proportionate to the density of their skulls. Anytime I really wanted to draw his attention to a behavior that was problematic, all I had to do was ignore him. There is nothing that attracts the attention of a bull terrier more than being ignored.

Once he understood the house rules, we decided it was time for Wally to see more of the world.

8

"Puppy Coming Through"

t was the fall of 1997, and my fourth book had just been published. We were off to Ottawa, Ontario, Canada's capital, where I was to participate in a literary event at the National Library. Travel advertisements in the *New York Times* describe Ottawa as "a bit of London, with a dash of Paris." Like so many things Canadian, it is not quite confident enough to simply be itself. The place is packed with civil servants on swivel chairs, who administer the country while politicians bluster and play gadabout. As a shepherd, I had an innate understanding of Ottawa. It is the place where the whole country gets fleeced.

In those days we rode the earth in an all-black Ford Bronco. It had oversize tires that made getting in and out of it an exercise akin to mounting and dismounting a horse, particularly for a compact person such as myself. One dog or two, it did not make much difference, the Bronco was packed to the roof. We always travel with everything we imagine we might need—and more—including food in its own refrigerator.

Years earlier when Mingus was still with us, we went on an expedition to a remote northern fishing lake. It was just past dusk in the middle of nowhere when the Bronco skidded out of control on loose gravel and rolled over in a ditch, leaving us hanging from our seat belts like parachutists lodged in a tree. The windshield had shattered into thousands of tiny pieces that lay on the roof of the truck below us.

We did an upside-down inventory of body parts and determined that all of our dangling limbs were intact and moving. Neither of us felt any pain. I squirmed out of the seat belt and pried open the door. Stephen was able to find his Buck knife in his pocket and began cutting himself free.

Our thoughts flew to Mingus and we called out his name. Rustling and thumping sounds could be heard coming from the backseat. Once liberated, I used a key chain penlight to find the dog behind the front passenger seat on the roof-turned-floor, covered in his dog bed and assorted fishing rods. He had been dazed by a pair of flying portable stereo speakers, but otherwise he was fine. Lids had come off cartons full of food, and half a case of wine shattered. I had Mingus outside and was wrapping him in a king-size duvet to ward off shock when Stephen hauled himself through the truck door and came lurching toward me.

"I'm hurt, Marsh, I think I'm hurt bad," he groaned, dropping to his haunches and sitting back, as though mortally wounded. "You've got to look."

My heart sank. False inventory. Dark as it was, I managed to find a real flashlight.

"Oh God, it's my head. Look at my head. I think it's my brains."

When I shone the light on him, it was apparent that some of the contents of a cooler containing salads had landed on him. He was wearing Caesar-flavored rotini pasta salad on his head; brains allegedly undamaged.

The only passerby we saw for hours was a short-haul trucker headed north who stopped, determined we were all right, and sent a CB radio call for a tow truck. By midnight, the police arrived, too. They found us camped out with the sleeping dog, listening to our Walkmans, surrounded by tea-light candles. I had cobbled together some prosciutto with brie on a sliced baguette so that we did not starve. The feather pillows that we had thrown in as an afterthought proved very useful on rough rocks.

When the police shone their powerful lights on the truck interior so that we could find some fresh clothes and dog toys to take back to a motel until morning, they were astounded by the sheer volume of stuff we were taking on a five-day fishing trip. We had a variety of fishing rods and tackle that could be used to catch everything from a five-inch sunfish to a sixty-pound muskellunge. There were suitcases full of clothes ranging from long johns to shorts, because you never know how the weather might turn.

Stephen enjoys an occasional martini, so I had packed an appropriate glass and shaker. From the way the police officer held the martini glass you might have assumed it was loaded. Then they found the pièce de résistance—a shot glass.

"You people are planning to go into the wilderness and you bring a shot glass?" exclaimed the officer with a shake of his head.

Years later, the doorman at the Westin Hotel in Ottawa had the same expression on his face when we pulled up on that crisp November day with Wally and Diva in a packed Bronco. The doorman's name was Ivan, and he knew something unusual when he saw it. While the baggage trolleys were filled, he focused his attention on three-month-old Wally.

"This is fighting dog," he said, in a thick accent that conveyed his Baltic origins.

At the time, Wally was about as tall as a quart of milk at his shoulder, and his floppy brindle ears were just beginning to stand up like an adult bull terrier's. After a long car trip, I was more interested in a hot bath than an argument, but the dogs came first. Ivan's black eyes followed us as we walked Diva and Wally across the street to a strip of park that runs the entire length of a man-made canal that cuts through the city. Both dogs stretched their legs and strained their leashes as squirrels took to the trees, chittering their complaints.

"Will be very strong dog," Ivan said conspiratorially, as he held the door for us back at the hotel.

In my opinion, the best hotels accept pets and make accommodations for their needs and those of the owners without relegating them to threadbare rooms or closet-size spaces that rent for full price. The Westin rose to the occasion. We had a lovely suite on the eighteenth floor, with floor-to-ceiling windows overlooking the canal and cityscape. Both dogs went immediately to the window, looking outside into thin air. I wondered if they had any sense of what height is or how they got that high. Diva was an experienced elevator traveler, but that meant nothing in terms of understanding. Wally's first elevator ride passed uneventfully in Stephen's arms. The "little room that moves" was no problem for him, although I have seen some dogs panic when the doors start to close, and others that require a push on the rump to get them inside.

Wally explored the hotel room nose-first. He noticed everything that was different from his regular home, including floor-length drapes and a mirror that reflected his own image. He looked at himself and looked again, expressing only mild interest and far preferring to harass three-dimensional Diva. In the early evening, we took them for a long walk beside the canal before going to the National Library event. It did feel a bit like Paris, with red maple trees.

I do not mind going onstage and talking or reading to a crowd.

People who attend such events have made a decision to invest their time in the belief that they will be entertained and enlightened, so the author already has the advantage. All you really have to do is get the words out without being a bore. I like to make it a bit of a performance, and I try to have some fun. At least I know I can get the words out.

As a child I had a lisp. When I was six, my parents sent me off for elocution lessons taught by a tightly wound Englishwoman. After two years of pronouncing aloud the mediocre poetry of Walter de la Mare and endlessly exercising what I had been traumatized into thinking was a "sausage-meat of a tongue," I was presented to an examiner from London's Trinity College Department of Speech and Drama. He was a slim tweedy sort who looked like he had never been a child and probably disliked the experience intently. I was determined to win him over. In a crisp but lyric tone I recited Walter de la Mare's only slightly memorable "The Little Green Orchard." It describes a scenario in which a seemingly empty orchard gives the constant impression that it is inhabited by a presence other than the droning bees and the cawing blackbirds.

Someone is waiting and sitting there,
In the little green orchard,

The poem is downright creepy if you ask me. I know teachers who have used it in Halloween programs. Whatever, my examiner loved it, including the mouth-to-hand gesture I made when whispering and the touch of hand to ear when "listening." Then I set off into a reading from the chapter in Anna Sewell's horse-narrated *Black Beauty* in which aged and broken-down Beauty meets his even more broken-down old friend Ginger at a cart horse stable in London, far from the green pastures of their youth. It is a shameless scene in which Ginger wishes for death and apparently gets it. I played it to the hilt and almost cried myself. Later, I received a bronze medal for my efforts and was invited to perform at some sort of energetic elocution event. After that, no one could get me to sit down and shut up, and I was finally able to repeat the tongue twister involving "seashells by the seashore" five times with proper sibilance.

I had a rousing good time "performing" at the library, and we raced back home to see what the dogs had been up to.

Wally was snoring peacefully in his crate, while Diva kept a watchful ear for our footfall. Room service and a moonlit walk with the dogs ended a long day. The night doorman did not say a word about the dogs.

Early the next morning, I took the dogs out, fed them, and crawled back to bed. Wally was demanding again at eight-thirty, and Stephen agreed to take a turn. He pulled on his loose black sweatpants and a black leather, biker-style jacket, topped off with a trailing black scarf and a pair of Jean Paul Gaultier sunglasses that look like futuristic goggles. I smiled and told him to brush his hair before leaving.

Stephen knew something was up on the way down in the elevator. Men in business suits poured in until they were stacked like lumber. Wally was squeezed against Stephen's shoulder, licking any ear he could reach. In the lobby, corporate types were variously mingling, checking out of their rooms, or looking for their conference room. Some sort of government summit was taking place at the hotel. Security and bodyguards paced the lobby. Suddenly there was this guy in black with bed-head holding a fur piece on his chest and proclaiming, "Puppy coming through."

The suits parted in stunned but obedient disbelief, and Stephen ran the gamut as though he were scoring a Super Bowl touchdown. Ivan had the door open, and Stephen and Wally hit the pedestrian crossing to get to the park. When you have lived on a farm in splendid isolation for some time, it is easy to forget that a huge segment of the population "dress" for their job and move en masse at specific times of the day.

A shaken Stephen called me from beside the canal and asked me to join him and Wally for a walk until the lobby cleared and it felt safe to return.

Ivan was waiting for us.

"What is that dog?" he asked, and we told him Wally was a bull terrier, a dog originally bred in England.

"Yes, yes," he said, "is a fighting dog."

"No, no," we said. "He's a puppy who lives on a farm."

We let Ivan hold Wally in his very large arms. As usual, Wally began trying to scale his way toward Ivan's ears.

"See he is coming to eat me," said Ivan. His thick eyebrows moved like darting mice, and I thought he might be on to something.

"I tell you what you must do with this dog," Ivan said, tucking Wally under one arm and holding his finger under his chin. "Once a year—for no reason whatsoever—you must take this dog and beat it."

Without subtlety, Stephen took Wally into his arms.

"No, no. It's not a bad thing," Ivan said, quite seriously. "Just a dog like this needs to be beaten so he knows who is who."

It was apparent that changing Ivan's thought on this matter would be the equivalent of convincing a vegan to eat bacon. I did wonder what it would be like to flog Ivan, though. After checking out of the hotel, I took the dogs for one last tour of the park. "Ivan the Terrible"—as we had taken to calling him—held the truck door open for them. Diva leaped in gracefully, but Wally's paws barely reached the running board. I went to scoop him up, but I could not resist pausing as he relieved himself on Ivan's boot.

Wally the Wonder Dog had spoken.

9

Cats and Bales and Puppy Dog Tails

The gradual walk-up to winter on the farm involves all sorts of things, from putting up the storm windows to rolling up the garden hoses. Barn doors are checked to be sure they will stay closed against howling winds. Heat lamp bulbs are replaced over the water pump, and the cobwebs of summer are dusted down. I put the garden "to bed," leaving stalks of sunflowers with huge seed heads for the blue jays to finish off. In the dead of winter, they stand in stubborn bas-relief against the stripped forest background, snowbound sentinels of summer memories when they are most needed.

From the beginning, we knew that Wally loved anything round. He worshiped balls. Like the barn cats that hear the crack of an egg from great distances and come running to their food bowl, Wally's ears were attuned to the *pop* that accompanies the opening of a fresh tin of tennis balls.

Any orb that moved delighted Wally. He had a selection that included many soccer balls in various stages of deflation. Simply running with balls and pouncing on them was not enough for Wally. Instead, he played his own brand of soccer, working his paws to drive the ball forward and taking headers at balls tossed his way. Many a plumber or FedEx delivery person put their time clock on pause to watch Wally field his balls across the front-lawn pitch. Spectators were soon engaged in play, captives of a puppy version of Pelé. He chased balls endlessly, until they had to be removed.

All of his toys lived in a box well beyond his reach and off the floor. If a comprehensive dog safety survey was ever done, I expect that it would show that more people suffer serious injury from accidents involving dogs' toys than do from dog bites. A near slip on a slobber-sodden tennis ball or a well-chewed Nylabone is graphic warning of what could happen.

Round, rolling items in any medium attracted Wally. When a neighbor brought over a wagonload of big, round bales of hay, Wally was overwhelmed. He immediately tried to scale one and succeeded, clawing his way to the top like a lizard on a sand dune. In the pasture, lambs play King of the Mountain on the manure pile. Just like them, Wally posed, full of himself, atop the hay bale. To his delight, he discovered a dead snake that had been caught in the binder twine. He poked it and pulled it, tossing it into the air and stomping on it to make sure that any vestige of living snake was gone. Then he rolled on it for good measure, performing a shimmy-shake on his back while his legs pointed straight to the noonday sun.

Stephen and I pushed the twelve bales from the lane to an area close by, where they would be protected but accessible during the winter. In terms of exercise, such labor is the farming equivalent of bench-pressing five hundred pounds, although once the bale starts rolling it is only a matter of maintaining momentum to get past ruts and low patches. I was wearing a red-and-black-checked shirt, but Wally looked more the lumberjack. As we rolled the bales he balanced on top, moving forward when he could and backpedaling when the bale got moving too fast. He was a study in balance and concentration, paws constantly moving, as though squashing ants.

Tired puppies are happy puppies, and the exercise kept Wally entertained and out of harm's way. He was curious about everything on the farm and quite fearless. I walked him on a leash through the sheep pasture, where he showed more interest in what comes out of sheep than in the animals themselves. He approached a couple of ewes, but as soon as he got close they turned away or stomped their hooves at him.

The ram would have been another matter. When Mingus was a young dog, an old, hardheaded ram named Jedi took a run at him and battered him against the steel-sided barn. Mingus's left side was flattened for about a month until his youthful ribs sprang back.

I had to carry a length of two-by-four in the pasture when Jedi was controlling the flock. That ram was so daft he would charge a fence post and nearly knock himself out. Once Jedi caught a helpful neighbor who had bent over to pick something up. The ram head-butted him high in the air, depositing him in a murky barnyard stew. It all happened in that unstoppable slow motion that renders the observer helpless. The new ram was more personable, but I kept him penned until Wally sorted out his relationship with the sheep.

The horses stuck to themselves. Nothing about any dog we had ever appealed to them, and Wally was no exception. For his part, Wally liked to watch them eat. Their chewing mesmerized him, big round cheeks in motion. But when a mare blew out her nostrils, Wally danced backward. He only sniffed a grain trough once before taking some threatening horse lip. Ultimately, he kept his distance, which was a relief.

There were other creatures, however, that did capture Wally's attention, bringing out the natural terrier in him. Squirrels and chipmunks that were preparing for winter had to beware of the brindle creature watching their every move. They frustrated him with their speed and climbing ability. A chipmunk once retreated into a carefully stacked pile of lightweight straw bales. Burrowing through them, Wally caused a chain reaction as one tumbled after another, disassembling the whole lot.

The chipmunk was long gone when I found Wally sitting on the pile of straw, much of it loose and scattered, having slipped the binder twine. He was panting and pooped, but so happy that he rolled over and rocked on his back until he slid down the straw and landed contentedly on his rump.

Our old barn cat, Webster, had a fairly tight rein on the vermin population, although Wally would occasionally surprise a mouse in the long grass. I did not want him having anything to do with rats, but they do come in from the fields during winter to contaminate the grain supplies. At age eighteen, Webster was getting a bit long in the tooth, and I worried that he might not be up to an onslaught of rats that particular year.

Bull terriers are supposed to be good ratters. Aside from the natural instincts of terriers to go to ground after their prey, bull-and-terrier breeds during Victorian times were sometimes pitted against rats as a form of betting amusement after the British Parliament passed the Humane Act of 1835, which prohibited dogs from being used for "sport" in the baiting of bulls, bears, and other large animals.

Peculiar sorts of men called "toshers"—think Bill Sikes the murderer in Charles Dickens's novel *Oliver Twist* who had a bull terrier named Bull's Eye—haunted the fetid, disease-infested sewers of London to catch the rats required. One hundred rats were needed for each fight. Chronicles and books of the period say that a world record was held by a bull terrier named Jacko who killed sixty rats in less than three minutes in 1862. That must have been before the bull terrier evolved into a "gentleman's companion."

I considered getting another cat.

Groundhogs are another pestilence on a farm, percolating fields with their underground tunnels and sneaking into gardens to nip off broccoli plants and anything else that strikes their toothsome fancy. A stumble into a groundhog hole can break a horse's leg. I do not like the mangy critters, plain and simple, and have done everything possible to encourage them to populate fields other than my own.

Guns are also something I could do without, and I used to be downright afraid of them. However, if the difference between a joyous, galloping palomino horse and a dead one is a hole-digging, broccoli-stuffed groundhog, a sixteen-cent bullet affords me a clear path to righteous action. Stephen has made a hobby of groundhog hunting, and eliminating them was one of the reasons I took a course in firearm safety and hunter education.

Without knowing the difference between a shotgun and a rifle, Wally bagged his first groundhog when he was about three and a half months old. I was in the barn when he came around the side toward the door with it in his mouth. It was a big, fat hog ready for a winter of hibernation in its musty hole, so Wally had to sort of drag it, because they were of almost equal weight.

The look on Wally's face was one of caution. He had done something, he knew that for sure. He had done something, and it felt right to him, so his tail wagged in a slow circle. Now he had something to show for it, but he was not quite sure how I would respond. His ears twitched and his brow furrowed, until I told him it was okay and he could drop it.

All of the dogs on the farm, even delicate Diva, have had a go at groundhogs and other small animals, such as possums, muskrats, raccoons and—always with disastrous results—porcupines. Canines have a natural prey instinct, just as horses have a natural flight instinct. Both are unavoidable and both become the responsibility of the owner to control. In Wally's case, when he is off his own property, he is on a leash, because to his triangular eye far too many fluffy little dogs resemble groundhogs.

Wally was not on a leash one early winter day when we were loading groceries into the back of the truck and he decided to bolt out of the back and launch himself into the traffic of the supermarket's parking lot. Dogs try to commit suicide in the most unusual ways and without any recognizable motivation. Stephen managed to catch him in midair and prevent the escape by latching on to the only thing available— Wally's tail. It is a wonder that the scream that followed did not split the pavement. Dumbfounded, Stephen collected Wally in his arms, and I thought the two of them were going to crumble in a mutual wail.

We got Wally home and assessed his tail. It was there, but it was not wagging. Stephen had "stopped" him near the rump, and Wally's tail rose from there and then went limp. I held a bag of crushed ice to the area while Stephen called the vet. It was five minutes before closing time on a Friday evening. Yes, we could bring Wally in.

The town veterinarian who first saw Wally was a burly fellow with a thick black beard and a bald head that dogs loved to lick. His practice was limited because of asthma and allergies to dog and cat hair, but he just had to have a few small animals to look after when he was not otherwise employed by the government, ensuring the safety of the food chain by inspecting meat-handling facilities. He adored bull terriers and had always wanted one.

We had taken Wally for a checkup to this same vet the day after we first brought him home. He let the puppy polish the dome of his head and paw through his beard, laughing all the time and pausing now and then for some examination. A listen to Wally's heart had caused a worried look, followed by a long listen as we held our breath so hard we could feel our own heartbeats. He heard a murmur in Wally's walnut-size heart. It was a slight one, he said; further testing when he was older could grade it more accurately. Sometimes puppies grow out of them as they become dogs; more often they stay and can become worse.

We had an option to take Wally back to his breeder—maybe trade him for the other male puppy or ask for a refund. Neither of those options were possible. After fewer than forty-eight hours, we were in puppy thrall. Wally's vet understood perfectly. He shook his chin, to get Wally's paws out of his beard. "He's going to break your hearts one day, this one is," he said. "So enjoy him every day."

Now the end of Wally, literally, lay limply on the examining table. The swelling was not too bad, but it hurt when touched. Wally held still for a rudimentary X-ray. We waited, paced, and self-flagellated while Wally curled up in a blanket and tried to chew the head off of a stuffed Garfield toy.

The tail was not broken, but a couple of vertebrae were slightly misaligned, showing signs of soft-tissue damage. The solution was to take Wally home and try to keep him "quiet." With an impossible task at hand, we left the vet's office greatly relieved.

Two weeks later the tail was back to full wag. There was a small crook to it when he was tired, but only an experienced and guilt-riddled eye would ever see it. Wally's tail healed.

Stephen's tale was just beginning.

10

An Odd Duck Calls at Christmas

When Stephen decided to leave the well-paid advertising world to write a book, our small world shifted on its axis. Ultimately, he let go of the city apartment as rents soared, and the units failed to turn condo as we had anticipated. Suddenly I had some darn fine artwork and furniture to accommodate at the old homestead.

The big boat drifted away, too, but nothing can dim the memories of those who fish and catch the big ones. It was the natural paring down of an expansive and expensive lifestyle in order to facilitate a new beginning. I pretty much had to drag Stephen kicking and screaming back to the farm to convince him of this.

The farm hardly ever broke even. It was much more of a hobby than an enterprise. I did some regular radio broadcast work telling stories about farm life. For a while I even had a segment on public television in which I dressed up in overalls and wore pigtails and offered cornpone opinions on burning rural questions such as "Do sheep fall in love?" I was relaying stories about my life on the farm to friends in the city, and Stephen convinced me to adapt them into newspaper columns and syndicate them to small-town, weekly newspapers. Then a foundation asked me to write vivid and lively anecdotal history columns for weekly syndication. Between that and running the flock, I kept busy in two quintessentially non-lucrative fields: writing and farming. With Stephen's help I obtained book contracts for compilations of my columns. One of those books won a prestigious literary award for humor. At forty, I had a whole new career.

Like the magazine journalism Stephen had written earlier, his book was nonfiction. He had no idea the scope of the project or exactly where it would lead us when he focused on a series of newspaper articles about the winter of 1993 arrest of an alleged serial rapist/murderer in the Niagara Falls region. The accused, Paul Bernardo, was a young accountant with sandy hair and boyish good looks who lived in an affluent neighborhood with his young attractive wife, a local girl named Karla Homolka, whom he had only recently married.

What captured Stephen's attention then, and what would prove to be the hellish vortex to the story, was the question of what the wife was doing while her husband was allegedly off raping and pillaging. That was the essence of his proposal to several publishers. Within a week, he had a book deal. His instinct proved unerringly, even eerily, correct about the female specter in the case.

Shortly after her husband's arrest, Karla Homolka confessed her culpability in crimes ranging from sexual assault to kidnapping and murder. A plea bargain was hastily negotiated in return for her cooperation. Her trial took place on a singular steamy July day in a courthouse just minutes from the mist of the Falls. The judge barred American media from the courtroom, fearing that they could not be trusted to obey a publication ban designed to protect the fair trial rights of her husband. It only served to fan rumors. Everything about it—from the weather to the agreed statement of facts—was incendiary. In the end, three teenaged girls were dead at or near the hand of the impenetrably still blonde in the prisoners' docket.

Prosecutors presented Karla Homolka as another victim of her sexually sadistic husband, albeit a victim with some culpability. Psychiatrists codified her as a battered woman, suffering from post-traumatic stress disorder and then used that tenuous diagnosis to excuse her inexplicable, murderous behavior.

A controversial plea bargain saw an aloof Karla Homolka, convicted on just two counts of manslaughter, drawing a tawdry twelve-year sentence. Just before he brought down his gavel, the judge imposed a sweeping publication ban on all details of the crimes and her role in them.

A few months later, the *Washington Post* succeeded in breaking the publication ban, and some of the rumors were proved true. There were no questions to cloud the minds of the Bernardo jury. The couple had videotaped torturous hours of their crimes, which were then analyzed frame-by-frame by overly zealous prosecutors. Though the jurors could see and hear the videotapes, the press and those in the gallery were restricted by court order to audio only.

When Bernardo's trial ended in an obvious verdict of guilty, Stephen moved to the farm to write full-time. It was a daunting task, not only because of the heinous nature of the crimes, but also because of his "inside" knowledge of the police bungling and political wrangling that had been deliberately and cunningly hidden from public view.

I attended many of the trial proceedings with Stephen, and together we played as a sort of Mutt and Jeff with everyone, from lawyers to police officers, prosecutors to cemetery directors—the whole cabal, including members of the murderers' wedding party. In the process, Stephen accumulated a large archive, encompassing the entire background of the case, police reports, witness statements, psychiatric evaluations, crime scene photos, and police audiotapes and videotapes of interviews with the wife, along with a hodgepodge of home videos, school records, and minutiae such as lists of books borrowed from the library.

We lived close to the edge during those months Stephen spent piecing together this dark story. There were times when I took my sheep health and lambing records to the barn and studied them closely, determining which of the least productive and oldest ewes I should send to the market so that we could pay the bills. As I watched Stephen's book unfold, there was no question in my mind that every sacrifice was worth it.

The book, *Invisible Darkness*, did well. It made best-seller lists and generated considerable controversy about the "deal with the devil," which would see the sinister wife set free in at most a dozen years. A national television network's investigative unit made a documentary based on the book and Stephen's archival material. It won awards and showed in an endless loop on *Court TV*.

That documentary reaired late in November 1997, after we had returned from our trip to Ottawa with Wally and Diva. It attracted the attention of a number of viewers who had missed it the first time, including a female columnist for a tabloid newspaper. Shortly afterward, another writer who had novelized a book about the case wrote an article in which she commended Stephen for his work but dared to suggest that he had made things up.

Stephen is nothing if not proud of the effort he put into that book. He was not about to let some literary poseur call him a fabricator. He wrote a letter, detailing exactly where he had obtained the facts in his book—the volumes of police material, the private psychiatric notes, the police videos—the jackpot that any first-rate investigator strives for. It was published.

In early December, the tabloid columnist called Stephen, introducing herself as a friend of an individual we hold in high regard. She said she just wanted to chat and was interested in the archive because she had been trying to get some of the video that had aired on television and had been "having no luck." She used her nickel-and-dime wiles, complimenting Stephen on the book that she later admitted to police she had not even read.

I imagine that Wally was curled at his feet while they spoke. She wanted to come to the farm to see what she could see of the archive. Stephen demurred.

Having once been a member of the press, I have always thought that the best counsel I could give anyone is "don't talk to them." I know how a quote can be skewed. I know how an hour-long interview can boil down into one garbled paragraph. I know that the more complex the issue, the more dumbed-down it can become in the media. I know that all media are not created equal.

Stephen's attitude has been the opposite. From the beginning, he embraced the press and cooperated with them, while maintaining his position as the symbolic Mennonite in the pack—separate and distinct, always dressed in black, and holding his cards close to his chest.

This particular caller was an odd duck to both of us. I did not like it, and I did not want someone whose drivel I considered birdcage liner visiting my home. Perhaps pining for someone to talk to about the case who did not know every detail as intimately as I did, or perhaps just toying with a notion, Stephen called the columnist during the week before Christmas and offered to let her see some of the material if her interest was in spotlighting the scandalous deal that had been made with a murderess. The columnist was vacationing in Mexico over Christmas, but she would be in touch later. That was fine with me.

The holidays have always been a time of renewal on the farm. No need to rush around, just gradually get things done. Twenty or so acres of pine and spruce trees offered prime Christmas tree hunting grounds. Thousands of them were planted as seedlings before we bought the place, and over a couple of decades they grew thick and tall despite the annual pilgrimage of local Christmas tree cutters. We watched families grow over years of tree cutting. Toddlers matured into teenagers ready to try their hand with the ax. There were even a few teenagers who showed up years later with toddlers of their own tucked into sleighs to make the trek into the bush.

I also found a regular complement of tree thieves near the fence line and surprised them by galloping through the forest on Lady. If I had been Roy Rogers, I would have had my six-guns blazing. Instead, it was just me, wearing a scalp-hugging toque and puffy down jacket. Invariably, the embarrassed interlopers offered to pay. One silly fellow shimmied up a thirty-foot tree in an effort to cut off the top five feet. It is hard to hide in a tree when you are wearing an orange hunting jacket.

Over the years, the trees finally grew too tall for most households, but we always brought one in that would scrape the fifteen-foot ceiling of the family room. Just to get the tree in the house, windows had to be removed and sheer force invoked to push it inside. To us, it was not really a Christmas tree unless the star at the top slipped sideways. Now we had to accomplish the feat with Wally bouncing at our feet.

We had the tree up and secured it with fifty-pound-test clear fishing line. As usual, there was more tree than there was space in the room. The fresh pine scent spread through the house. We draped lights and hung a few baubles at the top of the tree before standing it upright to get a jump start on the job of tree trimming. When the lights were lit, Wally's eyes widened, and he leaned back into the sofa, looking up, way up.

The cartons full of decorations we had accumulated over the years came out, and I perched on the ladder, filling thin spots in the tree with large ornaments and making sure the treasured ones passed down through generations had special places. There were so many round and shiny things that Wally's face glazed over. While Mingus considered it his "manly" duty to try to christen the Christmas tree, Wally kept a respectful distance. Every morning he rushed to the room to see if it was still there. In the evenings, he took to lying underneath an outward stretched branch, looking up at the lights and the baubles. I expect that is as close to hallucinating as a dog can get.

Without much effort, the farm takes on the spirit of the season, even in the fields. Lambs that are born in May get their start in December. To tell whether or not a ewe has been bred, I put a harness that holds a crayon on the ram at the center of his chest. When a ewe is bred, he leaves his mark, literally. Ewes have a two-week cycle, so the color of the crayon is changed every fourteen days. By Christmas, the ewes are decorated with red or green rumps. It really looks quite cheery. If Martha Stewart ever finds out about this, she will probably get a flock of sheep.

Well fed and warmed by fine wine, we enjoyed the season with friends and family. Wally served as entertainment, plowing through snowdrifts and wearing them indoors. It was impossible to build a snowman around a dog that was hell-bent on running head-on into anything that was cold, white, round, and rolling.

Times were easy, and I relaxed into enjoying a new dimension in my relationship with Stephen. We laughed more together. We accepted more. My writing had found a rhythm. Stephen had proven himself. Life had not been boring.

Little did we know how interesting—and dangerous—it would become.

11

A Mind of Winter

The only New Year's resolution I made for 1998 was to take Wally to puppy school. He was going to be a powerful dog and had already shown himself to be a gamesman extraordinaire. I wanted to have more of a handle on him than that crooked tail.

In some ways, Wally was self-schooling, simply by copying everything that Diva did. First thing in the morning, they went outside together and squatted side by side. If Diva kicked backward with her hind legs, Wally tried to as well, although sometimes he just dug his feet in, failing to execute the backward thrust and looking somewhat constipated. Diva would often give herself a little shake in the snow. Wally gave a shake so rousing that when it ended, his ears hummed like tuning forks, but his tail stood stock-still. If I asked Diva to sit, Wally sat. When I called her to come, he came.

Wally needed to learn for himself, from me. Stephen was hopelessly bonded to Wally, and they were more equals than anything. When they stared deeply into each other's eyes in the equivalent of a *Star Trek*

"Vulcan mind-meld," Wally could probably have convinced Stephen to roll on his back and bark for cookies.

There was an old fellow, Bill Brodsky, who had bull terriers all his life.

"I was twelve before I realized he wasn't my brother," Bill said of his first dog. Wally occupied an equally anthropomorphic role for Stephen.

I strove for some control, respect, and decorum. This is not something easily achieved when dealing with a young dog who finds a cookie box in a cupboard, eats every last cookie, and then wears the cookie box on his head, bumping into things until he finds safety by standing in his water bowl.

The first thing I did in the New Year was enroll Wally in an eight-week course for puppies three to six months old. The instructor told me he had never had a bull terrier in his classes and looked forward to meeting one.

"Aren't they the dogs with egg-shaped heads made out of cement?" he asked.

I started thinking that maybe this instructor knew more about bull terriers than he was letting on.

January is a month of planning on the farm. Seed catalogs begin arriving in earnest, and the garden covered in snow is a blank palette on which imagined gardens can be painted. Usually I scheduled one crop of lambs to be born at the end of February. Those ewes were separated and fed extra grain in the last six weeks of pregnancy. Lambing pens need to be checked for loose boards. I was also busy hanging all of my water pails from a shelf in the barn that Wally could not reach, since he had taken to carrying five-gallon pails around, and sometimes wearing them on his head. Such projects anticipate the future and can be done in a timely fashion without rushing.

One thing we had not planned on was a telephone call Stephen received in early January from the erstwhile, sun-bronzed tabloid reporter who had returned from Tequila-land to announce that she was writing a story about him. While their conversations had been tentative and friendly before, it now became confrontational. The columnist gave Stephen warning that she was going to announce in her next column that he had told her that he had seen videotape evidence restricted by a court order due to its sensitive nature and subject matter involving the sexual assaults on murder victims.

Stephen protested and advised her that such a bald statement was incorrect, and it was fanciful thinking to suggest he would say such a thing to someone in her position. Assuming that the woman had actually read his book, he explained some of the ways in which a writer who attended the trials and listened carefully to the evidence could describe the passages of the book concerning the subject matter of the restricted videotapes. He did not, and would not, reveal his sources. Nor would he set out his investigative techniques for publication.

There were hundreds of hours of videotape interviews with the murderer in which she described the crimes in detail to the police, as had been shown in clips on the television program that aired months earlier. The columnist was not to be deterred. Stephen sensed some shameless glee in her manner. He told me, and I was sickened.

The column was as expected—inflammatory and defamatory and spun without substantiation. Snippets of quotes were taken out of context from a surreptitious tape the columnist had made on a tape recorder that malfunctioned. Police officers who failed to prevent the crimes lashed out harshly at their harshest critic. A lawyer for the families of the victims expressed outrage over the contents of a book that had been published two years earlier. Politicians called for a police investigation.

I spent the day taking down the Christmas tree while Stephen fielded reporters' calls. There was pain just doing that. Wally adored the tree.

I have a writer friend who keeps a Christmas tree up all year long.

"Just because I like it," explains Austin. He keeps a few strands of Christmas lights hanging from his bookshelves, too. Once you have been to his space a few times, it seems quite natural. If a person likes something, why should they not want to keep it with them all year long? I am sure Wally agreed with Austin's school of thought.

I began taking down the lights and baubles, from the bottom up. With half the tree stripped, I started sawing off branches that I could throw through a window into the backyard for recycling as cover on the flower beds.

There was so much tension in the house, I am sure the dogs felt it. Diva curled up in her space on the couch and watched me. Wally spent time on a cushion in Stephen's studio, watching him talk on the phone until he was bored and came out to see what I was doing.

Seeing the branches of his favorite thing being chucked out the window was too much for Wally. He howled and tried to grab one for his own, sending prickle-sharp spruce needles flying to places where the vacuum would still be finding them in July. Finally, I let him outside and watched as he made a beeline for branches that had collected in a pile outside the window, still wearing traces of tinsel.

Dogs are not known as architects of anything much except their own good fortune—when it occurs. A dog will dig away at its bed until it finds a comfortable configuration, but it never goes out and builds its own doghouse. So I expected that Wally had no plan at all when he began moving the branches around the yard. Some were quite large, and he struggled with them through two-foot drifts. When he could hold a small branch high and prance with it he was most pleased with himself, although some "bad" branches required a good shake before they were laid to rest. It was good exercise, and the branches ended up covering various parts of the garden. Soon enough they, too, would be covered with snow.

When I had finally whittled the tree down to a manageable, spindly size, I unscrewed it from the holder and lifted it toward the window, hoisting it up and sending it outdoors with the same respect a javelin thrower might exhibit to a retired piece of equipment.

By the time I had finished, the phones had stopped ringing and Stephen emerged—dazed—to stare out the kitchen window as darkness fell with the suddenness that is winter. I felt the weight of the insult he was feeling and knew that anger was not far below the surface. Friends had called to offer support. Professional colleagues called to say they had seen this sort of thing from this sort of columnist before and it was usually driven by someone with an agenda. Knowing he had not a hope in hell, Stephen wrote to the editor demanding a retraction.

My mother called and said, "Stephen didn't do that, right?" I said, "Right, Mom." And she said, "I knew it. Did I tell you neither your father nor I can remember what we had for lunch?"

I knew exactly how she felt. I wished I was standing in a water bowl with a cookie box on my head. Where oh where was poet Wallace Stevens's "mind of winter" when I needed it?

12

Cracking the Rules

think I took the flurry of news reports more seriously than Stephen did. He had studied with Marshall McLuhan when the media guru was massaging media theory into his infamous messages. To him, newspapers today were fish wrap tomorrow. However, I had a nagging feeling this was not going to be the case.

Within a couple of days, a police investigation was launched. At least, that is what we read in the newspapers. No police officer knocked at the door or sent a letter. Apparently, three detectives were going to read Stephen's book. Stephen found it laughable and absurd that a book published two years earlier would suddenly come under the scrutiny of the police. Prior to its publication, he had spent a month nearly living with a team of lawyers who vetted the manuscript for the publisher. What could there possibly be to worry about?

Then we received a phone call from a well-respected civil liberties lawyer who insisted that any criminal investigation was a serious matter. He was adamant that Stephen retain legal counsel because this matter was not going to go away.

I missed Wally's first puppy class. Instead, we met with a law professor who offered his services over what he perceived as a potential infringement of free speech rights. The meeting was in a university building on a campus north of the city in a wasteland of strip malls and suburbs. A friend described it as "a place Mussolini might have ordered over the phone."

That morning, Stephen's infirm father passed away.

We drove home in silence while snowflakes the size of quarters fell in a blizzard of white slush. The dogs were there to greet us. Stephen and Wally played soccer in the wet snow while I cooked a late dinner and hoped that life could return to normal.

You cannot allow distractions to take your eye off of a bull terrier who is still testing his limits. After the Christmas tree came down, we felt sufficiently confident in Wally's behavior to remove the childproof gate between the family room and the kitchen area. Now, like Diva, Wally could sit with us while we read the papers or watched television. Sometimes he laid his head across my lap, other times he crawled onto Stephen's lap. If he was not under our feet, he wanted to be on top of us.

Diva had carved out her own space on a sofa near a window where she could perch on the arm and look out over the backyard and the bird feeders. I kept a few strands of clear outdoor lights on an old lilac bush whose branches hung low to the ground. Seeds that fell from the bird feeders scattered beneath the branches, attracting gray-brown rabbits that visited at night. Diva watched them with mounting excitement until she was dancing on all paws and had to go out. Wally had no idea what this behavior was about, but he was always up for a run outside the house at full tilt into the lilac bush. I doubt they even saw a rabbit flee, since there was so much advance warning. They always spent a good deal of time sniffing and staring attentively into the dark, neither showing a trace of hound dog.

There was only one rule about the family room, and Diva had accepted it without question, as had all of our other dogs. Perhaps I am odd but I do not like having a dog watch me while I eat. When we decide to have our lunch or dinner in the family room, dogs are not allowed. Simple. I say "no looking," and the dog is supposed to go to its bed or anywhere outside of the room where we are eating. Failure to act earns a "git."

This is one rule that confounded Wally after he had been permitted to free-range in the room. At first, he followed Diva without question, but soon he started to pause. When a bull terrier pauses, it means they are thinking or having a digestive dissidence that could have consequences. Wally tried leaving the room and then sauntering back in while we dined. A sharp "git" sent him scrambling back into the kitchen with a big grin on his face, like a mischievous eight-year-old caught showing the neighborhood his sister's bikini top.

Stephen's mantra was: "You must not laugh at Wally. You must laugh with him." When Wally pulled stunts like this, the lines seemed blurred. I tried to keep my "git" firm and my face stony.

On this night, we were struggling to absorb the legal issues that had been raised that afternoon in an airless, humorless room. As well, there were the memories of Stephen's father, who had lived in a retirement home in a nearby town until the later stages of his debilitating illness required round-the-clock nursing care. "No looking" seemed impossibly irrelevant, but when I said it, both dogs left.

I was thinking about the summer we took Stephen's father fishing on the big boat and how he stood at the stern and stubbornly refused to sit down even in rough water. He caught a few lake trout but never said much about it. Years later, at the retirement home, those fish had grown into monsters and the waves were ten feet high. I was smiling when I noticed Wally's head in the doorway.

"No looking," I said, and he turned his head away, interpreting the instruction literally.

A few minutes later there was movement in the doorway. Crouched on the carpet, Wally was crawling ever so slowly across the floor on his belly with his head turned toward the wall. When we stopped talking, he froze and tried to slink lower. When we spoke again, even to say to each other, "Can you believe this?" Wally resumed his stealthy dog paddle until he reached a chair he could hide behind. He could not see much from that vantage, so he belly-crawled behind a stereo speaker and began taking quick peeks at us, ducking quickly, before the word "git" was spoken.

It was impossible not to laugh. What sort of jackboot dog owner was I to enforce eyeball restrictions when I clearly had a puppy that believed he had an invisibility cloak? Both Wally and Diva joined us for dessert.

Rules that were made to be broken cracked further that night. Diva quickly forfeited her dog crate in favor of the couch or her regular dog bed. Wally slept in his crate with the door open, but this night we heard him on the stairs. He had patrolled the upstairs rooms before with Diva, dragging himself up each of the fifteen steps one paw at a time, and skittering down like a fat spider on an icicle, only to land with a thud.

Old stairs creak. It seemed to take forever for him to reach the top. Our bedroom door was closed but ajar. Pushed open, Wally's nose rounded the door.

"I will not sleep with a dog in my bed," I muttered under my breath.

The door swung open, and there was Wally, back-lit by the soft hall light. His tail slowly wagged his body, and he took a couple of tentative steps forward, as though the floor might drop off at any moment.

Stephen turned on his reading light.

"Just this once," he implored. Wally kept wag-walking.

I was learning that nothing, including the letter of the law, is written in stone, and nothing lasts forever except in memory, and even that is imperfect. What harm could there be to snuggle a puppy on flannel sheets while a winter wind rattled the windowpanes?

Stephen lifted Wally to the bed, and the puppy crawled all over us, first licking and then bouncing from pillow to pillow, tail held high, singing his dog purr, "Arooo, Arooo," which signified happiness that skips a heartbeat. Then he flopped over on his side and burped.

Lights out.

13

A Cuckoo's Nest

Our first puppy school lesson was forty-five minutes of barely restrained chaos in the gymnasium of the local high school. Everyone had to figure out a way to remove snow boots and winter outerwear while puppies leaped and barked their greetings. Oh yes, we were also all carrying mats of various sizes, which we had been told to bring, along with toys and chicken wieners or other "bait." In New York, I once saw a line of slender models in yoga attire carrying their private mats while waiting patiently in line to enter a tranquil room for their blissful exercise. This group looked nothing like that.

On the way to class, I had grabbed a two-foot-by-four-foot pink carpet remnant that was the only piece of carpet I could find at the Dollar Store, and it was four dollars. I read somewhere that dogs are essentially color blind, and I hoped Wally forgave me.

"And what is her name," said the woman next to us in the row of puppies on mats. I knew then that the pink rug was a big mistake and very hard to roll up.

I had not missed much in the first owners-only session, since I had already been through one course of obedience training with Diva. The point was that these eight weeks were a COMMITMENT.

The instructor entered the room with a black-and-white border collie that was in a wire kennel on wheels. He let his dog out and told her to sit. We watched in awe.

Meanwhile, a miniature poodle bounced itself out of its collar and proceeded to attempt an intimate act with a chocolate cockapoo that collapsed like a stuffed animal. An elderly woman with a Pekingese held her dog close to her chest. Without the bow holding the hair out of its eyes, it would have been hard to tell one end of the dog from the other. The only puppies remotely close to Wally in size were a brother-and-sister pair of yellow Labs who must have been entangled in the womb because they were still dancing impossibly inside and out of each other's leashes.

Wally looked big and awkward. I felt for him the way I had felt for the chubby boy with the funny little glasses when I was registering for kindergarten. Wally had never had a private mat. He had never seen these dogs or these people in sneakers before. Some black-and-white dog with the attitude of a hall monitor stood over in the corner watching all of the toys. And I smelled like chicken wieners. A puppy like Wally had to have time to mull all of this over to see if it meant anything. Wally rolled over on his back and chewed on the new choke chain I had bought him for "training."

The instructor strode to the center of the gymnasium with his border collie beside him like a shadow. She had one of those clever one-syllable border collie names like "Gyp" or "Fly," and her willingness to obey was as substantive as treacle. Deliberately and demurely, she dropped the rag tug toy she was carrying in her mouth and positioned it squarely in front of her paws when she sat. This prompted a Jack Russell terrier no bigger than a roller skate to leap from his mistress's arms and run to the center of the gym, where he stole the rag toy and ran off through the tangled legs of the Labs who were blissfully chewing each other's faces.

It was as though the nimble white-and-brown terrier was Randle McMurphy, the Jack Nicholson character in the film of Ken Kesey's *One Flew Over the Cuckoo's Nest*. He was wild; he was free; and he could have any darn toy he wanted. All of the puppies barked and wiggled their approval.

At the center of the room, the instructor tapped his running shoe toe lightly on the floor and folded his arms, surveying the loony bin of puppies and owners. Even the Pekingese was yipping. Puppies that were not engaged in the cheering were either licking their paws or licking their owner's ankles or peeing. Wally had his head in my purse, checking for chicken wieners.

"A-tten-shun," called the instructor, who had rigid posture.

All fell silent except for the Jack Russell, who was off in the corner with his owner, growling while he refused to relinquish the rag toy, which was now looking much more ragged.

After making sure all of the puppies had done their "duties" (our instructor's code word for toilet activities), we worked those puppies like fast-food restaurant trainees for the next half hour.

The instructor told us what to do and then came around to each of us, providing suggestions. I was on my knees with Wally standing toward me, while I put my left hand through his collar. The instructor told me to put my right hand behind my back, and he slipped an inch or so of moist chicken wiener in my palm. I focused on Wally and brought my right hand slowly forward, holding the wiener between my thumb and forefinger. Moving like an alluring siren, I let him see but not touch. Then I turned my palm down and lowered it to the floor right between Wally's front paws, close to his chest. Like a genius, Wally hit the floor in a perfect "down" position.

"Good girl," the instructor whispered to me. "You can give him the wiener now."

I had Wally eating out of the palm of my hand by the end of the session, and I wondered which of us had learned anything.

"So how did it go?" asked Stephen, when we got into the truck. Wally stumbled to the backseat and fell over on the blanket he shared with Diva. I pulled on my seat belt and mumbled something, realizing that I had chicken wiener on my breath.

Stephen had to carry Wally into the house. The little guy only rallied enough to crawl into bed, where he snored like a boar and backfired like a Harley-Davidson. Six weeks left to go.

We practiced our lessons five or six times a day. Sometimes Wally and Diva would do them together, and they took to anticipating requests, lying down before I gave the command and looking ever so smug.

Stephen and I took Wally out for walks on the deserted concession road where we practiced the "come" command. While Stephen held Wally, I backed up on the snow-covered road, holding forth the ever-desirable chunk of wiener. When I called "come," Stephen let go, and I ran away as fast as I could until Wally caught up and took his reward. It happened very fast and I kept backing up farther and farther before Wally was released because he could run like a quarter horse released from a starting gate. More than once, I hit a patch of ice and slid into a ball, there to be covered with puppy, tumbling on the tundra.

The training was fun, and it was something to do while we waited and heard nothing about the police investigation, except that it was "ongoing."

Several friends joked that it was taking such a long time because the cops move their lips when they read. We laughed, guardedly. Having spent a great deal of time with police officers when researching Stephen's book, we knew that in some cases it might be all too true. Police are only human, after all. The qualification is that they have guns.

I remembered one evening Stephen and I spent at a ribs and wings bar in Buffalo, New York, with a bunch of officers who worked out of the division where the murders he was writing about had taken place. Off-duty and ready to swill, they were celebrating approval for the use of new Glock 9 mm handguns. Forming their hands into pistol shapes, they waved at the ceiling, yelling, "Pow, pow, pow!" One of them, a big guy with a wide friendly face, started singing his own version of Bill Haley and the Comets' classic 1955 hit "Rock Around the Clock," substituting "Glock" for "Clock." *"We're gonna Glock, gonna Glock, around the clock tonight."*

The boys at the bar went wild, swiveling their hips and singing along, with "pow, pow, pow" punctuating their gyrations. It looked like a madhouse, something you might anticipate seeing at a terrorist celebration the night before a suicide bombing.

The singer was now a deputy chief. I wondered how the rest of them turned out.

14

Cabin Fever

It is easy enough to catch cabin fever during the winter on the farm without having a posse to worry about. I have always been able to figure out some way to shake the blues. Painting my office walls aubergine was a mistake. Painting my toenails a glistening papaya shade was the right thing. Sometimes all it takes is reading a cookbook and making some outrageously complicated confection that should have its picture taken before being devoured. I made Diva and Wally some pumpkin and liver dog treats that looked inedible but rocked their world.

You can feel trapped during a rural winter. Stockpiling food becomes de rigueur, since a storm might blow in and the roads could be closed. That snug feeling the woodstove provides early in winter starts to turn ugly. Wood ash accumulates, and cleaning the stove sends clouds of tiny, former wood particles into the air to be inhaled or to settle on window ledges and china. Hauling wood to the stove becomes a never-ending chore. Bark chips and dirt accumulate beside the stove, along with the soggy mitts and socks left to dry close by it.

So when it came time for me to give a reading from my most recent book in a city just a few hours' drive away, it seemed a spectacular diversion involving minimal planning. The adventure was all the more pleasurable because we were being treated to a night in a pet-friendly hotel, due to the possibility of inclement weather. It was a few weeks before the sheep were to have their lambs, and a neighbor would drop by to fill their feeders. They had a heated water bowl and lots of bedding. We would be away for about eighteen hours of something completely different. I looked forward to a Jacuzzi, the promise of a back rub, and no dirty dishes to attend to.

The hotel was a short cab ride from the reading venue at a sleek museum that shone like a jewel in the snowy night. However, the reading was taking place in a windowless back room lined with cold, gray concrete brick. There were two of us reading, and we made an odd couple. The young man who was slated to read before me had just published his first literary novel, which one reviewer described as "elliptical, nuanced, affirming and sad." My second book about life on my *Green Acres*–style farm was described by clever critics as "humor on the lamb," featuring stories about everything from a lusty duck to wayward sheep and the world's largest all-female marching kazoo band. I supposed it was a tad elliptical, too, but no one said so.

The bookseller hosting the event arrived to tell me that unfortunately copies of my latest book had not arrived. In addition, two major roads into the city had been closed due to whiteout driving conditions and accidents, so the book clubs would not be attending. In fact, he had driven past one carload of book clubbers who were stuck in a ditch.

The young author huddled in a corner of the room with his girlfriend, flicking through his book. Usually, an author picks one long passage or several short ones to give the audience a sense of the work in about twenty minutes. I assumed that was what he was doing.

Eventually about a dozen people straggled through the door, covered in snow, wondering aloud if the snowplows were out and fearing that they would never get home. Eight of my "fans" had carpooled to make the trek. They were jovial matrons who brought their own homemade cookies and "tea" in a Thermos to perk them up after the drive. The other four were tweedy academics who had obviously come to inspect the young author and adjudicate his work. They did not look as though stories about judging the snowmobilers' chili contest or ruminations on the fascination men seem to have with cement trucks would bring them to this darkened cove on a stormy evening.

After collecting a six-dollar fee from each audience member, the bookseller introduced the evening and began by reading part of a glowing review of the first-time novelist's book. It was such a good review. I could not have written better for myself. The young man took to the podium and began reading without further adieu. He read for precisely six minutes, said "thank you," and walked to the back of the room, where he sat down with his girlfriend.

What he read in that short time was nothing short of wonderful, but it was hardly even three dollars' worth. Our applause faded into the cement brick. My fans were scratching their heads. The academics appeared to have nodded off.

With little fanfare, the bookseller introduced me, and I started with a story about stupid sheep tricks and ended by playing "Roll Out the Barrel" on my kazoo. At least I woke up the academics.

The bookseller sold four books by the emerging author, and the evening ended when someone's cell phone rang and we learned that a third road out of the city was close to being closed.

Back at the hotel room, I was happy to flop on the bed, trying to forget the whole fiasco. Stephen had drawn me a hot bath. We would take the dogs for a brief walk, and I could come back to soak and swirl in the tub until our room service dinner arrived. Already I felt a winter of tension melting behind me.

There was blowing snow in the parking lot, but the low-rise hotel blocked much of it. A steel-mesh fence enclosed the area, including a small field. We decided to let Diva go for a run but kept the unpredictable Wally on his leash. Diva danced away lightly, and we saw her gliding through the snow to the far fence where she stopped. We heard the elemental sounds of a confrontation. Then we smelled the skunk.

Diva and the skunk might have been thirty yards away, but the odor mushroomed, not blown away by the wind, rather rushed toward the hotel like a tsunami of smell. We were enveloped.

"Skunk!" we screamed at the same instant.

Diva was barrelhousing toward us, the obvious victim of a direct hit by a white-striped rodent.

"Get to the truck and stay there with Wally," I yelled to Stephen, as though we were in some disaster movie and the earth was going to be spite by malevolent parking lot forces.

Fumbling for his keys, Stephen ran for cover with Wally.

Diva was beside herself and soon beside me. I had her sit and stay, which she did against every instinct. Once leashed, I tied her to the bumper of the truck, trying to comfort her without having her jump into my arms, contaminating my "go to town" jacket. Stephen passed me a dog blanket through the window, and I tossed it around Diva's shoulders.

This was bad. This was very bad. It was nine-thirty at night, and roads were closing. We could not take Diva into the hotel. We could not drive home with Diva in her current condition or the interior of the Bronco would be ruined. It was freezing, and all you could smell was skunk so close it climbed in your nostrils.

I am no Rudy Giuliani when it comes to handling emergency situations, but I knew we had to do a number of things quickly. Stephen and

Wally would stay "clean." Skunk juice is an oil, and it spreads to anything that comes in contact with it.

I asked Stephen to go to the front desk and tell them what happened. We needed hot water, towels, and large plastic garbage bags in the parking lot, pronto. The kitchen was also solicited for tomato juice for its potential skunk-odor-reducing properties. People were already emerging from the hotel and standing on their balconies, trying to comprehend the ruination of their evening as the smell saturated the night air. I ran for the hotel room.

That Jacuzzi looked awfully inviting, and Stephen had Frank Sinatra playing on the portable stereo. Instead I stripped out of my clothes, waded into the long johns I had packed "just in case it gets cold," and layered on a couple of Stephen's sweatshirts and an old pair of sweatpants that would have to be sacrificed. I swept up the toiletries, threw clothes in the suitcases, and went back to the fray. So long, Old Blue Eyes, this lady was about to become a real tramp.

The odor had permeated the corridors of the hotel and was seeping under doors and into rooms. Wearing faces wrenched with the stench, confused guests milled about as though waiting for a fire drill. Over the years, I had been close to a few skunkings but never experienced anything like this.

In the parking lot, the hotel manager and two assistants stood at a distance from the truck and waved to me. Kitchen workers were bringing five-gallon pails filled with warm water, and three cartons of tinned tomato juice arrived on a luggage trolley. Maids had a cart full of towels, facecloths, and a pair of rubber gloves. Someone handed me a package of industrial-size garbage bags that were large enough to hold a ten-year-old.

I used Stephen's Buck knife to cut holes in one of the bags and put it over my head, as though it were some sort of Ned Kelly bandit body armor against the scent of skunk. Tucking my hair under the complimentary shower cap I pilfered from the hotel bathroom, I tied it with a plaid scarf. There was no point in anyone standing around, so I asked the manager if they could fetch our bags. He handed me a can opener.

Stephen looped garbage bags over the seats in the truck and lined the backseat with fluffy hotel towels. Wally kept pulling them away. However Stephen's frustration was nowhere near what Diva and I were going through.

I used a pot from the hotel kitchen to ladle warm water over Diva and towels to wipe her face, trying to rinse her eyes, which were burning from the skunk's spray. She was patient, gracious, and shivering. I drenched her in tin after tin of tomato juice, creating a murderous red stain in the snow-covered parking lot.

Rinsed and towel dried, Diva still smelled of musky skunk, but it was not quite as pronounced as before. I rubbed her with white hotel towels and tried to keep her warm. My garbage bag costume, improvised headgear, rubber gloves, and one layer of clothing joined sodden towels and empty tins in one large garbage bag. Maids waved at us as we prepared to abandon a scene that looked as though it should have been cordoned off with police tape. I realized I was wearing only my long underwear and wrapped myself in a clean towel.

Stephen had swaddled as much of the truck in protective covering as he could. We put Diva in the backseat where she lay down in abject embarrassment.

Wally squirmed in my lap, licking any stinky part of me he could find. My back ached, and I realized I had not eaten since noon. Still more or less in a state of shock, Stephen shifted the Bronco into four-wheel drive and drove us through the winter storm with the determination of a man who wants to sleep in his own bed no matter what.

At home, I made a toasty fire and some grilled cheese sandwiches before taking a long, hot shower. Spoiled with cookies, Diva spent the night in her crate on an old blanket. I would sweeten her scent in the morning with Skunk-Off shampoo. Wally and Stephen hit the bed, and all movement ceased.

Looking out over the glistening white barnyard and snow-draped evergreens, I wondered how anyone could ever want to be anywhere else.

15

Puppy Logic

When lambing begins on the farm, it takes precedent over everything else. This is not something a juvenile bull terrier finds amenable or logical, since bull terriers believe that they take precedent over everything and everyone within their ambit. So every time I bundled up to head to the barn to check on the burgeoning flock, Wally insisted on following.

A dog is no help in the barn. Wally was a scourge. He reminded me of the little kid you tell not to stick his tongue on the metal screen door in freezing temperatures, but the kid does it anyway. He was always doing things like carrying my pitchfork around as though it was his personal toothpick. Then he would get stuck between a pen and a wall with it and stubbornly stand there until I came to retrieve the purloined tool of my trade. He repeated this several times a day, until I hung the pitchfork on a wall. He sat and stared at it, as though it were the Shroud of Turin.

If I had a dozen ewes segregated in their own pens with their new lambs, I had to give each of them a pail with their grain ration twice a day. In the years B.W. (Before Wally), I would set the pails out, meter out the rations, and take them around. Feeding time is a good time to have a look at the lambs because the mothers are preoccupied with eating. To me, looking at animals is one of the most important aspects of good husbandry. A thrifty lamb or one with a slight limp can be an indication of a larger problem to be nipped in the bud. And it is always entertaining to watch the young lambs butt heads and dance backward.

With Wally in the barn, I had to have eyes in the back of my head. I could not leave a pail of grain unattended, because the next thing I knew he would be wearing it on his head. Dogs do not normally eat grain, but ewes with nursing lambs are fed a rich blend that is flavored with molasses. Wally had a sweet tooth to go with his clown act.

Over the years, I have learned that nature is best left to its own devices more often than not. Sometimes I sit with a ewe that is having lambs for the first time, to calm her with sweet talk, not to serve as her Lamaze coach. I keep the offspring of good mothers and eliminate as many potential problems as I can think of by feeding them well and keeping a flow of fresh air. The barn door is open in all but the most inclement weather. I may fence it in so that the lambs do not stray into snowdrifts, but a blast of frosty air is far preferable to damp, sweaty conditions. Penned ewes get a touch of molasses in their water to keep it from freezing. Wally enjoyed sampling that, too.

Outside of the barn, Wally was in love with winter. Despite his short coat, he dove into the snow with gusto. Standing in the lane, Diva regarded him with disdain. Wally thought nothing of chasing a ball straight through a snowdrift. Piles accumulated when the snow was blown from the lane. Once a crust formed on it, Wally clawed the way to the top of his personal Matterhorn. Sometimes he leapt and rolled down, or he used his belly as a snowboard and skimmed his way down like a greased penguin.

There were things in the snow that fascinated Wally. Sometimes he walked across the snow and paused, listening intently on some wavelength I could not decipher. Then he pounced, cracking through the crust and thrusting himself headfirst deep into the snow, leaving only the wagging tip of his tail visible. What he was hearing was the sound of meadow voles, tunneling through the snow in search of bits of grass and seeds. Often he barked before nose-diving into a suspected vole tunnel, as though deafening his prey might give him an advantage. I do not think he ever caught one of the short-tailed rodents, but he had hours of fun peppering the field with potholes.

We persisted at puppy school. The "sit" command was no problem for Wally, but the action itself perplexed the instructor, who was of the opinion that a "sit" was only correct when the dog's bottom rested firmly on the ground. As an anatomical rule, bull terrier bottoms never touch the ground in a formal sitting position. It is as though the dog's haunches are spring-loaded, waiting to go into launch mode at any instant, and the tension keeps their butts hovering in anticipation. The instructor's eyes narrowed while he examined Wally from all sides, finally concluding that he was sitting, even if he was not actually sitting.

Wally applied his cardinal rule, "If it isn't fun, it isn't worth doing," to everything, and puppy school was no different.

"Sit, down, come," what fun was there in repeating that?

The instructor was watching as I put Wally through that exercise when the all-fun-all-the-time light went on over Wally's domed head. He was in the "down" position and I was standing about six feet away.

"Come," I said confidently, having repeated the exercise ad nauseum at home.

Wally gave me that look of pure mischief that shoots out of the triangles where his eyes live. Then slowly, painfully slowly, he began to crawl toward me in what we have come to call the "commando crawl," head low, butt raised, and bowed front legs dragging the rest of him forward while his tail wagged in a slow circle.

The instructor pursed his lips and grew red in the face. I had to reward Wally, because he had done as he was asked, although his interpretation of "come" was creatively shaded.

"Amazing animal," said the instructor. He moved on to check the Jack Russell, who seemed to think "come" also involved undoing his owner's shoelaces.

To say that Wally squeaked through puppy school would be putting it mildly. I was never embarrassed for Wally but constantly embarrassed by him. At week four, we were instructed to bring our dog's food bowl to class. Wally had been enjoying the same blue plastic bowl for a couple of months. He loved his food bowl almost as much as his food. He carried the bowl around. He took it to his dog bed and licked it and chewed it long after any trace of food was gone. It was a mess of tooth marks; the only smooth surface being the actual bowl, which Wally could not fit into his mouth.

The instructor shook his head. I do not remember what lesson we learned using the food bowl. I just recall Wally lying on his pink puppy mat, chewing his bowl, and making great, loud scraping sounds.

Wally was learning in his own way. I could take him into the barn and tell him to wait while I went into a pen, and he would be there when I came back, although he might also be rolling on his back. He was always testing the limits. I kept reminding myself that there are no bad puppies, just ones filled with beans and wit.

To deal with dominance issues, the instructor told us to have the puppy sit when it wanted something, instead of barking or licking or doing some other less-than-desirable behavior. When Wally wanted something, the need was palpable, so he fell into the sit-means-I-want pattern quickly. He sat at the door to go outside. He sat before he was allowed on the couch. He sat before his food bowl was put down. It seemed to be working until one day I saw him sit and stand, and sit and stand, while looking at a shelf. I had no idea what he needed, but his sit-and-stand routine was unrelenting. Sure enough, behind a knick-knack there was an old tennis ball that he wanted. As it turned out, puppy logic was irrefutably logical.

Toward the end of our puppy school training, we entered the gymnasium to find a variety of dog toys, balls, socks, and other irresistible items strewn around. Anything that was plush and squeaked drove Wally to a level of pleasure that bordered on erotic fetish. These were the forbidden fruit he lusted after. At the veterinarian's office there was a furry cat toy that sat on top of the magazines. Wally strained on his leash to get into the vet's office for no other reason than to rush to find that toy and maul it. The "decorated" gymnasium approached paradise.

Our instructor told us that this minefield would test each puppy. Each puppy was to sit at one end of the gymnasium while their handler waited at the other with a treat. The puppy was to come when called, ignoring the beckoning pleasures laid out at its paws. If the puppy stopped, it was to be called and reminded of its mission. My heart sank. Wally's eyes were bright with excitement. The plush Garfields and rag octopuses might not all squeak, but he surely wanted to see if they would.

Many of the puppies flew across the gym to their masters. These were puppies that I thought had not an ounce of sense of self, but they certainly responded to chicken wieners. I had to call Wally's name and the command about twenty times. He never backed up; he just never developed any sense of meaningful forward propulsion. He paused. He lingered. He stuffed items in his mouth, arriving at my side with all things plush trailing from his meaty gob.

The instructor gave me a withering look. Our puppy school examination was one week away.

Lambs once dependent solely on mother's milk were now dipping into the molasses-flavored feed. Snowbanks melted into muddy puddles. I wondered where the voles went when their tunnels wilted, but the frost was still in the ground. Wally was looking more like a dog than the ungainly, all-paw, big-headed puppy that first showed up for school.

The actual test was unnerving, for me at least. There were long sits, long downs, long stays, and a round of fancy figure-eight heeling. Wally cracked when the instructor tossed a tennis ball in front of him, sending him bouncing around the gymnasium in chase like a brindle heat-seeking missile. Chaos erupted, and many of the puppies reverted to form, chewing one another's faces and snagging shoelaces. Our instructor had something much more dignified in mind, but he bent to the will of the puppies and let us toss our leashes in the air.

By some miracle, Wally earned his graduation diploma and was spared the indignity of puppy reform school. Spring was in the air.

16

These Dogs Hunt

I have always embraced the seasons on the farm, even knowing the extremes of heat, cold, dust, and mud that they herald. Sometimes spring happens so quickly you almost miss it. One day sludge-laden snow melts in a warm rain that greens the pastures. The daily diary became a litany of garden notes: "one row corn planted, potatoes mounded, need more peas."

Day-old chicks are ready to be picked up at the farm supply store. Peeping balls of yellow fluff with the specific gravity of marshmallows join the lambs in the barn, where they huddle under the winter heat lamps that warm them until they feather-out. Black-necked geese cruise the flooded pond with awkward goslings trailing behind. At dusk, the air—now fragrant with the smell of earth—is filled with the cacophonic chorus of peeper frogs singing their lust.

Wally liked the pond. I took him down there and sat on an old maple tree stump while he pranced along its edges, charging into the chill, clear water whenever a frog jumped. The edge water was not deep, and he could wade through its grassy reaches easily, sometimes snapping at a spot where a frog had disappeared.

He grew bolder and started swimming in the pond, always on the hunt for hopping amphibians. His head poked above the water while he cruised, looking more alligator than dog—beady eyes in search of frogs' legs. We called him "The Wallygator." To my knowledge, he has never caught a frog.

There were other hunters out there whose skills we questioned more closely than Wally's. We heard from friends and family that the police were sniffing around, asking questions about Stephen and his work and inviting various friends and acquaintances to be formally interviewed.

It seemed obvious to Stephen and to the lawyers that the investigation could be wrapped up if the police did a little research into how professional writers write. After all, the techniques of detection and storytelling had similarities. The law professor who was advising Stephen had also attended many of the legal proceedings involved in the case as a media consultant. He knew the volume of material that was presented at trial. Like many others, he suspected that this investigation had less to do with the actual content of the book than it did with Stephen's sources, those individuals who had given up the information that condemned various authorities involved in the botched murder investigations and subsequent prosecutions.

A meeting was arranged for a "casual" discussion with the investigating officers. The law professor accompanied Stephen, and they all met in a grim-looking building. For the first time, Stephen learned that his investigators were from the Major Crimes Unit, which seemed a bit of overkill, since he was a writer, not a murderer. All they wanted was for him to name names. Journalists' ethics and the sanctity of sources were irrelevant to them.

Wally and I waited in the parking lot. It was a sultry afternoon, and we found a shaded patch of grass where we could practice some dog obedience exercises. After puppy school, Wally went straight into an adult dog obedience class. I found that educating him was a welcome distraction. He was doing well in a class with big dogs who were more laid-back than young puppies, but every once in a while the instructor accused him of turning the gymnasium into his own private comedy club. If the crowd was willing to give it up, Wally worked the room for laughs.

As time stretched by, I imagined that Team Stephen could have used a little Wally-levity in their windowless interrogation chamber.

I was right. When Stephen and the professor emerged from the other building they were both blowing steam out of their ears. Nothing had been accomplished. The interview ended in a standoff.

Later, a friend who had experience with police boards told us he was not surprised.

"This isn't just going to go away," he said. "These dogs hunt. That's what they do."

17

Anonymity at the Other End of the Leash

A couple of weeks after Stephen's police interview, I was named a YWCA Woman of Distinction in Arts and Culture.

On the evening of the presentation dinner/gala, my parents and friends sat with us along with a local politician. Mother and Father beamed, as they always did when their daughter served them proud. While I caught up with my friends I noticed Stephen bending the ear of the politician about his case. She looked decidedly uncomfortable. It was a common reaction. People routinely believe that if the authorities—police, the tax man, homeland security, whatever—decide to take a look at an individual, that individual must be guilty of something and the blight could spread to anyone they so much as nod at. It seems not all that much has changed since Salem.

We spent that summer in restless anticipation. The fact that Stephen was under police investigation was very public. Reporters called regularly for updates. Our social calendar shrank noticeably. When we did attend an event or a dinner party at the behest of the faithful friends who stood by us, conversation invariably turned into a status report. It became wearying.

We needed a diversion. It had to be something that would take us far away from our regular circle of friends and acquaintances, off the farm, but with dogs. I wanted it to be a hobby in which nobody knew or cared who we were or what we did. Then I remembered my experience with Diva at dog shows. Nobody paid any attention to me; all eyes were on the dog.

Wally had champions in his background. He had British, American, and Canadian champion genetics going back for generations, dogs like Monkery's Buckskin, Burundi Black, Aricon Eye Spy, Jocko's Caesar of Magor, and a bull terrier whose name practically defines the breed, Bullyrook Batteries Included. Before Wally's ears were up, we had been told he had "championship potential." We could go for short day trips and remain totally anonymous while enjoying all the chicken wieners we could eat.

I called the bull terrier club I had joined and asked about show schedules. Shows that were strictly for bull terriers were months away, so I decided to enter Wally in some all-breed shows, where we could also be entertained watching a variety of breeds strut their stuff. I did so against the best advice of the bull terrier club secretary.

"You'll be up against Willy," she sniffed. "He's being campaigned everywhere."

I had no idea who "Willy" was, but he did not scare me. I booked us into the first show available. It was about a month away and cost me all of twenty dollars. The show would mark Wally's first birthday. He was booked in the "Open Dog" class, which had a Jack-the-Lad kind of ring to it.

Finding a filigree-fine show chain and lead took a day in itself. We went to a store that specializes in all things dog and show related. I always wondered where those impossibly small bows that hold the bangs away from a Yorkshire terrier's eyes came from. There were bags of them for sale in all colors.

I had to practice with Wally, confusing him to no end, since dog shows have a protocol that is different from obedience training. For instance, it is bad form for a dog to sit in a show ring. They are supposed to stand, and stand with force—chest out, head up, eyes alert, and paws firmly fixed. Leaning against the handler or restless shifting of hips is taboo. What surprised me as we practiced was how quickly Wally could go from a standing position to rolling on his back.

According to the breed standard, a bull terrier "must be strongly built, muscular, symmetrical and active, with a keen, determined and intelligent expression, full of fire but of sweet disposition and amenable to discipline." The mere scent of a chicken wiener brought out the sweet and amenable in Wally. He was strong, muscular, and active enough to run into a woodpile without noticing that only chipmunks could fit through the spaces between the wood blocks. I thought he looked symmetrical, if a constantly wagging tail was considered enough to balance his whomping headpiece. His intelligent expression shone when he was keenly and determinedly trying for another piece of chicken wiener. Of course, I thought there was nothing standard about him at all.

If you have never been to a dog show and you like dogs, by all means find one and go. The Westminster Kennel Club Show in New York City is the pinnacle of North American shows and has the wonderful attribute of being a "benched" show, which means that all of the dogs appearing in the show are available to be admired by the public throughout the entire show. However, at the majority of all-breed conformation shows, dogs are judged by breed in alphabetical order. So show people with dogs like affenpinschers and Afghans often get the least sleep, and members of the general public who like to sleep in on dog show weekends often miss the early classes.

I was not prepared for my first all-breed dog show. The sheer chaos of the parking lot outside of the arena was unexpected. There were people off-loading crated dogs onto wheeled trolleys along with their grooming tables and boxes filled with clippers, hair blowers, and all manner of coat-enhancing, taming, detangling, and shining products. At the back of the parking lot, a mélange of mobile homes, live-aboard pickup trucks, vans, and SUVs were arranged in a tribal village of dog show exhibitors. People from the Hound Group were parked beside people in the Toy Group. Working Dog people and Non-Sporting-breed types mingled in loose camaraderie around outdoor card tables and lawn chairs where exhibitors exchanged notes on judges, shared old war stories, and out-and-out gossiped.

Stephen dropped me off with Wally and drove over the horizon to find a parking space. In a cordoned off "dog relief" area, I walked Wally, and he reluctantly performed his "duties" only after all other dogs had left the area. A passing borzoi tried to sniff his hindquarters and that sent him airborne. Then Wally saw another bull terrier, except it was all white. He froze the way he does sometimes when noticing his reflection in the door of the refrigerator or in a mirror.

I registered and obtained an armband with my number. We were 009, and I realized I had been one of the first to pay my entry fee because according to the catalog the armband numbers went into the 500s. There were only four bull terrier entries, and Wally was the only male. The judging took place in Ring Two, where we stood waiting while the American Staffordshire terriers were being judged and the Australian terriers half their size assembled for their class.

Stephen found us and adjusted my armband, pushed my hair out of my eyes, and gave Wally a pat. I dressed specially for the event in a bright yellow jacket that I would never have worn otherwise, but I thought it set Wally's orange-brindle stripes off nicely. His ears were clean, toenails clipped, and I had showered him with the garden hose to spiff him up.

Dog show order differs from that of lifeboats—males first, judged from the youngest to the oldest, with a couple of other categories in between. Then it is time for the bitches, a perfectly acceptable term at a dog show. So I was surprised when the steward, who handles everything from paperwork to calls for ring cleanup, asked for the junior bull terrier puppy bitches to enter the ring. The girls trotted past Wally, wiggling their bottoms while the handlers pretended I was not there. My bright yellow jacket and a dog with a grin as goofy as Wally's are hard to ignore, so I took the liberty of tapping the steward on the shoulder while the bitches stood prettily in the ring. He was startled that I should suggest he was missing an entry on his list—but there I was with an armband, a receipt, copies of my dog's registration papers, and a catalog clearly listing our entry.

You would have thought that someone had tried to swindle Mother Teresa. The judge was impatient. He had thirty-five terriers to judge between 9 and 10:30 A.M. So far he had only judged four breeds and nine dogs. The steward checked everything twice with the show secretary and the chief steward. Wally was officially entered, no doubt.

The bitches left the ring and the steward called for "Open Dog bull terrier 009."

I jiggled my hand around Wally's jowls and whispered in his ear, "It's showtime."

Off we went, free trotting into the ring, where Wally stopped and froze like a statue while the judge looked him over. Without making his usual attempts to lick any hand that gets near him, Wally held his pose—intent on my hand, which I held close to my chest, granting him just the tiniest of glimpses of a stuffed squeaky mouse that I had managed to keep a secret. The judge patted him down, checking the lay of his shoulder and the spring of his loin. I slid to Wally's side and held his jaw, allowing the judge to examine his pearly whites.

"Down to the corner and back," said the judge.

I was so glad that I had watched the previous classes. I set off with Wally at a fast walk on a diagonal across the ring, where we did a neat turn and headed forthrightly back to the judge. Wally caught a glimpse of the stuffed mouse inside my jacket as we turned and he gave a crowd-pleasing kick with his back legs. When we pulled up a few feet from the judge and I held out the mouse, Wally's every muscle was poised in anticipation and he was grinning from ear to ear. He looked like there was so much dog inside of him that he was going to burst.

"Around you go," said the judge, and we trotted off around the ring. Wally was up on the balls of his feet, moving like a jaunty riverboat gambler about to collect his winnings. I was just along for the ride and happy that I had remembered to batten down the sports bra.

I thought Wally won his class handily, even though he had no competition. We waited while the bitches strutted their stuff. Stephen had started to show some interest. I watched how the other handlers held the leash, sometimes wrapping it loosely around their shoulder while the judge examined the dog. They were always looking, both at their dog and at the judge. Some had dried liver treats that they kept in their own mouths until they needed to use it as bait. I did not think I could go that far. Wally was tugging on his leash, trying to get at a dog cookie someone had dropped on the floor near the steward's table. The older bitch puppy with a professional handler won over a younger one. They were both adorable.

"My little witchy is a losing little bitchy," said the young puppy's owner as she left the ring in a bit of a huff. I do not think he meant to, but Wally almost tripped her.

Now there were three bull terriers called to the ring to determine who would be the Best of Winners—a puppy bitch, an adult bitch, or Wally the Wonder Dog. I looked at Wally and could tell he was fading, lulled by the weight of chicken wieners in his stomach. At the squeak of the mouse, he rose for one last grin and wiggle as the judge ran his hand down along his back.

"Best of Breed and Best of Winners," said the judge, a kind-faced, reedy fellow who looked a bit like Farmer Hoggett in the movie *Babe*. I thanked the judge profusely and picked up traces of dried liver while shaking hands with my fellow competitors.

We had barely started our new hobby, and already we had a couple of ribbons and two points toward Wally's championship title. An hour later, we were back in the ring for the judging of the Terrier Group. Only fifteen terrier breeds were represented, although there are more than two dozen listed by the kennel club. Many of the dogs (and bitches) had been the only representatives of their breed in the class and were called "Specials" because they already had achieved the status of champion. Most of these dogs had professional handlers. You could spot them easily in the parking lot, where their vans and trailers generally contained a number of different breeds of dog that they were "campaigning" for an owner.

It is done all the time. For instance you do not see media mogul-comic Bill Cosby prancing his champion terriers around the show ring, although he has co-owned two Welsh terriers and a wirehaired fox terrier that won the Terrier group at Westminster. These are generally dogs that have a lot of money riding on their merit as future breeding prospects. They are not dogs like Wally, who would rather be hunting groundhogs or banging his head on a ball.

There was serious tension in the show ring, which now seemed like a confined space, with dogs butting up against other dogs' butts. Wally was particularly concerned about the smooth fox terrier behind him who had a curious nose. When we were told to take the dogs around the ring, Wally was constantly looking over his shoulder to see if anyone was gaining on him. With his ears flattened and his tail between his legs, he looked more like a Wal-Mart shoplifter than the "gladiator of the canine race" he was supposed to be. The judge ended up raising his finger in our general direction, and I started to drag Wally into the middle of the ring until the horrified steward motioned me back. It was the otter-faced border terrier that was being called for closer examination. In the end a salt-and-pepper gray miniature schnauzer with silver white eyebrows and Santa Claus–style whiskers took the top prize.

We were exhausted. Stephen was sure Wally could have taken the schnauzer if he had tried. We spent the rest of the morning admiring dogs and absorbing the dog show process. Some of the silky toy breeds were painstakingly groomed, strand by strand. The eyes of Old English sheepdogs were uncovered and covered over again. In crates draped with towels, thousands of dollars' worth of genetics snoozed before their close-up with the judge. A little girl looked at Wally and cried, "Look it's a Bodger dog." No one cared who was at the other end of his leash.

18

Riding the Trail

Roy Rogers died that summer. I wrote a tribute to my favorite "saddle pal" for the public radio network where I had been telling country tales for almost a decade. Roy was really Leonard Franklin Slye. The "King of the Cowboys" grew up in Duck Run, Ohio, where he rode a brown horse to school and learned to yodel.

I remembered the rocking-horse days of childhood when the squinty-eyed cowboy with the white Stetson and silver spurs came into my living room and kicked up dust riding a palomino and chasing the bad guys. I wished my singing cowboy hero "Happy Trails," just like the ones he and his ever-smiling wife, Dale Evans, sang about in the show's theme song.

According to Roy Rogers's Code of the West, we all have an obligation to take good care of animals and treat children and old people right. It is hard to argue with homilies. I also remembered a line from one of the songs Roy and Dale sang: "It's the way you ride the trail that counts." That meant something to me when I was a child, and it meant more and more to me now.

Wally and Diva made fools of themselves all summer, running in circles and figuring out new ways to entice us into play. When Diva tired, she lay down under her favorite tree and ignored his antics. It was good for the older dog to give her bones a shake and show the youngster a few tricks.

For the first time, Wally experienced the antics of lambs. Once liberated from the barn, the lambs have the entire pasture as their playground. They butt heads, run in packs, and dance backward when fluffy dandelion seeds blow their way. They also do everything in their power to escape from the pasture and venture into the lane. Usually this involves belly crawling under a gate or finding a flaw in a fence. Once one lamb finds a route to "freedom" all will follow, since following mindlessly is a part of the Code of Sheep.

Wally found them one dewy summer morning, about fifty knee-high lambs crowded on the grassy circle at the end of the lane just outside the barn and beyond the pasture. His immediate response was to come running back to me with the news.

Chasing sheep is bad-news behavior in dogs, so I leashed Wally for his first encounter with the walkabout lambs. Their heads popped up in unison when we rounded the corner. They looked like teenagers who had been caught smoking behind the shed. In seconds all of the lambs were scurrying to get under the gate and back to their field. Wally found this frenzy quite exciting. We went over to the gate and watched the lambs scatter back to their mothers, where they bumped up to their respective udders, trying for a quick feed.

Ewes that took exception to a dog in their vicinity came over to stomp their hooves at Wally. He ignored them. Wally's interest in sheep was strictly limited to what came out of them, a scatological problem that plagues all breeds from time to time.

The lambs grew bolder. Each time Wally found a passel of them in the lane, he came to me with a worried furrow on his brow. All I had to do was clap my hands and the mischievous little monsters ran for the safety of their field. Like Wally, they were of boundary-testing age.

One morning I was watching from a window in the second story of the house as a crew of lambs crawled their way under the gate. Then I saw Wally approaching them with his soccer ball.

Balls are sacred objects to Wally. They are what the double helix was to James Watson and Francis Crick in 1953, a very big deal and unique in their own right. Wally contemplates balls, nudges them, nuzzles them, and chews them. Watching him play with balls is a wonderment that invites the question "Is there anything more fun than chasing a tossed ball?" Some dogs hit a high note over Frisbees, but Wally has always stuck with orbs.

His game is soccer, and he handles the ball with the expertise of a World Cup striker. Had he not already grown to know and appreciate his name, Wally could easily have been recast as Pelé or Beckham. He uses his bully front paws as adeptly as Oscar Peterson uses his hands on the piano, feathering with his left and fanning with his right. He can turn a ball back and use his hindquarters on it, too. He jumps in the air to make a header and has bounced tennis balls off his nose since he was a puppy.

Now he was trying to find out just what sort of stuff these lambs were made of. He pushed the ball toward them. Nothing. They barely glanced up from grazing. He pushed it more forcefully, and a bold young ram stood his ground and stomped. Three more times without a reaction and Wally was ready to take his ball elsewhere. It was only then that a strumpet of a ewe lamb ambled his way and offered herself to him in a most suggestive manner, for a sheep that is. At the thought of a "sheebull" or a "lamb terrier" in the barnyard, I opened the window and shouted, sending the lambs running to the field and Wally running to the house.

I recall that summer passing as one long series of glimpses of Wally running past a window either chasing his soccer balls or scooping them into a shallow pail and racing around a cedar tree in sweeping figure-eights. There was joy in that. Diva watched him from her bed on the porch, her head turning from side to side like a spectator at a tennis game as he crisscrossed the yard with endless energy.

The other thing I remember about that summer is the relentlessness of waiting for the police to conclude their investigation. The original announcement suggested a three-month time frame. Eight months had passed without a word. I plodded on, finishing another book. Stephen was stymied. No one was going to talk to an investigative journalist who was under police investigation. In late September, Stephen's lawyer sent a legal letter requesting a resolution to the matter within thirty days. Precisely thirty days later, he received a request for his client to present himself at a police station to be formally charged with two criminal counts of breaching a court order, which carried a maximum penalty of two years in prison.

Word reached us in the late afternoon as I was preparing to give a speech to a conference of rural ministers. While driving to the event, Stephen worked his cell phone, calling contacts in the media and alerting associations representing the writing community.

I am told my speech was well received and there was a lot more laughing than usual in that Lutheran church hall. Some of the ministers even managed to work some of my material into future sermons. At the end of the evening, I sat at a desk, signing books for the reverends and listening to their stories. Many of them shook Stephen's hand and thanked him for being such a help to me on the farm. I could only imagine what they would be thinking the next day when they read the newspaper.

I had another speech to give the next day, autumn being the time when many groups have an annual meeting and celebration. Although I desperately wanted to be with Stephen and his lawyer when they went to the police station, I headed off to a hall filled with farm women who were having a networking day with the theme Expanding Our Horizons. When he was finished at the station, Stephen joined me once again to assist in the book-signing process. I told the women a couple of stories involving Stephen's misadventures on the farm, and they greeted him like an old friend, some of them gamely poking him in the arm while others offered a friendly hug. I imagined how their horizons would be expanded when they watched the six o'clock news.

The police planned to hold a press conference at the police station, but they chose to forgo it once they saw the front-page news reports, in which issues of free speech were raised. That very day, the Writers' Union of Canada issued a letter to the government stating, "Investigations of this sort—attempting to elicit a writer's confidential sources—constitute encroachment on the freedom of expression that is an essential aspect of a free and democratic society."

Stephen found the process of having his mug shot taken and being fingerprinted humiliating, which is what it is intended to be. I took a deep breath before watching the news that evening. I should have videotaped it. There was a fine shot of Wally and Stephen playing a game of soccer across from the police station before his lawyer arrived. Whatever the trail ahead held, we had Wally riding shotgun.

19

Natural Instinct

Og shows are all about appearance, but function should also follow form. Greyhounds are built for speed with a purpose—to hunt deer and gazelle, even rabbits. Inuit peoples used the Alaskan malamute as an all-purpose working dog for everything from tracking polar bears in snowstorms, to hauling heavy sleds and warming children through bitterly cold northern nights. Deerhounds, foxhounds, and all manner of retrievers and pointers have their work cut out for them in their name. Toy breeds are as delightful as their genus suggests. Bull terriers have been refined from cruel beginnings, but they still have the natural instinct of all terriers to find out what the heck lives in a hole.

Wally checked his groundhog holes routinely, traveling from hole to hole, sniffing and circling, looking for signs of life. I once observed him making a definitive statement to the resident groundhog by defecating on what might be considered the doorstep of an underground burrow. Sometimes he carried a ball with him, and if he hit on a pungent odor or one that held particular interest, he often dropped the ball down the hole, where they rolled out of reach, entombed with the grimy groundhogs. He dropped so many balls down holes that I fantasized about the groundhogs having an underground bowling alley at the end of their tunnels, into which Wally's balls threaded like errant pinballs.

Wally's ball collection was a motley assortment of beslobbered tennis balls, volleyballs, basketballs, and soccer balls, all in various stages of decomposition and deflation. Early on, I wearied of weekly trips to the sporting goods store to replace limp balls. I simply could not have the life chomped out of my bank account every time he punctured a pricey ball, as much as I appreciated the need for the sporting goods store manager to send his kids to college. Wally was trained to use a hard rubber toy called a Kong as a mouth guard anytime he played soccer or bandied about his bigger balls.

Bull terriers are well known for their selective hearing, but when it comes to the privilege of associating with balls they will obey any rule to have the divine right of access. If Wally drops his mouth guard in the middle of a game, he dashes to retrieve it, no matter whose kneecaps get in the way. When that happens, Wally's bone-hard head becomes a swinging sack of cement, and I have had more than a fair share of bruises.

I experimented with all manner of balls. It became a sort of mindless obsession. Wally loved rubber balls and the wildness of their bounce, but he could swiftly tear them into a nightmare of chewable pieces. My father donated cricket balls he had saved from his English childhood, but they had no bounce, and removing the random "prey" imitating action of balls rendered them uninteresting. A friend sent me a dense rubber Cressite ball made in England, but it was too heavy and large for fast play. I needed to find a substantive smallish ball that would stand up to the power of Wally's jaw.

Narrowing it down to lacrosse balls, I began testing the mettle of various brands, since all balls are not created equal. Finally I found one that would last, at an upscale store specializing in lacrosse equipment for championship play. Joy of joys, they also came in colors other than white, which was a disaster when lost in a snowdrift. There was even a glow-in-the-dark ball. I fancied those would come in handy when searching for balls that rolled under the buffet.

Wally was trotting along with a ball in his mouth on a walk through the woods with Stephen in the late autumn. Paths carved through the evergreens are lined in soft fallen pine needles. It is a peaceful place that commands a contemplative state. I know of city people who say they cannot imagine spending five minutes in the country in all of that quiet. If they were pointed down the path through the evergreens, they might have a change of heart.

Lost in his thoughts in that silent world, Stephen was suddenly re-moved from the mystic by screams from Wally that he had never heard before. This was not the surprised yelp of a puppy nipped on the nose by Diva for being a tedious bother. It was not the soulful "arff, arff, arff" we heard after Wally fell over the edge of a sheer wall of a gravel pit and slid three stories on his tender backside. It was not the wounded wail we heard when he ripped a front toenail running on a snow-covered concession road, making our first videotape of him more *Straw Dogs* than *Wally's First Winter*. These were bloodcurdling screams that did not let up.

Confused, Stephen ran in the direction of the horror to find Wally beating his head into the ground, his front section covered in porcupine quills. Meanwhile, the silver-gray pincushion that had inflicted the damage was limping off into the woods. Stephen scooped Wally into his arms and ferried him to the house, to the truck, to me, and to the vet.

The media were often quick to note that Stephen is a "big" man, and that is exactly what this situation demanded. Years of training with weights and lifting barbells in the parlor/Ping-Pong room he had con-verted into a private gymnasium allowed Stephen to carry a seventy-two-pound dog that was writhing in pain across thirty acres of pine

needles and pasture. I found them just outside the pasture gate, both exhausted and panicked.

Wally wanted to roll his quill-covered muzzle in the ground to get
rid of them. I held him while Stephen brought the truck around. In the
backseat, I wrapped a towel around Wally's shoulders to try to keep
him from swiping at the quills with his paws, causing them to break or
pushing them in even farther. He had quills that went straight through
his tongue and quills that spiked in the roof of his mouth. Some were
perilously close to his pain-wracked eyes. I took a few quills myself, as
collateral damage while holding him.

It took the vet an hour to pluck poor sedated Wally clean. Stephen
could not bear to watch, and should probably have been sedated himself. I stayed while Dr. Kim, close to full-term in her pregnancy, wrestled
the quills out with a scissorlike hemostat, pulling them clean away with
impressive strength. Wally woke up wagging his tail. Contrary to popular myth, there is no "venom" in quills, and they are not hook shaped.
The quill tip is a tight corkscrew with a backward projecting barb designed to penetrate, rather than withdraw. The vet added that it was
somewhat of a challenge to get the quills out of the muzzle, due to the
"gristly" texture of a bull terrier's muzzle. Harrumph. I did not mention
he has kisses sweeter than wine.

The puncture wounds healed cleanly, and I only needed to daub a
few with a veterinary ointment, which I also used on myself with success. A number of quills gradually worked their way to the surface,
where I pulled them with the pliers on my Swiss Army multitool. One
particularly ugly quill lay flat beneath the skin under Wally's left eye.
We were taking the dogs in for their rabies booster shortly and I wanted
a professional to remove that quill.

A few days before the appointment, I noticed Diva moving slower
than usual. Something in the way she held herself was off, and her coat
lacked its usual blue-black luster. She ate but without gusto. Rabbits

were clustering under the lilac bush in the December snow, and she had no interest in hoisting herself on the sofa arm to watch them. I stroked her soft cheeks and she gently licked my hand. There was something wrong.

Wally had his quill removed, and a general check of his skin showed that he was warding off infection and ready to go back to the woods on a leash. Previously, he had only received needles from the lovely Dr. Kim, who was now on leave, preparing for the birth of her child. I do not like needles much myself. As a child, I would only allow Dr. MacKenzie to needle me, because he confided that he had a special rubber needle that he used only on me. Perhaps Dr. Kim had suckered Wally in the same way. When another vet gave him the vaccine, he yipped and howled and had to be carried to the truck thrashing all the way. Bull terriers vacillate between being absolute stoics and absolute wimps.

I called about Diva earlier in the week, but since she had no fever and seemed in no distress, we waited. The vet drew blood, and it was thick and dark. Other tests and X-rays were tried. Nothing was obvious, but he wanted to do an exploratory surgery after she had been stabilized on intravenous overnight.

My dear girl gave me her catlike paw, and I collapsed around her, hugging with every ounce of my being. Squeezing everything else out—the clinic smell, fluorescent lights, the mewing of caged cats, and the scent of fear between us—I remembered a winter night when Diva and I were alone at the farm. Something outside had excited her, so we walked into the soft snow. The Northern Lights streamed across the open sky as I have never seen them before or since. They flowed in ribbons shot with red and green, forming a canopy over the old farmhouse. I lay down, watching the show, waving my arms and legs to make an angel while Diva licked snowflakes from my face. That was our perfect moment.

The vet called the next morning to announce that Diva was brighter and hugely playful. He thought he was seeing an entirely different dog than the one that had slowly walked away from me the day before. Although she was twelve, he thought her prognosis looked much better. How I longed to be with her, but Stephen had a court appearance, and there was nothing I could do but wait anyway.

Diva died on the operating table, riddled with cancer. True pack animal that she was, she hid whatever weakness she may have felt until the end.

Stephen had been mug-shot. Wally had been mugged in the woods. Diva-dog was a sweet memory.

That Christmas was unusually quiet.

20

Nothing Too Outlandish

have to admit that I was glad to see the end of 1998. It seemed to me a downward spiraling year, starting with an ice storm that paralyzed much of the northeastern United States and Canada. The Russian economy collapsed. Hurricane Mitch devastated Central America, killing more than ten thousand souls. A disaster movie, *Titanic*, swept the Academy Awards, and Céline Dion delivered a chest-thumping rendition of its theme song "My Heart Will Go On" to more than fifty million television viewers. A Saudi named Osama bin Laden was said to be behind explosions outside the U.S. embassies in Nairobi and Dar es Salaam. When Old Blue Eyes left the building on May 14, that was the day the music died for me.

I wondered what sort of sign it was that my first speaking engagement of 1999 was at the psychiatric unit of a downtown hospital. The program brought poets and authors into the ward; it was hoped that comingling patients with staff would be an entertaining session and a brief respite from the loony bin. My travel expenses were paid, and my publisher agreed to pick up the hotel tab for this worthy cause. I approached the assignment with some trepidation, not knowing what to expect.

After my childhood experience with a broken limb, I thought of hospitals with some fondness. Twenty years later, a bout with early-stage cervical cancer, followed by disastrous surgery to try and amend fertility issues, had changed my views. I saw the burden on the staff and the infrastructure that permeated large treatment centers. I saw the politics. I found myself in hospital rooms that were not clean, let alone sanitary. Anytime I was a patient, I checked my own name on my chart to be sure they had the right body in the right bed. Taping pictures of family, my farm, and my dog on the walls emphasized that I was human and had a life to go back to.

Wally and Diva sometimes stayed at a neighbor's kennel when we traveled. They had a wonderful romp. Sheila cared for them as if they were her own, and they had a huge yard to play freely in. I have a feeling that neither of them ever slept in the kennel area, and I am fairly confident that Wally mastered the stairway to the guest-room bed. We always felt a touch betrayed when the dogs perked with excitement as we turned down Sheila's side road. They trotted off to the yard without even looking back. When we picked them up, Wally barked and "Arroood" all the way home, telling us the story of his stay.

Sheila retired, and I hesitated to leave Wally with anyone else. It was not as though he was suffering grief over Diva's departure. He sulked a bit for a day. The next evening, he casually leaped onto the sofa, taking her place. I did not take this as a sign of insensitivity. Dogs, better than us, seize each day and celebrate what exists in it. Rather than grieving over that which is no longer, they move on.

That left the matter of finding a hotel in the city where Wally would be accepted and where we would be comfortable at a reasonable rate. Court appearances and attending sessions with what was becoming a team of lawyers was going to require a base. As it happened, there was a pet-friendly hotel within walking distance of both the courthouse and a park.

The Metropolitan on Chestnut Street in Toronto is an oddity in the chain-dominated hospitality industry because it is privately owned. This means management has some discretion and the option of indulging eccentricities and preferences. Thus the owner, Henry Wu, a Hong Kong businessman and chemical engineer with a love of food, created a Chinese restaurant, Lai Wah Heen (translation: Luxurious Meeting Place), that *Gourmet* magazine noted has a "sense of Hong Kong's new culinary design." The *New York Times* hailed the dim sum as "maybe the best in North America." The lobby floor is polished black marble. The linens are Frette; the artwork distinctive; and no request is too outlandish.

Stephen named a preferred rate behooving lowly writers. He also wanted a one-bedroom suite, explaining that Wally requires room in which to play soccer. Negotiations commenced. We wanted one fee, including parking and taxes, but as everyone knows taxes cannot be avoided. We compromised, and the deal was done. I could come back from the psych ward and have a Jacuzzi.

The reading took place in a room that was used for hospital staff training sessions. It was comfortable and cheery enough. The patients wore their own clothes rather than hospital pajamas. One woman came wrapped in a bedsheet. Unlike farmers, who generally choose to sit in the last rows of any meeting, the patients were determined to get as close as possible to me, while their minders self-segregated at the back of the room.

I started to introduce myself and my stories, when one clearly excited middle-aged man's hand shot up. He was squirming like the kid in class who knows the answer to a teacher's question.

"Yes?"

"I have a question."

"Go ahead," I said.

"Are those your real teeth?"

I assured him they were.

They were an attentive and appreciative audience. I told a story about trying to housebreak a piglet for a television show, and the room erupted in pig-snorting sounds, which I believe was actually started by one of the orderlies.

Then I made a casual reference to skinny-dipping, because I believe that every country kid within bike riding distance of a pond has skinny-dipped. It was as though everyone in the room suddenly wore clown noses. The excitable man immediately stood up and told a story about going skinny-dipping with his brother and having their clothes stolen. The young woman in the sheet began removing it seductively.

"I would like to try skinny-dipping," announced a tall man with a quizzical expression.

Everyone had a story about being naked somewhere, sometime. One rather sad-faced woman said: "I once walked down Main Street naked and nobody noticed."

I thought it was a disaster. The organizer assured me that it had gone very well. The man who thought he might like to try skinny-dipping had never spoken up at a group event before. My host said she planned to recommend me for the dialysis reading program.

It was a bitterly cold and stormy day. The hospital was three blocks from the hotel, so I hiked it, wishing I had worn the long johns that are a fixture of my winter farm attire. Stephen was with his lawyer, and Wally needed to be taken out.

There is a rule that bull terriers are mindful to enforce. If they do something once, they expect to be able to do it forever, whether it makes sense or not. For instance, when Wally first rode home from the breeder's with us, he spent part of the time lying on a blanket at my feet in the truck. Subsequently, he grew to be a knee-high chunk of a lad, broad of chest and dense with muscle. He tried to take his place at my feet every once in a while, convinced he still could fit.

Wally had stayed at hotels without incident since his initial encounter with "Ivan the Terrible" at the Westin. Still, memory runs deep in the brain of a bull terrier, even though they have an uncanny ability to forget that you just fed them and expectantly demand more.

The doorman at the Metropolitan wore buffed leather boots and a long black coat with epaulets and brass buttons, just like Ivan's. My goal was to get Wally past him without incident. I wanted to teach Wally that he was not to squat or raise his leg in front of the hotel, rather he had to move along a reasonable distance, even if it meant running.

Everyone who worked at the hotel was happy to have Wally as a guest. The concierge saw us coming and had the door automatically open for us. Wally's determined stride told me he meant business. I watched his eyes narrow as he saw the doorman's boots, and he headed for them. Fortunately a flight crew bus pulled up in front of the hotel, and the doorman was busy herding a bevy of Dutch beauties from KLM into the hotel. I directed Wally to a spot in front of a billboard away from the hotel proper. This became his protocol and earned Wally a respectful nod from the staff.

We fought our way through the snow to a park area complete with chestnut trees and two pines under which Wally decided to stand for the longest period, trancelike. I have never had another breed do such a thing, but Wally and other bull terriers tend to go into a meditative sort of state when soft branches or trailing grasses brush their head. In the middle of a snowstorm, Wally had taken Japanese haiku master Basho to heart: He was learning about the pine tree from the pine tree—the "Zen thing," as one of my friends put it.

The snow did not let up that night. Morning found the city choked by thick snow, coming down and piling up, buffeted by howling winds.

Traffic disappeared. Nothing was moving in or out of the city. It was a white apocalypse, the sort that happens every few years. We hunkered down in the room and hoped the storm would abate. It did not. A neighbor checked on the animals at the farm. Given that they had a heated, automatic water bowl and those big round bales of hay, everything was status quo. If chickadees with legs the size of blades of grass can brave a brutal storm, stocky sheep covered in lanolin-greased wool with a sheltered barn at their disposal should have no problem.

We, on the other hand, were storm stayed. I think we would have been welcome to camp out at the psych ward, but the publisher agreed that in such an extraordinary circumstance another night at the hotel was in order. The only problem was that I had no food for Wally, and the nearest supermarket was a mind-numbingly cold seven blocks away, through snow so deep it had stopped streetcars.

"So call room service," said Stephen.

Nothing on the room service menu quite fit Wally's dietary requirements, so I called the restaurant directly. No request was too outrageous for the kitchen of Lai Wah Heen. I asked for a good-size portion of lean ground beef, lightly cooked, with a side order of rice and a few steamed green beans and carrots. It was a meal that would closely approximate my home cooking.

Wally's room service supper arrived in a heated trolley graced with a single orchid. It came in a layered, lacquered Chinese food box. The aroma was delectable. While Stephen signed for Wally's supper, I stirred the meat to cool it. I could not resist a taste. The ground beef was sweet and more succulent than any fast-food purveyor could ever dream of. I stirred fluffy rice into it and chopped in the bright vegetables. After I put Wally's dish down for him, watching as he courted the food bowl in his ritual up-on-the-balls-of-his-feet walk-up, I caught a glimpse of the receipt.

With tip, Stephen had rounded the figure to sixty dollars, billed directly to the publisher. Later, I told the story to a fellow bull terrier owner who is also a writer and understands the reaction publishers can have to unusual line items on hotel bills, such as "dinner for Wally."

"You have balls of Cressite!" exclaimed Dede. I hope someone remembers that when I need an epithet.

21

"Saw You on TV"

Dwelling on what we came to call "the trubbles" accomplished nothing. It was the sort of thing we had to compartmentalize, putting it into a box tucked away in our brains to bring out only when it was required. I had two books published in 1999, one of historical anecdotes and one of country life stories. In terms of the book world, I was on a roll.

I had not suddenly become a workaholic, but I needed to get books to the marketplace to keep the Good Ship Wally afloat. There was a dog-eat-dog book world out there to capture. *Monica's Story* was on the bookshelves, a biography of "that woman" who was central to the near-impeachment of President Bill Clinton. My stories and anecdotes had to compete with prose such as, "like blood seeping from under a closed door, the truth began to dawn." I had my work cut out for me.

One of the perils of being an author is publicity. Some writers abhor going on the circuit and promoting their work. I am exactly the opposite. One of the first things I did when my first book was placed in my palm by an exuberant publisher was to rush right out and buy myself a classic Liz Claiborne "author's uniform." It is a terribly simple outfit—navy with small white flecks, a long, pleated chiffon skirt with a slimming V-necked topper and oodles of little buttons. I wear it with a necklace made of hand-painted glass bananas that never fails to prompt a conversation—and sensible shoes. I think it makes me look rather like the mother of the bride. I never wear it for anything other than book promotions and speechifying.

Authors have publicists who work very hard to get them out and about, and particularly to get them on television. People seem to believe you are a really serious writer if you appear on TV. I have yammered away on radio programs for years, but just one television appearance elevates an author to the status of celebrity.

"Saw you on TV," strangers say in the supermarket, in a familiar manner, as though they know you because they have seen you in their living room or at the foot of their bed on TV. And, since so many TV programs in the multichannel universe now run their programming in never-ending loops, it is possible for someone to see you on a television program that was actually made months or even years earlier. This can be somewhat unsettling, since you never know which program it was and whether or not you were any good. At least I always know what I was wearing.

But getting on TV is by no means easy. A publicist needs something to work with other than—"This book has a blue cover, lots of pages, and it is not written by someone named Monica."

So it was on a hot summer day that I found myself in a television studio with Wally in tow. Since the boy became such a large part of my life, he also subsumed part of my writing. Stories about him appeared in my new book of rural tales, so naturally I wanted him on the cover.

A professional photographer (and friend) arrived at the farm to take the book's cover pictures. John has roots in farming—his father raised crops and pigs and painted everything in sight with creosote on the farm where he grew up. So John is accustomed to the vagaries and odors of livestock, but he is not really fussy about dogs. Turning his lens on Wally was not a priority. Nevertheless, while he was off in the field taking pictures of sheep and guinea fowl, I rigged up some bales of straw behind the Dutch door entry to the barn. This is the place where the "author's portrait" for my book covers has traditionally been taken. The door frames me holding a lamb with a rooster perched on my shoulder or me holding a lamb with a horse looking over my shoulder, that sort of thing. The soft light, combined with John's talent, seems to be just right for knocking fifteen years and fifteen pounds off, which suits me kindly.

As John strolled back toward the barn, I called Wally and grabbed the smallest, cutest lamb I could find from the pen. Wally does not like standing on his hind legs. Bouncing on his hind legs to catch a ball is another thing. Otherwise his front end is cumbersome and weighty, as I know well from the many times he has sprawled across my lap.

While John set up his camera, mumbling something about getting a turkey in the shot this time, I was coercing Wally to crawl up the bales of straw behind the bottom of the door. I fancied that if I could get him on his hind legs, his front legs and shoulder would drape over the door, while I held the lamb in a similar pose on the other side. I had not considered that this meant me single-handedly lifting and positioning said dog, while holding a squirming lamb and trying to look at the camera with a pleasant smile. I dropped the lamb on the bales quite a few times, and Wally bolted and wiggled. John kept saying the turkey thing was really the way we should be going, but I was determined. Finally, we got the shot—big old Wally's grinning, tongue-wagging face beside an adorable lamb, with me sandwiched between them looking surprisingly carefree, considering that the lamb was not wearing a diaper.

Finally my publicist had something to work with. "This person wrote a book, and she will bring her dog into the studio." Bingo. TV producers love any alternative to some author droning on about their book. TV show hosts instantly realized that they would not even have to read the book—they could just talk about the funny-looking dog.

Our first appearance was booked on a cable network show that had a special weekly book segment after the news. The hotel we were staying in was close enough to the studio for us to walk. However, with a summer heat wave in progress, I decided I would melt wearing nylon stockings. Instead, I bought a tube of that pour-on tanning lotion and watched in awe as my legs turned a golden bronze.

Off we went: me in my author's uniform, with a pair of strappy sandals, and Wally in his blue collar.

After breezing through security at the TV station, we were guided down a very long corridor by an efficient young woman with a thick clipboard of papers who had the perspicacity to offer Wally a dog biscuit. She earned his undivided attention. We were dropped off in the "green room." This is a sort of holding pen for guests that is seldom actually green, although the lighting in such rooms tends to be unflattering in the extreme, causing one to look a little green. This was particularly true on this torrid day because the station's air-conditioning was malfunctioning.

Watching the green room television, I could see that the female news reader who would be conducting the interview was a perky, blond sort who was probably twenty-everything less than me—twenty pounds, twenty years, twenty IQ points, etc. As soon as the sports announcer took over, she bolted from the studio and assailed us in the green room, fairly sliding across the floor on her knees to greet Wally at his level. Obviously, she was much smarter than I had allowed. I liked her a lot. Wally gave her a saucy grin and sniffed her ears.

We tiptoed into the darkened studio as the weatherman was explaining the air pollution index and promising no relief from the heat wave.

The interview set consisted of two swivel chairs and a sort of cube-style coffee table on which the book was displayed. I was wired with a chest microphone, and Wally planted himself firmly on my feet, back to the camera. We tried to get him to look at the robotic camera, but given a choice between looking at something with ears and something without, Wally always chooses eared creatures. In sync with her subject, the interviewer began rubbing Wally behind the ears, and sure enough, when we went live to air, Wally was framed in a full shot, with his back leg thumping wildly while his newest best friend made cooing sounds about the "most wonderful doggie in the world."

The camera pulled back, and we began talking about the book, sort of. If I tried to tell a story about my first experiences hatching chicks, the interviewer turned to Wally and made a kissy face, saying, "And how did the Wally doggie like the baby chickies?" Wally quite enjoys it when humans turn into squeaky toys. He crouched down in his "ready to play position" and gave a perfectly timed bark. The interview was going exceptionally well. By the time we got to the commercial break, the entire viewing audience knew they were watching a woman who had written some sort of peach-colored book. More important, there was a dog named Wally on TV that always thumped his hind leg when you rubbed him behind his ears. Wally liked to lick human ears, and he did not quite fit on the cube-style coffee table, but he gave it a good try, considering he had to knock the book off first.

Fully aware that he was the center of attention, Wally had no idea how many people were watching him humiliate me on television. After readjusting the set during a commercial, the interviewer asked me a question, and I was in the middle of a semiwitty reply when Wally let out a great sigh and slowly lowered himself to the floor. There, he discovered my naked, artificially tanned ankles and began licking them, gently and quietly.

I am so accustomed to having my ankles licked that I thought nothing of it, save that it gave me a chance to talk about the book. While

I chitty-chatted on, I noticed that the TV camera seemed to be zooming in on Wally's display of affection toward my ankles. When one is of a certain age and sweltering under hot lights in an already overheated TV studio, having the camera focus on something other than your own glistening brow can seem like a blessing.

The interview ended just as Wally decided to abandon my ankles and sample the interviewer's. Great howls of laughter and another fine bark. The camera turned off, and I patted Wally while the microphone was retrieved and pleasantries exchanged.

Then I saw the state of my ankles—my very white ankles, as they were now. Wally had licked the tan totally away. The entire event had been captured on TV.

The producer of the show provided me with a tape that I could watch at my leisure. There I was, in voice-over, telling stories about stupid sheep tricks and my eccentric rural neighbors, while the camera clung to Wally's face and his devotion to cleansing my ankles of any vestige of artificial tan. Below the straps on my sandals there was tan, and my round, firm calves were tanned—but the ankles were as carefully cleaned as an egg in a carton.

I walked back to the hotel with Wally, wishing that I had worn ankle socks. The "tan" was easy enough to patch up, but I swore I would wear nylons to any future filming and my ankles would be off-limits.

The following month, I was strolling the supermarket and a woman whom I had seen several times before stopped me to say, "I saw you on TV." I smiled as though television was a miracle and I wondered which program she had seen. But I did not need to ask.

She was looking at my feet.

22

Dirty Tricks

Wally enjoyed his time in the limelight. In every city we visited, he met a new publicist with a fresh bag of dog cookies. Wally was loose at one casual television studio with hip VJs and roaming video cameras, playing soccer in the studio and running the ball down a long hallway—oblivious to his surroundings.

"It's not even 2000 and this dog has World Cup-itis!" declared the host. He soon discovered how seriously Wally takes his soccer playing when the ball rolled under his chair.

One television crew came to the farm and treated their audience to footage of Wally running around with his soccer ball in a pail. Some lambs were in the lane, and one decided to butt Wally. He cried out in pain, whimpered, and ran off to hide behind my knees. So much for the notion of "bull-and-terrier" breeds being aggressive, nasty creatures.

We entered the new millennium without incident. Computers kept functioning and airplanes stayed in the sky. All of the fears of Armageddon were put to the lie. It was just another excuse for major fireworks displays.

Our whole household had World Cup-itis that summer. It was a great tension leveler—watching men run up and down a playing field with a ball controlled variously by their feet or their foreheads.

The wheels of justice rolled like flattened tires. After more than a year, the only "evidence" that the police were able to find to support a charge of disobeying a court order was Stephen's book itself. They alleged that twenty-seven passages in the 648 pages of *Invisible Darkness* could not have been written without a viewing of the toxic videotapes that were restricted by court orders. They offered no theory of who, what, when, where, or why someone would have shown the tapes outside of court. Furthermore, they had destroyed the tapes they intended to rely on in a bonfire designed to provide closure for the victims' families.

In what seemed a topsy-turvy case, the law professor who was representing Stephen proceeded methodically, arguing erudite constitutional and free speech issues. If the prosecution was allowed to enter the book as "evidence" against Stephen, he could be questioned, and if he refused to name names he would be held in contempt and jailed.

The late Jack Olsen, hailed as the "Dean of True Crime Writing in America," was quick to come to Stephen's defense. Having written thirty books in the genre, Jack's affidavit stated that Stephen's book "deftly assails the ineptitudes and bungling of the police and the Justice Department." He added: "This cannot make anyone in a position of authority, either in policing or in the administration of justice, very happy."

David Kidwell, a justice reporter for the *Miami Herald* who had been sentenced to seventy-seven days in jail for refusing to name his sources, noted that his refusal to breach the confidentiality he had promised had helped him professionally and sources now trusted him more than ever.

All thirteen affiants wrote with passion. The judge grew twitchy and terse, cutting off Stephen's lawyer as he tried to read portions into the record and holding short shrift for the notion of protecting confidential sources. When I saw the judge handle Stephen's book as though he wished he had a pair of tongs, I had a profound sense of doom.

"This guy is going to put you in jail," I told Stephen.

Some people respond to stress by withering away. Stephen's response was the exact opposite. Suddenly he was on a raft of medications for high blood pressure and all manner of stress-related disorders.

These sorts of experiences are life altering. Novelist Dashiell Hammett, who crafted the hard-boiled detective Sam Spade in *The Maltese Falcon*, was already physically fragile when he was ordered to jail for six months for refusing to name names in 1951. He served five months of his six-month sentence and came out of jail a broken man. His partner, playwright Lillian Hellman, wrote that he was "a thin man thinner, a sick man sicker."

That fall, the professor resigned from the case. He had nothing more in his bag of tricks to offer to the court. All his learned constitutional and free speech arguments had failed. The Writers' Union, PEN, and an association representing journalists were crying into a void for the case to be dismissed, and their support was welcome, as well as the donations that poured into a defense fund. Some very successful writers contributed proportionate to their abilities; however, most moving to me were the smaller donations from poets and struggling writers who wanted to show their solidarity.

What no one could have predicted—and what the prosecution did not see coming—was that the lawyer replacing the professor would be one of the most respected criminal defense lawyers in North America, Edward L. Greenspan.

Stephen and Eddie had been acquainted for many years, but I had never met "the legend." He turned out to be soft-spoken, elegant, and able to catnap through a conversation without missing a beat. We met him at his office in a renovated turn-of-the-century bank, where he pads around in his stocking feet surrounded by legal books, some of which he has written.

Lawyers may not be everyone's cup of tea. Like dentists, most people do not want to need their services and complain bitterly about the cost of enduring what is often painful time with them. However the great ones, the Johnny Cochranes and the F. Lee Baileys, all share a similar trait that they somehow transmit. As their client, you feel safe.

Eddie was planning to have a chat with the prosecutor.

Time to get on with life. We loaded the truck with as much stuff as it would hold and headed off on a research expedition that took a circuitous route through Maine and the East Coast of Canada at the peak of the autumn leaves. Wally kept busy in the surf, barking at waves, spitting out salt water, and "retrieving" seaweed on rocky beaches. If there was a rotting fish or a dead seagull to be found, he embraced it.

I was researching a Presbyterian cult in nineteenth-century Cape Breton, a curious tale that I was trying to craft into an historical novel. While I hunkered over historical records, Stephen and Wally met with local characters. The man and the dog were inseparable. At night we all dined in a cabin with a magnificent view of Bras d'Or Lake, where Alexander Graham Bell inaugurated experimental flights using monumental kites in the early 1900s. I collected rocks, dirt, and the bark of trees to take home with me to keep the sense of place of that Gaelic highland.

We were days away from turning to home when our friend Harvey called early one morning. Harvey and his wife, Sandra, were escaping the city and staying at our farm for a restful weekend. I think they were looking forward to being alone. On previous visits, Wally had burst into the guest room and spun his dervishlike Tasmanian devil act on the bed, with them in it. We were having some work done on the house, and I told them to just ignore the slight chaos of the place.

"Stephen, I'm wondering where your big TV is," Harvey began.

The family room television had not been involved in any of the renovation.

"In fact, there don't seem to be any televisions in the house," Harvey continued. Do not ask me how or why, but for some reason we had accumulated half a dozen or so televisions of varying sizes. They seemed to be in every room. Not one second of a World Cup soccer match was missed in our household.

As gently as he could, Harvey told Stephen that it was apparent that we had been robbed. The door to the house had been unlocked when he and Sandra arrived late the night before. They had noticed oddities but were tired and went to bed. In the light of day, it seemed all of the electronics in the house had disappeared.

"Oh yes," said Harvey, "there also don't seem to be any sheets or blankets." Of course not, the thieves had wrapped and cushioned their booty carefully. My guests had slept under towels.

Harvey called the police, and they made careful notes of the areas where an outline of dust showed something had been removed. This was a professional job. The thieves took items that they knew they could dispose of quickly and easily. They did not touch the antiques. They did not take my silver Medal for Humor or our collection of hand-blown glass swizzle sticks. Stephen's computer, printer, scanner, and copier were gone, but he had backed up all his files.

I got lucky. My older model computer was left behind, along with a couple of aged televisions. The backup to my machine was spotty at best, and I was terrified that I had lost all of my research, writing, manuscripts, and ambient thoughts. Too old to steal was just fine by me.

Through skilled detective work, the police placed the time of the crime at just a few hours before Harvey and Sandra arrived. That was a stroke of good fortune, since the whole event could have gone awry had they interrupted a heist in progress. What was missing was just stuff, although I mourned the loss of the quilts my grandmother made.

By the time we returned to the farm we were ready to liaise with insurance agents. The police said there was no hope in hell of recovering any of our stuff. It had probably been presold and was gone for good.

We were in a store buying replacement linens when Mr. Greenspan's office called. "You must come to the office immediately. There are developments in Stephen's case that must be discussed in person." After receiving that cell phone call, we did not immediately abandon the project. I bought the required linens in a record fifteen-minute spree. Wally has this thing about high-thread counts in his bedding, and I was not about to short him.

At his office, Eddie leaned back in his chair, so far back that I thought it might tip. His cigar ember glowed with burnt-orange anticipation. I sat on the office sofa, a low-built affair designed for client comfort that Eddie's wife, Suzy, had been plotting to replace for years. Stephen removed himself to a side chair, and Eddie's junior, Marie, who had done the grunt work, sat next to him.

"I have good news," Eddie said, pondering the soaring ceiling. "I talked to the prosecutor. His wife is a huge fan of Marsha's books and he has been told to abandon this prosecution so that Marsha doesn't have to suffer further."

"What, what?" Stephen and I cried like true bastions of literacy.

"Seriously," said Eddie, leaning forward with the sparkle of a scamp in his eyes. "They know they can't win. They are backing down totally. Stephen will receive a full acquittal."

I wept, losing all sense of anything in that moment. To be liberated from such a horrendous accusation was cataclysmic. Eddie smiled softly.

Stephen frowned.

"You owe me twenty-five bucks," crowed Eddie. He and Marie held a private bet on Stephen's reaction. Eddie bet that Stephen would be royally disappointed that the prosecution let themselves off so lightly when they deserved a public pillorying.

The court date was weeks away. We planned a party for supporters at the gracious home of our friends Barry and Claire, who are superb hosts. Barry helped spread the word, while Claire schooled me in the nuance of caterers and service providers. Stephen's publisher supplied the wine. It was going to be a fabulous party.

The only contingency that the prosecutor demanded was that the announcement of the acquittal be kept out of the press until the day that it was read into the record. Any leaks and the deal was off. Our friends were duly cautioned, including a reporter who moaned and said that this was exactly the sort of news that always got leaked.

Sure enough, the day before we were to go to court with an armada of supporters, the story appeared in a newspaper, written by a reporter who held unrestrained animus toward Stephen. The prosecutor was on the phone to Eddie in a flash. Eddie went ballistic and refused to even take Stephen's telephone calls.

Thankfully, Marie listened to Stephen when he explained that he had not spoken to the reporter and it was common knowledge in the media that neither man liked the other—a sentiment Stephen expressed with some color. Marie followed up with a few phone calls and announced to Eddie that Stephen could not possibly have been the source of the leak. Further, the language was wrong. The article announced a "stay" of the charges, which is quite different from the vindication of an acquittal. Eddie spoke to the prosecutor. The leak had not come from Stephen. It came from disgruntled police who wanted to sour the deal and knew just the reporter to plant the story with. I had seen dirty tricks over the years, but this one was low.

The court was packed and there might have even been a jovial air, had it not been for a bench full of scowling police officers at the back of the room. When we all rose and the judge took his place, it felt like a hallelujah.

In a subdued voice, the prosecutor mumbled something self-serving about "the public interest" and stated that he would not be calling any further evidence. The judge looked as though he was going to blow a gasket, his face contorted cartoonlike in shades of angry red that ran the spectrum to almost purple. When a prosecutor withdraws and offers no evidence, the judge must acquit the defendant regardless of their personal opinion of the case. Stephen was exonerated.

Edward L. Greenspan rose to the occasion and graciously thanked the prosecutor for ending the prosecution.

"At the center of this case was the risk that for the very first time in our long and great history, a writer could face going to jail for the crime of merely writing," he said in measured tones. "That is something one sees in Iraq, Iran, or China. It is not something we should ever tolerate in a free and democratic society."

Oh yes, we partied that night. It was a gathering of friends that had clearly separated the wheat from the chaff in our lives. I was proud to be among them. In this literate agora there was bound to be speechmaking, and words of thanks.

"Don't tell me I did this pro bono," cried Eddie.

23

Do the Hucklebutt

tephen's acquittal coincided with our twenty-fifth stay at the Metropolitan Hotel, and we were upgraded to their luxurious London Suite, complete with a dining room table that seats ten. We woke up in the four-poster bed as one happy family, with Wally ensconced between us and snoring so loudly that the curtains quaked.

Stephen had some media interviews to do. The elegant space was ideal for the television crews that rolled in and out like patches of fog with cables. My job at such junctures is to keep Wally out of the way. Whenever he sees people he tries to cut one out of the herd and make them his soccer-playing foil. Group participation would suit him just fine if he could get it. Wally believes that life should be a ball.

The last interview was almost complete. I had kept Wally in the bedroom with me, and we rolled the ball around the room, as quietly as possible, to Wally's frustration. When I peeked out and saw the lights had been turned off, I opened the door, and we went out to greet the visitors.

The crew was fine with dogs, so I let Wally off his leash and he began licking the ears of the soundman who was trying to pack up. Stephen sat on the sofa, and something funny must have been said because all of a sudden both he and the interviewer were laughing hysterically.

Something in that moment set Wally off. I like to think it was the sheer joy of hearing such unrestrained laughter again. He went into his ready-to-play crouch and started making the odd singing sounds he emits in anticipation of something that is just too good to be true—like a game of soccer or a walk in the woods. It is not the "arroo, arroo," of storytelling, but rather a gurgling muddle somewhere between a bark and a whine that we call a "snarfle."

With that warning, Wally launched into a perfectly articulated hucklebutt of the entire room. Driven by his powerful butt end, the brindle muscle-mass on paws propelled himself nose-first like an anteater on Ritalin, racing across the room at top speed. At the dining room table, he threaded his way through the chairs as though they were agility weave poles. The table quivered as he tickled its legs in tight turns.

Then it was over to the living room, where he leaped in the air and twirled like an unbalanced helicopter before launching his right shoulder into a wing chair, with the rest of his parts following in more or less the correct anatomical order. He bounded from the chair and onto the ottoman, careening off the wall into a perfect bank shot toward a display case featuring Murano glassware. Without knowing the dimension of his cone of uncertainty, I deflected him toward the foyer, where he jitterbugged on the marble floor—his paws dancing as fast as Lionel Hampton's mallets on a vibraphone. Then he tore over to jump onto Stephen's lap, taking a television light stand and some cables with him. He sat there looking as harmless as a NASCAR racing car in a garage.

I do not know who coined the word *hucklebutt*, but the tone of the word matches the action. I suspect the origins lie in an infamous song of the mid-twentieth century, which refuses to die. It was called "The Hucklebuck," composed by Andy Gibson, featuring saxophone riffs created by Charlie Parker. The bluesy beat and honking sax of Paul "Hucklebuck" Williams sent it to the top of the rhythm and blues charts in 1949, where it remained for a year spawning a frenzied dance craze. Roy Alfred added frisky lyrics, and the song took off again in the 1950s with a recording by Frank Sinatra featuring instructions involving synchronizing a hunched back with the movement of one's sacroiliac so that the dancer appeared to: "Wiggle like a snake, wobble like a duck."

I may even have watched the 1956 episode of Jackie Gleason's *The Honeymooners* in which Ed Norton attempts to teach Ralph the moves to "this hot number." In fact, sometimes dancing the hucklebuck got downright suggestive. However, its image was cleaned up in the 1960s when artists as diverse as Annette Funicello and Count Basie recorded it. By the 1970s it was elevator music. There have been jazz versions and rockabilly versions and even a punk-reggae version of the song. Whoopie Goldberg rendered a mean hucklebuck in her 2005 HBO special. I reckon any song that strikes a chord in the sacroiliac has staying power.

I do not think the television crew in the hotel room knew quite what had hit them during Wally's thiry-second hucklebutt performance. Again there was laughter, and my quiet thanks that no one and nothing had been damaged.

The classic story about a bull terrier hucklebutt was written almost a decade ago by Californian Robert Bollong and subsequently became legend throughout the dog-loving Internet community. Among people who own bull terriers it is simply known as "The Cosmo Story."

Robert wrote:

It happened a few months ago when Cosmo was about six months old. I woke up that morning feeling down, but being the dedicated employee I am, I went to work anyway. (I hate using my sick time when I'm sick!) When I got home I was looking forward to going straight to bed, as by now I had a fever and body aches. But, to my dismay I had forgotten my daughter's softball practice. I could not press my wife into taking her because she was already taking my son to ice hockey practice.

So I left home with my daughter and returned some two and a half hours later. The first clue something was wrong appeared when I opened the garage door. The garage was flooded.

"Where did that water come from?" I asked my daughter.

I walked to the door leading to the house from the garage and opened it. I heard the sound of running water coming from my daughter's room.

What in the hell, I thought.

I lurched into my daughter's room, and was met by the sound of water squishing in the rug under my feet. I peered around the corner, to her eighty-five-gallon aquarium, which houses rare and exotic Rift Valley African Cichlids from Lake Tanganyika (and yes—of course—expensive). The tank was nearly empty. The water had all escaped, wet the rug, and seeped out through the drywall into the garage.

"My god, my god, my god," I yelled. "My fish!"

My daughter followed me as I went to open the equipment cabinet under the aquarium to see what kind of mechanical defect had caused this tragedy. I opened the cabinet door, and to my disbelief, there was Cosmo inside the cabinet.

He had the aquarium water out-flow hose in his mouth and was drinking the last few ounces of water from it, as he shook it like a madman. He looked up at me, with a look of surreal satisfaction—his little, black, beady eyes glinting in the dark cabinet. He had a strange look, almost a smile on his face.

A million thoughts ran through my head. How did a dog get inside a closed aquarium equipment cabinet? How did he get inside the house? It did not take me long to place the blame—on my wife! She had forgotten to put Cosmo away when she left for hockey.

I picked Cosmo up and walked him to his crate, my feet squishing in the soaked carpet. As I walked I surveyed the destruction. He had been in the house over two hours, by himself.

He had systematically clipped all the electrical cords from their plugs, leaving the plugs sticking out of their outlets with little piggie tails. Why he didn't get electrocuted, I don't know.

Cosmo also chewed up my son's brand-new hockey helmet and, in an attempt to get a toy out from under our couch, he ripped most of the fabric off the lower portion of the sofa.

He'd emptied the kitchen trash can and had strewn the trash throughout the house.

But the coup de grâce, the pièce de résistance, that little touch only the evil mind of a pig-dog could think of, hit me last, and sent me over the edge.

As I walked through my bedroom I began to smell something, and notice stains on my walls, leading from my bathroom to my bedroom, through the hallway, and into the kitchen. I entered the bathroom and the full realization sank in. One of my children, one of my precious, lovely children, whom I love . . . but who have the bad habit of not flushing the toilet, had gone "number two" and did not finish the job by flushing, nor were they troubled by closing the lid.

Cosmo had found this interesting object floating in the john, and plucked it out. He then ran hucklebutt through the house, throwing it in the air as he did, as evidenced by the streaks on the wall.

That was it, I lost it. Just as my wife came home. I began to cuss and couldn't stop. I never yell and was now doing so at the top of my lungs. My neighbors came out in dismay. I finally calmed down, nearly cried, mentally and physically wrecked, and spent the next four hours cleaning the mess up. A professional rug cleaner was called at extra $$$ for the late night emergency call. My children were forced to clean the "artwork" off the walls.

Late that night after I had fallen asleep, I awoke with a start. I had a sudden realization of what that mysterious look on Cosmo's face was when he was in the aquarium cabinet.

It was a shit-eating grin!

I double-dog dare any owner whose dog hucklebutts to tell a better story.

24

Goofy Guts

learned a lot about the different phrases bull terrier owners use to describe the sometimes wacky behavior of these dogs from an Internet list of people from all over the world whose singular bond is their choice of dog breed. It was comforting to know that I am not alone. Other people have dogs whose feet smell like corn chips. Other people refuse to buy a sofa or chair that a ball can roll under. Other people have seventy-two-pound lapdogs that use their heads as battering rams.

Wally's "Zen thing," the meditative state he goes into when soft tree branches touch his head, is also called "trancing," "jungle dog," "primordial pooch," and "doing drapes." The "commando crawl," in which the dog drags itself around by the forepaws, is variously called "creeping," "creepy crawls," "G.I. Joe," "sneaky snake," and "slithering." Bull terriers almost universally "frog dog"—splaying themselves like squashed bugs and rubbing their bellies. This is the way Wally crawls off the bed, not hopping, just "froggin' " until he thuds to the floor on his own special throw rug.

"The chin," as in "She gave me the chin," refers to the endearing habit bullies have of putting their chin on your leg or arm and gazing longingly at you while you eat. They drool simultaneously. The dogs themselves have been dubbed bull terrorists, pig dogs, hog dogs, devil dogs, and hell hounds. Everyone agrees the description "three-year-old in a dog suit" aptly suits the bull terrier. Everyone wants their dog to last forever.

I had barely introduced myself to the group, which numbers in the thousands, when Wally became terribly ill. It started with a bout of "urka gurka"—the term used to describe the sound of dog stomach contents being returned. This was uncharacteristic. Wally had only vomited once in his life, and that incident involved a rabbit's foot and tons of grass and weeds. Dogs sometimes eat grass voraciously when they feel the need to rid their stomach of an objectionable substance. Without the aid of vets or books or search engines, they know that suddenly becoming an herbivore will trigger a gut reaction.

Then Wally did not want to eat. He did not want to do much of anything. If his face could get any longer, it did, and the mischief was gone from his eyes.

"Hey, buddy, how ya doin'?" asked Stephen in the hail-fellow-well-met dialect that he uses when talking to Wally, who always responds by wagging his tail.

There was no wagging response.

Wally refused his ball.

We were off to the veterinarian. Initially, we learned that Wally had a temperature, and some line items in his blood work were a bit off. The vet gave him a shot that boosted his spirits and caused great running around, as well as some antibiotic. The next day we were back to vomiting and lethargy. All sorts of disease possibilities were bandied about—pancreatitis, Cushing's disease, Addison's disease, even hepatitis. Between the definitions in my *Merck Veterinary Manual* and Internet search results, I was approaching catatonia. I called Wally's breeder, who suggested X-rays and an ultrasound to check for an internal blockage.

In my experience, animal emergencies seem always to occur on a weekend or worse, a holiday. I had a ewe prolapse—expelling her uterus—on a Saturday night when all of the Kiwanians who happened also to be veterinarians were at the biggest fund-raising hoedown of the year. I suspect they drew straws to determine who would head out in the dark of night to repack a sheep in my chilly barn. When she was eight months old, my palomino filly, Karma, nosed a porcupine—on a Sunday. It was during a Labor Day weekend that Lindy, my Limousin cow, began exhibiting the classic signs of rabies. Wally was running true to the formula.

That Sunday morning, we rushed Wally to the Ontario Veterinary Clinic at the University of Guelph, a world-class facility that has all of the diagnostic aids known to internal medicine—human or canine. His temperature was worrisome, and an X-ray showed a possible mass outside of his intestine. He was admitted to the intensive care unit, and we were sent home.

There are people who do not understand the emotional attachment that forms when you love an animal. They snort at the notion that a human-to-dog bond is akin to the love and fear a parent feels for a child. To them, a sick animal is a lost cause, and it is not worth throwing good money after bad. We are not that sort of people and authorized the university to do every test they thought necessary and commandeer every expert opinion they wanted to save our boy. Stephen slapped down a credit card and told them to keep it on file.

The silence was desperate during the ride home, our minds stumbling through memories. I nearly tripped over one of Wally's balls, and I wept thinking that he was alone in a cage without his beloved ball. For the first time in years there was an empty space in our bed. If I felt dark, Stephen was living in a black hole.

The veterinarian called first thing in the morning to let us know Wally had come through the night and was alert. His tests were booked, and he was having a neurological consult. We were welcome to visit him and review the results of his tests that afternoon. In his weakened state, the ICU was the best place for him. Stephen got off the phone sobbing from relief.

The ultrasound showed no mass or any other readily identifiable problem with his organs. A complete blood panel and urinalysis left no one any the wiser. The echocardiogram revealed no signs of infection, and the heart murmur Wally had as a puppy was still mild. The vets were stymied. Wally wagged weakly when he saw us. I left a ball with him that night, and we went home to cling to each other in the king-size bed that now felt like a vacant plain.

In the meantime, I had the counsel of some of the top veteran breeders of bull terriers in the world at my fingertips through the Internet list. The perceptive information I was receiving sent the vets on a learning curve about bull terriers. They were talking about performing an exploratory surgery and possibly tapping Wally's joints for clues when my Internet sources presented an alternative—a barium swallow.

Following barium through Wally's intestinal system would show whether or not he had an organic blockage that did not show on other tests. One breeder cited the finding of a "floater" in one of his dogs. It happened to be the tongue of a leather shoe the dog had chewed as a puppy. It had drifted around in the animal's stomach for years, occasionally gumming up the works, until it was finally swooshed through by a sludgy barium swallow. We tried it on Wally. He was clean as a whistle, sparing him invasive and expensive surgery. The vets added a new technical term defining Wally's condition. One of my Internet advisers put it succinctly: "Wally has goofy guts."

By his third day in the ICU Wally's fever was diminishing. Even though he had an eight-foot intravenous tube feeding into his right front paw, he dragged us into the clinic hallway to play soccer. The home-prepared food I brought him was greeted with mild gusto. Some of the technicians and college interns who saw it in the refrigerator had Wally-food envy.

Four days later and almost $2,000 lighter, we brought Wally home with a bottle of antibiotics.

Some people might question whether it was worth it. We are not that sort of people.

25

Off to Jail

With Wally fully recovered and winter melting into spring, there was a general sense of well-being in Wally's world. Stephen and I were ticking along with our projects in the writing worlds. I was becoming familiar with the Presbyterians in my cult novel, as well as idiosyncratic things like the Gaelic interpretation of the nature and color of winds. Stephen had uncovered a Jamesian "figure in the carpet" during the hours of review he went through assisting in his sweetly resolved criminal case. He discovered the real reason behind the tawdry, twelve-year sentence the murdering wife in his first book had received, and he decided to build it into another book. Next thing I knew he was writing to the vixen in prison. More remarkably, Karla Homolka was writing back.

It is creepy having the man in your life receiving twenty-page letters from a she-monster who would have already been given the needle in Texas without a second thought like Karla Faye Tucker. Sometimes she wrote to him on pale pink stationery decorated with flowers and drawings of Winnie-the-Pooh. Sometimes she typed single-spaced letters in small script printed on both sides of the page to preserve her precious printer ink and paper stash. They never spoke about the crimes, but the discussion ranged widely from her taste in reading materials (Dean Koontz to Sylvia Plath) to her opinion of the lawyer for her victims' families: "What a jerk." The correspondence provided a remarkable frame for a book that promised to be as damning of police, prosecutors, and politicians as his first.

Part of Stephen's research involved visiting jails for women prisoners, particularly those inhabited by his lethal pen pal. That summer we visited two of them, both in the province of Quebec, north of cosmopolitan Montreal. While journalists are normally only allowed into prisons on carefully orchestrated tours, Stephen cultivated the interest of a high-level politician whose job it was to inspect any jail he pleased, and he could bring anyone with him he wanted. Off we went to jail—with Wally, of course.

The first prison was dubbed Club Fed by the media because it featured town houses in which the inmates lived cooperatively. It had a gymnasium for team sports, a day care center, and a canteen where the inmates could buy food supplies ranging from fresh lettuce to jelly beans. The women wore their own clothes and worked at various prison jobs, including sewing underwear for male prisoners. The warden gave us an overview and took us on a personal tour. What might sound like a gentrified place unbefitting to its purpose was anything but.

The door swings closed in jails, and that is the immutable truth of incarceration. A person can live in that controlled world—where the medicine (largely antidepressants) is doled out twice a day and security cameras survey every nook and cranny—but it sure as hell is not anyone's idea of "having a life."

I cannot imagine that living in a house full of strangers—some with mental health and drug problems that made them a danger to themselves and others—could be anything but punishing. Further, with rare exceptions there are no dogs allowed in prison.

When we finally left, I felt a sense of relief and could not wait to get back to the comfort of the Ritz-Carlton Hotel, where Wally was regally reclined on a feather duvet.

The days we spent in Montreal before the next tour were spent walking in neighborhoods with Wally. Stephen discovered that when he walked Wally by himself, they became "team babe magnet." Saucy French-speaking women with pillow-soft Bardot lips thought nothing of approaching them and leaning over to Wally-level.

"*Asseyez-vous*," Stephen instructed, and Wally sat to be petted.

"*Son nom est Wally*," said Stephen, always bringing a laugh, and—more often than not—a response in English.

When I walked Wally by myself, we attracted homeless people who had a dog somewhere in their past. They just wanted the comfort of petting Wally, and something for their pocket.

The Ritz-Carlton is a dog-friendly hotel, exuberantly and elegantly managed. At the Ritz, you do not wander down the corridor to find an ice machine. There are none. Instead, room service brings you ice in silver buckets. Whatever *Madame*, *Monsieur*, and *Le Chien* require is only a phone call away.

One evening the elevators were crowded with convention-goers, and I decided to take Wally down the stairs a few flights for his walk. Far from simple, the staircases of the turn-of-the-century beaux arts building turned into a maze of corridors and locked doors. When I finally reached a door that would open without triggering alarm bells, we emerged at the far end of a stunning ballroom. Tables were being set and a band arriving for what was obviously a swank private affair.

"Wally!" cried one of the managers who had welcomed us to the hotel when we arrived. He threw his hands in the air and came gushing over to provide a personal escort across the polished dance floor to the front door. I felt as though I was in the company of a celebrity.

The comforts of the Ritz were in stark contrast to the maximum-security prison for men we toured next. This was a jail that few ever get inside without committing a heinous crime. One wing held the nastiest of the nasty—notorious biker thugs and child killers. Another area served as a clearinghouse for evaluating new inmates. In one small enclave, there were cells occupied by six dangerous female offenders, including Karla Homolka, who had recently added Stephen's name to her visitors' list.

This was a prison like something out of an old James Cagney movie—set well away from civilization surrounded by flat acres of cornfields, encased by high metal fences topped with rolls of barbed wire. Inside, doors clanged at every corridor. For purposes of our tour, the prisoners were locked up. The only cells we saw were those inhabited by prisoners who had earned the privilege of working for the prison. Their cells were directly across from the identical unit in which the women were held. These were cramped spaces, with views of cornfields or parking lots. Still, they were preferable to solitary confinement, with mattress-less beds and stainless-steel toilets.

There is something about the concrete used in the walls of a prison that imparts a feeling of density. The only place that felt human was the prison library. We were outside of it, walking one of the many long corridors, when the prison went into lockdown. The doors slammed shut at either end of the corridor, and we stood waiting while a dangerous prisoner shuffled in shackles from here to there. If it had lasted one second longer Stephen's claustrophobia would have kicked in. I was glad to hear the final clang of those prison doors and most happy to return to the lap of luxury, to having my ears exquisitely washed by a dog who always knew that doors would open for him.

That night in a Montreal bistro I thought of ordering frogs' legs, a garlicky dish that is popular in French Canada but seldom served elsewhere. Something about seeing the inside of a jail changes your attitude toward living and living things. Frogs' legs sounded brutal, and I settled for thick onion soup and ratatouille.

The next day we returned to the godforsaken place. It was visitors' day, and Wally and I were not invited. While Stephen was being cleared through the secure entrance beside a turret where armed guards with machine guns surveyed the perimeter, I played soccer with Wally on a patch of scrub grass. The sun beat down. Wally ran his ball and fielded headers. I imagined the prisoners who had this view were glued to their windows, watching something different—anything different—to relieve the monotony. They would never have seen anything like Wally.

After hard play, both of us were panting. In typical Wally fashion, he wandered into the grass and managed to find the only mud puddle for miles. I found him wallowing like a contented pig. He was stretched out full length, belly crawling his way toward me, grinning from ear to ear.

I do not know what they put in penitentiary mud, but it smelled unsavory. I could not possibly put him back in the truck, let alone walk him through the lobby of the Ritz. So it was then that I entertained the watching prisoners and the guards in their high perch by giving Wally a "bath" with two bottles of Perrier and a facecloth.

By the time I was done, I came to think that Wally had earned his brindle stripes honestly.

26

The Kindness of Strangers

The year 2001 will always be scarred by the events of 9/11. I remember being at my desk that morning and glancing over at one of the ubiquitous televisions that pepper the house. It was tuned to CNN, but silent. I noticed the crawling news line across the bottom of the screen. It said that all air traffic in America was grounded. I called out to Stephen that something was terribly wrong.

That day my heart sank and I was as afraid of the world as I had been earlier in the year when millions of cattle, sheep, and pigs in Britain were burned and buried in the foot-and-mouth disease epidemic that threatened the world and made me fear for my flock.

Fifty years earlier, J. D. Salinger's bildungsroman *The Catcher in the Rye* was first published. In current events, I finally understood the depths of what Salinger's angst-ridden protagonist, Holden Caulfield, meant when he told his sister, Phoebe, about his aspirations and in the process explained the book's title:

"I keep picturing all these little kids playing some game in this big field of rye and all . . . I'm standing on the edge of some crazy cliff. What I have to do, I have to catch everybody if they start to go over the cliff—I mean if they're running and they don't look where they're going I have to come out from somewhere and catch them. That's all I do all day. I'd just be the catcher in the rye."

So many needed protection. So much was at the edge of a cliff.

That was it. We needed a break from reality and from work. Typically, I thought of going to a dog show, but just to watch.

Wally's show career ended with Stephen's acquittal. He never enjoyed being in the show ring as much as he enjoyed bouncing tennis balls off his nose for the crowds outside of the ring. When bored in the ring, Wally tried making things interesting by sticking his head up the skirts of judges who looked like trees. The clown white makeup and cornstarch I applied to cover the ball-calluses on his nose did not sit well with him, and I ended up wearing more of it than he did. Of course, you are not supposed to use makeup on show dogs, but if you ever get a chance to peek into a grooming box you can bet you will find more than combs and brushes.

Showing did have its moments. During my final turn around the dog show ring, I got tangled in the leash and tripped over Wally. He took advantage of this opportunity to give me a good ear licking, which is when I discovered that my nose was bleeding profusely on my bright yellow show jacket. I lurched to my feet and soldiered on, retrieving Wally's makeup sponge from my pocket and stemming the flow with it while streaking my own face with clown white. The judge was a dear fellow with a sense of humor.

"Looking more and more like your dog, miss," he said with a twinkle.

I vowed that the next time I took Wally to a dog show it would be on Mars.

And so it came to pass that one mid-October day we loaded the truck and headed for Mars—Pennsylvania. The dog show I wanted to attend was being held at the Mars Four Points Sheraton about twenty miles north of Pittsburgh, and the only dogs showing were bull terriers. The show is called Silverwood, and every year, in some North American city, hundreds of owners, families, and dogs make the pilgrimage to go around the ring for top-dog trophies, party like maniacs, and buy anything that has a bull terrier on it at whatever price. People come from as far away as Australia, Japan, and England. I wanted to see it, and we could introduce Wally to the demimonde.

That would not have been enough for Stephen to invest in a vacation, so I threw in a visit to Frank Lloyd Wright's ethereal architectural wonder, Fallingwater, a few hours from Mars, as well as the possibility of a Steelers game or a visit to the Warhol Museum. Pittsburgh is Andy's hometown. Then, in a lovely coincidence, Stephen got a call to do some television work in the United States—in Pittsburgh. Not only could we take a vacation, go to the dogs, and see the sights, but the network would also pay a large part of the expense.

I heard about Silverwood through the Internet bull terrier list whose members offered advice when Wally was so ill. By now some of these people had become e-mail buddies, although I was more acquainted with their dogs than with the details of their lives.

I was also going to be a vendor, having received permission to buy the tough lacrosse balls Wally loves so much at wholesale. Then I set down to the business of making a sticker to put on the balls, branding them as official Wally Balls. Master ball chewers from California to Maine had tested the balls to ensure they held up. I packed boxes in different colors to display in a huge glass vase. My stickers were silver foil, and it took me about thirty hours to design a smiling bull terrier head with a ball in its mouth.

Since this was a last-minute decision, I feared there might be no room at the inn, however, I managed to book the last room available at the Sheraton—the John F. Kennedy presidential suite. We made the trip a leisurely drive, stopping off in Buffalo, New York, to fill up on the city's namesake chicken wings where they originated, at the Anchor Bar.

In 1964, the restaurant's owner, Teressa Bellissimo, whipped up the first batch of deep-fried wings folded with a spicy hot sauce that is ideal with blue cheese dip and crunchy celery stalks. In those days, they also came with the down-and-dirty jazz vocal stylings of Dodo Green, the first woman who was ever signed to Blue Note Records and something of a legend.

The next day we stoked it to Mars, arriving precisely with everyone else. We were not the only ones who knew how to pack an SUV to the roof rack, except many of these vehicles were jammed with dogs in their crates, who also wanted very much to be out of them. Barking and howling filled the soaring atrium of the Sheraton, which turned out to have acoustics worthy of Carnegie Hall, prerenovation. While others packed their luggage carts with dogs, Wally and I strolled across the lobby to check in.

"Welcome to Mars," said the desk clerk. I felt as though I had arrived somewhere outside of the galaxy. While Stephen wrestled with the baggage, Wally and I went to check out the presidential suite on the fifth floor. We rode the glass-paneled elevator with a white bull terrier that looked just like Spuds MacKenzie. They were everywhere.

I could not help humming "Hail to the Chief" when we got to the room—a spacious and well-appointed suite overlooking all of the action in the atrium. One distinctive feature was an obvious difference in shading in the carpeting, where a throw rug had been removed, no doubt to prevent anticipated dog damage. It left a fine clear space for Wally to play soccer. I set up his food and water bowls in the wet bar area and watched Stephen struggling with the bags beside a woman who had four dog crates and at least as many zebra-striped dog beds strapped to her luggage cart.

I felt as though I knew many of the people and dogs at the show. Some of them recognized me from the photographs on my books, but I was at a loss to figure out who they were unless they told me their dogs' names. A conversation might go something like this:

"Hi, Marsha, is that you?"

"Yes, great to be here."

"I'm Lynn, Pacman's mom."

"Great to meet you. How is he doing?"

I also met people who knew me only by the e-mail address name I had chosen—one that I may never live down—"Hucklebutter." One person who had been most helpful during Wally's illness was a breeder who called himself TOM in capital letters in his e-mails. He was a retired naval officer with a clever wit and a judge's eye for dogs. When I saw a figure in a navy baseball cap sitting alone on a bench in front of the hotel watching the dogs arrive, I figured it had to be him. Wally was finishing a walk, and we approached.

"Tom?" I asked. He nodded. "I'm Marsha. You helped me so much and I want to thank you."

"What's your handle?" he said, not taking his eyes off of Wally.

"I'm the Hucklebutter," I admitted.

"Ah, then this must be Wally." They sat on the bench together and had a perfect visit.

I also met up with Marty, the westerner who was letting me peddle my Wally Balls at her booth. A big-hearted and direct woman, Marty had everything from T-shirts to sculptures of bull terriers on surfboards to sell. We had a corner booth, and I brought Wally down to keep us company. He was a crowd pleaser, winding his way through corridors crowded with shoppers and dogs, carrying a ball in a pail.

Wally took over Marty's chair and proceeded to "arrooo" at my vase full of his balls. I dipped into the inventory and gave him an orange one to chew and nudge. He nudged it right off the chair, where it rolled under the skirted table next to us, featuring hand-painted bull terriers on ceramics and glassware. The whole table shook when Wally beelined after his ball. I ended up with one handleless mug as a souvenir.

After returning Wally to the room, I watched a wedding party photography session in the atrium. I met some of the bridesmaids in the elevator. They had nothing to do with bull terriers but offered that the bride and groom shared an allergy to dog dander. Now they were having a difficult time getting a picture taken without a dog in the background. I do not imagine that the question of whether or not a dog show is being held at the hotel is one that occurs to many wedding planners. Perhaps it should.

CNN was on the television in the lobby with the sound off. Now the scrolling news line said that anthrax had killed some postal workers. The world was mad, and I was at a dog show selling balls.

That afternoon Stephen came back from his business meetings, and we went into Pittsburgh to visit the Andy Warhol Museum. All was whimsical and well observed until we took a side tour of an exhibition of photographs and postcards taken during the era when African Americans were routinely lynched. These disturbing images seared my mind. The world had been mad before 2001.

Marty dined with us in the evening at a steakhouse where they served drinks bigger than your head and meat portions so large they hung off the plate. Stephen was initially wary of "Internet people," fancying the potential risk of meeting serial killers and other demented sorts online. Once Marty started telling stories about her bull terrier, Rocky, Stephen started in on Wally stories. I hardly got a word in edgewise.

The next morning was the day of the big show. I got up early to take

Wally out for his constitutional before Stephen left for another day at the studio. It was a Steeltown grim, rainy day, and I had no umbrella.

A grassy area had been fenced off for dogs to do their business, complete with cleanup bags. We scooted across the parking lot, and I could tell from Wally's demeanor that he had business to conduct. With other dogs in the area, his attitude changed. Wally is not what you would call a shy dog, he simply prefers his privacy. In the interest of responsible dog ownership, I retrieve what-comes-out, but he prefers me to avert my eyes while it happens. The idea of other dogs watching him derailed his will.

We walked around and around without any action. My sodden running shoes squished on the wet grass and I must have looked as miserable as my feet felt.

"Having trouble?" a voice asked, and I looked away from Wally to see a pleasant fellow sporting three earrings in one ear.

I explained that we had spent twenty minutes in the rain and I knew Wally had more than his bladder to empty, but he refused to void himself in the company of other dogs.

"Have you got a match?" asked the stranger. I thought he had not heard me properly through the earrings, so I repeated my dilemma.

Lo and behold, he produced a match and advised me to insert it in Wally's voiding aperture.

I am not the sort of person who accepts the advice of strangers without considering the source. However, this fellow had a handsome bull terrier at the end of his leash. A sturdy male, the tawny, reddish colored dog had black commas as "eyebrows" framing a streak of white that ran down his forever-smiling face. Wally and the red dog sniffed each other amiably. I figured anyone with such a good-looking, friendly dog probably had good intentions.

"Just insert it into his anus and that should do the trick," said the stranger, holding forth the match in the rain. "Don't let go of it."

With mixed feelings, I withdrew Wally to a space between two cars and dutifully inserted the sulfurous end of the match, withdrawing it quickly and hoping no one had seen my act of indignity.

We returned to the grass and continued walking to no avail. At the other end of the enclosure, I noted the red dog succeeding where Wally failed. I shrugged. I was given another match and told to leave it in place longer than my furtive two-second attempt.

The jaunty dog and his owner were halfway across the parking lot when the match worked its wonders. Like Blanche DuBois in *A Streetcar Named Desire*, I was beholden to "the kindness of strangers."

In the hotel lobby, Wally gave himself a great shake, all over a nicely turned-out and carefully groomed bitch owned by another of my e-mail friends, Naomi. Her girl, Six, was the sixth in her litter. A dark brindle beauty, I swear she flirted with Wally, and he was smitten. Later, I saw Naomi in the grooming area smoothing Six's dampened coat while all of the groomers joined in a rousing chorus of the Baha Men's "Who Let the Dogs Out."

You could hear them as far away as the hotel restaurant where the honeymooners were sneezing over breakfast.

"Who let the dogs out? Woof. Woof."

The Silverwood show was a grand event, parading champion dog after champion dog. I was fortunate enough to sit beside a woman who told me she had been in the breed "since the Ice Age." Quite the character, she regaled me with whispered comments on dogs and their handlers.

"Look see that bitch needs more fill to her face," she said. "And so-and-so should know better than to bring that undershot dog into the ring. And will you look at that botched ear set."

By the time it was over I knew every flaw Wally could possibly have.

At the banquet that evening, I regaled my new friends with the matchstick story. They howled, and I learned that it is an old trick used by handlers at shows and obedience trials. Rubbing a leash across the area is another method of stimulation. After hearing that, I found my-self looking at dog handlers' leashes in a different way.

I also found out who my kind stranger was. The Silverwood winner was the red dog, Ch. Rocky Tops Sundance Kid, popularly known as "Rufus." The stranger was Tom Bishop, one of his owners. Five years later, I saw Tom again. He was celebrating in the ring at the Westmin-ster Kennel Club Dog Show, where the same grinning dog won Best in Show.

I sure can pick them.

27

"Let Old Wrinkles Come"

The remaining sojourn was spectacular. Fallingwater, architect Frank Lloyd Wright's triumph on Bear Run Creek, is a marvel. A feeling of Zen and natural trancing occurs inside that woodland retreat, with its cantilevered concrete terraces suspended over water, polished floors of quarried stone, and eye-of-the-forest views through seamless windows. The autumn leaves peaked as we ambled home through a national park.

The serenity of Fallingwater stayed with me for days. I wanted to hang on to it forever but knew I could not. Arriving home, I made an immediate appointment with my doctor.

I think I knew something was amiss for a while, but it was the single-ply toilet paper in the roadside motel where we stayed one night in less-than-Sheraton circumstances that prompted actual bleeding. Empowered by Eve Ensler's play *The Vagina Monologues*, I can admit that there was trouble with my vagina. There were subtle changes in the skin, and a patch was raised with a pearllike surface. What I had tried to convince myself was that something natural to do with aging had turned into something suspicious.

My family doctor is also a friend who has the finest wine cellar in town. He keeps a pair of Clydesdale draft horses that he harnesses for parades and handles with pride. His wife is a nurse who leaves him for months at a time to travel to the far north to minister to the ills of aboriginal people. In doing so, she also befriended the stray dogs that abound there—dogs that are often shot or face starvation. She established a program called Friends of Animush to bring veterinarians from the south to remote communities where they conduct open clinics—neutering, vaccinating, and educating. Her home is an open door to distressed and abandoned animals.

I knew from my doctor's friendly face that the diagnosis was not good news. He called it squamous cell carcinoma in situ—a form of skin cancer. That was a new one on me. I now imagine that you can even get cancer of the fingernails and nose hairs.

Telling Stephen was the hard part. When they were still married, his ex-wife had been hospitalized for two years as a consequence of a cancerous tumor. All of the other patients who had the same form of the disease died. Three times, Stephen was told to expect not to see her again. The treatment involved so many intense drugs that her personality changed significantly. When she recovered she hopped into a travel trailer with a West Coast sports promoter, leaving Stephen and her children behind. The words *cancer* and *hospital* are trouble to Stephen.

A biopsy by a skin specialist confirmed the condition. Now I was getting scared. Due process would have sent me to a gynecologist, followed by an oncologist. Stephen was having nothing to do with due process. He was on the cell phone to Erica as we drove out of the medical clinic parking lot.

A brunette dynamo, Erica and her husband, David, are an attractive and vivacious team capable of holding their own in any conversation. Erica is also a physician who keeps abreast of who is doing what best in the medical community. Anyone who knows her and has a hint of illness calls on Erica for advice and referral. The woman has been sainted by many. Erica got me an appointment with an oncologist in a couple of weeks.

"I would send my daughter to him," she said. That was good enough for me.

Naturally, I was doing my own research, following spidery Internet links that gave meaning to the term World Wide Web. I also found a support group of about a hundred women suffering from the same condition. These voices of experience held back nothing, sharing their surgical and recovery stories freely and openly, often with dark humor. They came from Australia, America, Canada, England, Scotland, and the Bahamas. Some were educated, some not. All were bonded by cancer and what they cavalierly called their "DVs." When I asked what they referred to, a wickedly chortling chorus shouted out in e-mail: "Designer Vaginas, of course."

I was speechless, even more so when I learned there are plastic surgery clinics that do nothing but perform variations of such surgery for purposes of vanity. I have always been more partial to the theory of the Nurse in Shakespeare's *Romeo and Juliet*: "With mirth and laughter let old wrinkles come."

My oncologist was a smallish man who did not look directly at me, preferring to stare at the edge of a table or a jar of cotton balls. His assistant was more chatty—a young Dane who had just returned from a stint working with Doctors Without Borders in Africa. He was passionate about the work and told me all about it while taking more samples and setting me up for a colposcopy, allowing the oncologist a magnified view of the area. I had gone through all of this many years earlier when precancerous cells were removed from my cervix. The same catchall phrase applied: "This is going to pinch a bit."

The diagnosis was vulvar intraepithial neoplasia staged at level III. I was scheduled for laser surgery, and the nurse could answer any of my questions.

"Ninety percent of the recurrences I see are smokers. You should quit," said the oncologist almost hopelessly. Then he was gone.

"You'll have such lovely pink skin once it's healed," the nurse confided. A small reward for undergoing second-degree burns and not being able to cross my legs for two weeks, I thought. Giving everyone in the office copies of my books and leaving a signed set for the oncologist was my way of putting a face on my vagina.

That evening when I wrote to the "Gyngals" about my appointment, I learned that a member of our group died that day. Statistics suggested a five-year survival rate of anywhere from 90 percent to 50 percent, depending—always depending. Gobsmacked by the reality of what I was facing, I dedicated my house as a smoke-free zone in Terri's honor and vowed to quit in the six weeks before my surgery.

Stephen had not smoked in years, and some of my friends were not even aware that I smoked because I tried to respect the air space of others. However, the ashtray in my office was seldom empty. When words did not come easily on the page, I smoked and they came. I later found that even without a cigarette, the same words came. I took a break from the intensity of writing a novel and returned to short stories.

Addiction is powerful, but I had the ideal circumstance in which to quit my habit of thirty years. The motivation was to save my own life. I could not cheat in the house without it being noticed, since Stephen has the nose of a plott hound. It was December, and smoking outdoors was chilling. Gradually, I cut back. Stephen joked that if I had been told that secondhand smoke could be harmful to Wally, I would have quit years ago.

My last cigarette dwindled to ash outside of the office of a doctor who practices hypnotism on his entertainment industry patients. He can place suggestions about remembering lines in insecure actors' heads and remove the "block" from screenwriters stuck in a rut. Now he was going help me quash my addiction once and for all.

I remember my hypnosis quite clearly. It was almost an out-of-body experience. I listened to my breathing and the doctor's voice. He had me imagining I was in an elevator going down. My head slumped forward. Down I went. Then I was to picture myself on a beach alone. I felt beautiful. I drifted into the clouds, where I put my last package of cigarettes into a shimmering box and watched it float away. My health was important, and I would protect it. I could return to this safe place anytime I had the urge to smoke or had any tension to alleviate. I got back in the elevator—up and out.

I tried inducing the state a few times before the surgery. It worked. Thanks to my support group our household was more than prepared for my recovery. I had books to read, movies to watch, and chocolates at my bedside. The freezer was stocked with homemade chicken soup. I was not allowed in the barn for at least a month, so Stephen had been versed in chores and stupid sheep tricks.

Wally knew something was afoot, something not to do with him. He took to crawling under my desk and lying across my feet. The morning we left for the hospital, he played frenetic soccer on the front lawn. Everything about it was, "Look at me. Look at me." I had to laugh. He was irrepressibly goofy.

Tagged and gowned at the hospital, Stephen stayed with me until they wheeled me up to the surgical floor. He was told to call in after an hour and a half, when I would be ready for discharge. The emotion was intense. I told the big lug to be sure Wally had water, and we hugged good-bye.

An orderly left me a few feet from the operating room. After telling me it would not be long, a nurse draped me in a crisp cotton sheet. Then I waited, writing stories in my head, since there were no magazines or books in the clinically clean environment. A flurry of activity in the corridors followed. An accident involving multiple injuries took precedent over my impending bonfire. I was moved to another corridor and abandoned.

Vowing to ride it out without panicking, I sent myself into a wholly pleasurable hypnotic state that led to blissful sleep.

Stephen was off visiting friends with Wally, pacing and calling the discharge station every half hour to see if I had been delivered. He increased his calls to every fifteen minutes after an hour and a half. Then he raced to the hospital and started asking questions. Nobody seemed to know where I was.

They checked the morgue. Finally, one nurse took it upon herself to search the mazelike surgical floor corridor by corridor and she found me—fast asleep with the sheet pulled over my head like a good parrot. Wheeling me over to the elevator area, Stephen was allowed to come up to assure himself that I was not on some coroner's slab.

When it finally came time, going into the operating room felt like going onto a television set. Surely this is not real, I thought. Those huge lights, people in masks, and that sound—that sound that is the patient's heartbeat, my heartbeat. There was a doughnut-shaped mold made of gelled plastic on the operating table. I told them they would need a larger one to accommodate my firmly packed buttocks. This brought a round of muffled giggles, since it was intended to cradle my head. They could laugh. That was a good sign.

The room fell suddenly silent when the oncologist—who I had taken to thinking of as "Dr. God"—entered the room looking intense and weary at the same time. I deeply wanted to greet him in my best George

Jones country-and-western voice—"Hello, darlin' "—but I resisted and simply asked if he had received the books I left for him. The tiniest curl started in his lips.

"Yes, I did. Don't have time to read much though," he said. "But I might move to the country myself one of these days. So thank you very much."

From behind her mask one of the nurses winked at me. Positioning my head in the doughnut, she whispered, "He *never* talks in surgery."

Satisfied that I had made myself a person, I followed the anesthetist's request to count backward from one hundred. Just before I blanked out, I blurted: "I quit smoking." Fading into oblivion I heard a faint, soft applause.

Stephen was with me when I shook my groggy head and reentered the world. Everything had gone well. All I had to do was heal. Stephen had a body pillow laid out for me on the truck's reclining seat. The ride home was bumpless, and Wally rested his head on my shoulder.

Throughout the following six weeks I was pampered, fussed over, and fed well. Under Stephen's care, the sheep grew round as they prepared for lambing season. Wally was gentle around me. While he normally jumped on the bed and dove under the covers, without concern for anything that might be in his path, he lay contentedly beside me.

Soon I was back at my desk, where I finished a book of short stories. I gave them all what I fervently hoped for myself—a happy ending.

28

Addressing the Bone

Though I survived that winter, our chickens and exotic pheasants did not. A killer mink laid siege to them. A bold creature no longer than my forearm, it lived in an underground den beneath the barn. Fueled solely by bloodlust, it systematically killed pen after pen of helpless birds no matter how much we fortified them with steel mesh. It always found the one weak link and edged its way through to the killing field. Too quick to be shot and too wily for Wally, we called it the Taliban Mink. When it was finally trapped there was no gitmo.

The mink had teeth like daggers, much worse than Wally's piranha puppy teeth. Now when I rolled Wally on his back and gazed into the chasm of his mouth I noticed that his canines were flat. It was as though the four normally fanglike teeth had been clipped off.

Perhaps that is why our twenty-two-year-old black barn cat, Webster, never minded it when Wally picked him up in his mouth and carried him around like a stick. Nothing surgical caused Wally's teeth to be blunt; he simply gnawed so many balls and hefted so many plastic pails that he'd worn them down.

Then there is dog breath. On a farm, a dog can get into eating all sorts of breath-altering items that do not fall into any food group. Wally prefers raccoon droppings. He likes to go for walks through the trees next to a cornfield where the black-eyed creatures have corn-eating orgies. His nostrils go on alert, and next thing you know he is head over teakettle in 'coon dung.

Consequently, I invested in a vastly overpriced sort of latex finger puppet with soft rubbery bristles. After fitting this device over my index finger, I smeared it with Doggydent toothpaste—also vastly over-priced.

Wally clamped his lips shut when I tried to rub the brownish paste over his teeth. Then he discovered that the toothpaste tasted like meat, and he could not get enough of the stuff, which made the brushing pointless.

As part of his diet, and to help clean his teeth naturally, I started giving Wally raw beef bones. At first, he ignored them, sniffing warily and backing away. Then he allowed himself to sample one. Ever so gin-gerly, he stood over it, gnawing, never lying down and capturing it with his paws, as other dogs do. His oddest bone behavior was "addressing" the bone. He strutted toward it as it lay on his dog bed. Pausing with his head held high, he gave it a singular bark. I had no idea what this shout-out was about. Perhaps he was just making sure that there was not a cow hiding in there or something.

When I pointed out Wally's flat canines to the veterinarian, we agreed that they warranted the attention of a specialist. Just like hu-mans, dogs can require root canal treatment—sometimes they even get crowns.

Eddie, the Jack Russell terrier on the old television sitcom *Frasier*, had seven root canals performed on his little teeth, due to wear caused by a tennis ball obsession. Known offscreen as Moose, his handlers only discovered the problem when the dog refused to pick up a Barbie doll in a scene from the show. Animals cannot tell us exactly where it hurts. With a dog like Wally, who does not flinch when he crashes into doors headfirst and wags his tail even if a baby carriage is resting on his paws, well, it can be hard to tell what he is feeling at any given moment.

I called the dental vet's office to make an appointment, and Dr. Fraser Hale answered the phone himself. We had a pleasant chat about Wally's mouth, the procedure involved in checking his teeth, and, of course, the potential impact on my bank account.

Having had a dentist for a father, I understood pretty much everything Dr. Hale talked about. And I have had a few root canals of my own. In fact I seemed to need a root canal every time my father came back from another course in what is technically known as endocrinology. It is not a procedure I would wish on a dog—and now here I was booking an appointment for Snoopy-nosed Wally.

In order to examine the teeth and take X-rays, Dr. Hale was going to put Wally under a general anesthetic. Wally fasted for twelve hours before his appointment. By morning, he had the look of a starving child in a CARE poster. Stephen shared his pain and made me take Wally's breakfast with us so that he could eat as soon as he was sensate.

Dr. Hale has treated everything from ferrets to fur seals, performed orthodontics on Siamese cats, and installed ceramic crowns on German shepherds. If it is a tooth, Dr. Fraser Hale can handle it. He also has a great dog bedside manner—open, friendly, well spoken. I would have let him pat my head if he wanted. Fairly quickly, Dr. Hale became simply Fraser.

We talked dog teeth for a while and looked at tooth diagrams and pondered the mystery of why dogs grind their teeth into oblivion. Fraser's assistants ran their hands over Wally continually, and he was obviously smitten.

Then the time came to actually do it. First Wally was given a sedative. Stephen and I sat with him in the waiting area, watching his eyes glaze over. A woman walked by with a large cat in her arms. Wally barely acknowledged them. I patted his head, and the tail that never stops wagging slumped to the floor. Then he pretty much crumpled into a heap.

Stephen carried all seventy-two pounds of Wally to the operating room. Fraser welcomed us to stay and observe the proceedings, or we could wait outside until he completed his exam and had a treatment plan to discuss. Stephen left immediately, probably needing a sedative himself. The sight of his beloved Wally rendered unconscious was far too disturbing for him. I watched while Wally was hooked up to all sorts of monitors and the anesthetic was administered.

In all of his years, I had never seen Wally the Wonder Dog so totally still. I rubbed his paws and stroked his ears, comforted by the heart monitor, which told me he was still in there and he would be back.

Fraser and his team moved efficiently, checking and charting each tooth before beginning the X-ray process. I do not know how many X-rays were taken. On the itemized bill all it said was "X-rays—lots."

Fraser showed each one to me, pointing out highlighted areas and places where pockets of infection could exist. Every new angle was a revelation. Finally it was narrowed down to eight "teeth of concern": four canines and four molars—all potential root canals.

The teeth in question had thick roots, even though dental roots are supposed to recede and slenderize in the aging process. Fraser said that five-year-old Wally had the roots of a one-year-old dog. How sexy is that? Unfortunately, when he first saw them on the X-rays, he also thought all eight teeth were as dead as canaries in cats. Examined closely, however, there was no sign of infection. I just have a big bull terrier with fat roots in his worn-down teeth.

Wally had a few problems with his gums, which were likely the cause of his unsavory, un-raccoon-related halitosis. Fraser treated those and set about a complete cleaning.

When it was over and done, Wally was wrapped in a blanket and moved to the floor, where he was duly hugged. By this time, the whole dental team was humming my nonsense "Wally Boy Wally" song, which has limited lyrics and virtually no melody.

Gradually the light dawned in Wally's eyes. He wagged his head instead of his tail, dopey but lovable. I imagine that certain cats could come out of such surgery with real attitude, but not Wally.

Fraser explained that Wally was still experiencing the narcotic effect of his sedative. The solution was to give him a shot that would reverse the narcotic. Fraser warned that the effect would be dramatic.

Well, it was Stephen King dramatic. Within thirty seconds Wally turned into a bull terrier on crystal meth. His ears perked up, his triangular eyes widened. Arching his back and hunching his butt, he launched across the waiting room like a bat out of hell with radar.

In the space of seconds a once near La-La-Land Wally had leaped to the top of the reception desk and was licking the ears of the office assistant, sending pet insurance brochures flying.

Then he was off again, sliding across the floor for a direct hit on the dog food display. One large bag of Science Diet cracked open, spilling kernels of puppy chow across the floor. With Stephen clinging to the leash, Wally wove his way through the waiting room chairs, knocking a few over and tangling his leash around at least one chair leg. He wound up at the dog toy display, bouncing six feet straight in the air to grab the leg of a stuffed Garfield toy. I added dog food and a toy to the check and considered asking for a reversal of the reversal drug.

After a while, Wally got back into his skin and licked the dental team good-bye. His teeth were polished pearls, his gums a lovely pink, and the grin was the one all dogs wear when they have just swallowed your wallet. And I loved him so.

29

Spelling Trouble

I n 2002, reality television turned its cameras on brain-fried Prince of Darkness Ozzy Osbourne and his family, including Minnie—a white Pomeranian with diamond-encrusted fangs.

Queen Elizabeth II made New York mayor Rudy Giuliani an honorary knight, and Martha Stewart lied to the feds about a stock sale. Enron and WorldCom led a wave of corporate scandals, while the Catholic Church was rocked by allegations of illicit sex and molestation.

"Axis of evil" and "weapons of mass destruction" became popular catchphrases in the "war on terror."

Meanwhile, sniping incidents in Maryland turned suburban gas stations and strip malls into hunting grounds, killing ten and wounding three. Serena Williams defeated her sister Venus at Wimbledon.

I could add to the list that Stephen Williams finished his second book, *Karla*, since that too was destined to bring headlines.

It started out badly, with Stephen's commissioning publisher going into bankruptcy, leaving the work temporarily homeless. Despite ongoing interest in the murder case and what one reporter called "the scoop of the century" in the correspondence Stephen had with the jailed succubus, publishers backed away from the book. Some of them would not even read it.

"My sense is that publishers don't go looking for trouble, and this book—and Williams himself—spell trouble," opined a professor of journalism, who had not read the book. One publisher called the book "excellent," but some of her colleagues threatened to resign rather than be involved with it.

Finally, a small French-language publisher stepped forward, and the book was published in a language in which neither Stephen nor I are fluent. A few days later, at the prompting of the lawyer for the victims' families, the attorney general ordered a police investigation into whether or not Stephen's correspondence with Karla Homolka violated the sweetheart deal his predecessor had made.

It was a typical knee-jerk reaction.

The media swarmed like blackflies, and the public hailed the idea that the case might be reopened, allowing for an appropriate sentence to be passed. Next thing you knew, Jerry Springer was sending producers to Canada to try to get jailhouse interviews.

The controversy made the book a French-language best seller, even though it was a tempest in a teapot. The conditions imposed by the so-called deal with the devil merely restricted Karla Homolka from discussing or profiting from her crimes "for the purpose of any book, movie or like endeavor." She and Stephen never discussed her crimes.

The police investigation had stalled because there were no French-speaking officers available to translate it. They got their chance early in 2003, when it was published in English. Reviews were stellar, citing the book as "solid investigative journalism uncovering ineptitude on a massive scale." There were comparisons to Truman Capote and Norman Mailer.

If the book's critical reception was positive, its public perception was poison. In an unprecedented theatrical twist, the lawyer for the families of the victims held a press conference that was televised live on two national networks. The lawyer fumed and fulminated about the book, suggesting that its contents were illegal and urging bookstore owners to voluntarily remove it from their stores.

The rant sent the book to the best-seller list and the investigation was transferred to the Major Crimes Unit.

There is no "normal life" when the centurions are circling. I found it difficult to focus on my own novel. Stress had never affected my work before, so I asked my doctor for a CAT scan to see if there was something physical distracting me. He called to say that yes, indeed, I had a brain and it seemed to be functioning normally, at least from a physiological perspective.

Stephen and I vowed to be kind to each other. It sounds simple, but it took effort we had never needed before. I had appearances and speeches to keep up while promoting my own work. We made these events into mini trips away from the new "trubbles." I was reading with a friend at a lakeside community, and we all went out afterward and got silly over a superb dinner. The next morning we walked Wally along an empty beach that stretched for miles.

It was strange to be living with the best-selling author in the land and also having him hung out as a pariah. And then there was me: "nice person and funny lady, friend of animals." If my readers or broadcast listeners connected us, how did they reconcile that difference between us? A newspaper columnist summed it up: "She's funny, and he's not." Yet I still found great humor in Stephen's company. How could I not when I watched him play with Wally? Grabbing those pointed ears and twirling them around while saying, "You need an attitude adjustment, fella. Neener, neener, neener." Whereupon Wally twirled backward, whacking his head on a table leg and falling down in adoration.

I noted that even the most crusty media people had a hard time falling for the "evil Stephen" line when they saw man and dog together. Writing a profile that appeared on the front page of a newspaper that serves a city of several million, the reporter who visited the farm began his story: "Wally is as stubborn as they come, a concrete-block of a dog who wants to play and won't take 'no' for an answer."

At the end of April we had two engagements: a party thrown by my publisher in the city and a reading I was giving in a gentrified rural town. Our expenses were paid; we had money in our pocket, and the highway stretched out for mile after graceful mile.

At times like that, all you need is a leash and a dog like Wally to find nirvana.

30

By the Book

During the months of controversy, Stephen was as restless and busy as a puppy. When he was not giving interviews, he was in his office, toying with Web sites he was creating for both of us. They were works in progress that spanned several years.

My Web site was all sunshine and lollipops, pictures of the farm and Wally and excerpts from books. Stephen's was larger, containing background on his books that included excerpts from discovery material, police interviews, and statements. He bought *Creating Web Sites for Dummies* and a software program, twiddling with the technology when he was bored and consulting a helpful webmaster. Every once in a while he e-mailed me a link to what he was doing and I took a look, although it clashed with my novelist's immersion in the ambit of a Scottish Presbyterian cult in the 1800s.

A couple of days before we were to attend my publisher's party, Stephen engaged in an exchange with a reporter of his acquaintance. The pair constantly winged quips and jabs at each other. The reporter suggested Stephen was up at the farm staring out the window. Stephen countered that, in fact, he was at work on something quite interesting, and he mentioned his Web site. A few hours later, the reporter called to say that he was going to do a story about it—no matter that the Web site was "under construction" and no matter that it was not listed on any search engines.

The resulting story was disjointed and lurid, suggesting that Stephen eventually planned to post videotape with sexual content to the Web site, along with extensive details of the investigation. The Web site address was provided in the article, otherwise no one could have found it.

Among the first, and by far the most prevalent, to log on to the Web site that day were the police. While tens of thousands of people visited one or two pages of the site, few could be bothered dealing with its slowness and the many dead links. I had Stephen show me his Web site. When he opened the first page of a police statement, scrolling through it I saw the name of a sexual assault victim whose identity was protected. My gut twisted. Stephen immediately e-mailed the Internet service provider, instructing that the entire Web site be shut down then and there.

I left to walk Wally. He trotted down the hotel corridor without a care, and I longed to replace my turmoil with his blissful ignorance. We walked through the familiar park across from the courthouse, an all-too-familiar building that I thought of as a part of my past.

At the party and at dinner afterward my thoughts roiled. Mistakes like that happen in newspapers all the time, without intent. There have been incidents in which a person who was in the witness protection program has been identified, to their mortal jeopardy. The news organization apologized, and the judge advised them to be more careful. Responsible media do not set out to identify victims of sexual assault, and Stephen had made it clear in the author's note to his first book that he had changed names to protect "the privacy of the many innocent victims." What was done was done, and the remedy was made without a moment's hesitation. Somehow I did not think that would matter.

The next day, as we drove to my speaking engagement, Stephen's lawyer Eddie Greenspan called. If Stephen had made a mistake, Eddie said he had done exactly the right thing. Eddie told him that he was already on the record and would handle any discussions about charges with the authorities.

"Tell Marsha to stop worrying. You aren't going to jail," Eddie said. With a laugh he added, "Besides, if you do go to jail she can visit or she can leave you."

The Tri-County Literacy Festival was a great success. I signed more than one hundred books with the help of the organizers, since Stephen stayed at the motel, trying to contact the webmaster to make sure his instructions had been followed.

A full-blown spring day followed. We started the weekend with a coastal drive to a village by a bay where there is a company that makes replicas of antique tin tiles I'd thought would be ideal at the farm. We puttered along, taking back roads and stopping at empty parks where Wally could play, running up the slide steps and flattening himself across my lap while we slid down. At home, I had an hour before sunset to plant a row of radishes and lettuce, while Stephen barbecued and the lambs grazed in the lane.

The next morning we started going about our business when we heard *pings* from the security system, indicating something was in the lane. Three police cruisers pulled up in front of the house. Five officers emerged, three with guns drawn running around to the sides and back of the house. My first thought was: Where's Wally? My second was, Where's Eddie?

Proceeding by the book, one local officer and one "soother" were sent to arrest Stephen. Having "secured the perimeter" and discovered that he was not armed or dangerous, the others left.

"What is this, Henry?" Stephen asked, recognizing an outfielder from the Master Batters baseball team in the slow-pitch league he had played in years earlier.

"You're being arrested and charged with breaching a court order, Stephen. We've been told to bring you in," said Henry.

"Here's the charging document," said the soother in his best "I'm just the messenger" voice. Henry told us they always send a soother when the higher-ups think the arrest might be confrontational.

"Just call me Bill," he said with a thin smile.

We fudged and plodded as much as we could. The guys were okay with Wally, but he lay on his bed and did not even try to play with them. Uniforms are intimidating things, as are guns, even in their holsters. No adopted tones of voice or faux manners complement paramilitary fashion.

Stephen left a message at the offices of Greenspan Partners, and Henry went for the handcuffs.

"Whoa," said Stephen, "I thought we were just going in to the local station for another set of mug shots and fingerprints and then release on my own recognizance."

"We're going to town first, but after that we have no instructions," said Bill, who was obviously perturbed that he was being kept in the dark and treated like a pizza delivery boy.

"Just to warn you, it could be an overnighter."

"You've got to be kidding," I said, but Henry shook his head.

"Well, he's certainly not going anywhere dressed like that," I responded.

Stephen went to change from his shorts and T-shirt and I went to pack his suit bag. There was no way my man was going to appear before Lady Justice half dressed with hay in his hair.

In another bag, I packed toiletries, combining a mélange of the many pills Stephen now took—stomach pills, blood pressure pills, nerve pills—all ones he knows by sight. Then I threw in some cottage cheese and fruit, wishing I had baked cookies instead of planting radishes the night before.

The handcuffs came out and bile rose in my throat. They hauled Stephen off like a drug dealer, cramming him sideways in the small backseat of the cruiser. His face jammed against the window because a man his size wearing handcuffs simply does not fit.

In torturous foreign regimes, writers, intellectuals, and teachers have routinely "disappeared," for expressing opinions and publicizing facts.

Now I knew the frightening feeling of seeing my own loved one hauled off by the very authorities he had been so critical of. Wally sat quietly with me all afternoon. He did not interrupt me by dropping balls at my feet or whacking my calf with his nose when I was talking on the telephone.

Late in the day, we went for a walk through the woods. Chasing his balls, Wally made mad runs through the trees, zigzagging his way so close to the bark that he should have been seared. Everything about him screamed, "Look at me. Look at me." It was as though he thought he could make everything all right, or at least make me feel better. Dogs do not even have to try to be endearing.

What would be would be. I had no power to change a thing—just rage, and even that was growing weary.

31

Tunnel Vision

Without Stephen that night, our bed might as well have been the size of a football field. Wally likes to lean against his "dad," pressing Stephen to the edge of the bed. I am not as malleable. Sharing a bed with a bull terrier is a mug's game. They maximize their space creatively, stretching horizontally atop the pillows, or diagonally across the bed, keeping their legs as stiff as newel posts. Wally is a "tunneler." Several times a night, he wakes up under the covers, realizes he is suffocating, slithers to the bottom of the bed, and slides to the floor with a thud. I have long since abandoned any thought about tucking in the bottom sheet, lest he be caught like a sausage in a blanket.

After a brief snooze on the rug that softens his fall, he shakes himself awake, stretches with a groan, and plods through the darkness to his water bowl, submerging his entire lower jaw and lapping up as much water as he sloshes around. Then he burps—an all-too-human sound, reminiscent of a burghermeister who has just consumed a full stein at an Oktoberfest beer hall. Getting back into bed involves scaling me first, then stretching over to Stephen's shoulder and whacking him upside the head with that anvil of a nose. Awake or asleep, Stephen automatically responds by raising the covers so that Wally can tunnel between us until he almost suffocates again, and the process repeats itself.

Wally does not attempt to wake me because he knows it is futile. I am a power sleeper. I once slept through a fog-bound flight in a light aircraft filled with former Vietnam fighter pilots who were accompanying the governor of Louisiana on a fishing trip to Costa Rica. We were flying through mountains west from San Jose to Parismina on the Caribbean in fog as thick as vichyssoise. The plane had no instruments, and radios did not work in the mountains. The pilot, who looked to be about twelve, was listening to marimba music on his Walkman. All around me men were alternately cursing, praying, or retching. Stephen kept asking me, "What should we do, what should we do?" Then he noticed that I had pulled a vest over my head and was fast asleep. I woke up just as we were landing, zigzagging down the pitted runway to avoid sea turtles.

So I slept through Stephen's outrageous night in jail. Wally and I in the king-size bed with the super-size duvet we had made so that we'd have a chance of some covers, even when Wally hogs them. Not by choice did I stay at the farm. I simply do not have the driving skills to wade into urban traffic. I felt like quite an idiot. Here I was, ace sheep wrestler, fearless speaker and catcher of a nine-pound bass on a light line, but four-lane highways were beyond my ken. I wanted to stand proudly beside Stephen. Even more, I wanted to post his bail.

The prosecutor was demanding a pledge of $25,000 to secure Stephen's release, and that had to be done in person. I was in touch with our party host friends Barry and Claire all day, and then I put the real touch on them. Having once been detained in a South African jail during the apartheid period, author/broadcaster/poet/raconteur Barry Callaghan is all too familiar with the treatment that those who delve in what he calls "the word" can confront under dictatorial and fascist regimes. He was not about to see his friend languish in jail and agreed to provide Stephen's bond.

Stephen spent his night behind bars in his underwear on a concrete slab without a pillow or a blanket. A light was trained on him at all times, and a female civilian was brought in to sit outside of the cell, watching him all night, averting her eyes only when he required the toilet. Although the police thought Stephen's claustrophobia was fake, they left the outer door to the station house area slightly ajar.

As a young child, Stephen's mother used to tie him to his bed to prevent him from wandering into the parental bedroom. One day when his children were still with us, we visited their grandparents. Stephen's mother was ironing, as usual. This time was different only because she was pressing Stephen's baby clothes, which she kept for some inexplicable reason and laundered religiously once a year.

Curious to see the clothing that their father once fit into, the children asked what the strips of blue leather were for. Stephen's mother did not even look up through the steam.

"These were your father's tie-down straps," she said' matter-of-factly, and the story rolled out about the necessity of keeping a three-year-old confined to his bed. After that, I never questioned the reality of Stephen's claustrophobia.

Breakfast was the apple I sent with him. He was not allowed soap, a towel, or his toothbrush, and the police forgot to return his vintage Porsche watch. Dogs in a pound are treated better, and I understand Stephen communicated that sentiment. The handcuffs were put back on.

Before the bail hearing, he was held in the basement of the courthouse where the cells are filled with desperate souls and abandoned hopes. By this time, everyone in the courthouse knew who Stephen was because the media had flooded the parking lot with camera crews. A friendly guard removed Stephen's handcuffs and put him in a large private cell.

"I'm your biggest fan," she said. "If I had known they were bringing you here I would have brought my book for you to sign."

Recuffed at the insistence of the police, Stephen was paraded before a justice of the peace. The prosecutor laid out her bail stipulations. Then Mr. Greenspan took the floor, sharing a brief jest with the J.P., who had been a student of his. He spoke to Stephen's education, good character, and lack of any previous criminal record. Outside of court, Eddie lambasted the attorney general, calling the circumstances of the arrest "a stain on the democracy that we live in."

Eddie also questioned the appropriateness of the prosecutor's involvement, noting that she had been portrayed "in a light she can not have enjoyed" in Stephen's first book, *Invisible Darkness*. As a junior prosecutor, she'd had an affair with her married boss, a senior prosecutor. He was one of the architects of the deal that gave a flimsy twelve-year sentence to a murderess. Now they were married, and her boss was her husband. He assigned her to Stephen's prosecution, and she made sure Stephen spent an unholy night in jail. When the cuffs finally came off and Stephen walked out of the courthouse, he was surrounded by reporters.

"I've always thought there was a vendetta being exercised," he told them.

Still furious about every aspect of the situation, Eddie drove Stephen downtown to his favorite watering hole and refuge, Bistro 990, and told him to have a decent lunch. Then, in an elegant gesture, he sent a limousine to ferry his weary client home to the farm.

We collapsed that night between clean sheets, with our heads on feather pillows. Wally tunneled, thudded, slurped, and burped all night, happy to have his world returned to normal.

32

Wally at the Met

Now we were news in our own neighborhood. In fact, we were news even before Stephen's arrest. Unbeknownst to us, police cruisers and unmarked cars had been patrolling in front of our lane for two days before we got home.

"Oh yeah, they were just watching and waiting for you to get home," one neighbor offered. "It was like they were swarming."

One message left on our telephone answering machine might have foiled the whole ugly mess and Stephen could have simply surrendered in the presence of his lawyer. We said nothing, knowing that when most people see any police activity they back away, shut up, and shun—in about that order.

Simultaneous to the laying of the criminal charges, Stephen was ordered to surrender his archive of discovery materials and computer files immediately. A challenge had to be lodged.

Although Stephen never set out to be a poster boy for freedom of expression, he had no choice but to defend himself. Never mind his archives and lofty journalistic principles, we stood to lose everything, including the farm and Wally's bed to the "unspecified damages" that senior government prosecutors harped on in a pernicious civil lawsuit. I do not know if there are angels, but I do know that good friends have stood by us above and beyond anything I could ever have imagined. They stood up by using their words. They stood up by providing unwavering support. They stood up by writing big checks when our coffers were bare.

Even though it is technically against the law for the government to sue a citizen while conducting a criminal prosecution on the same grounds, governments do what they want. Only time and money can stop that steamroller. We tried to assist the lawyers, but in those early days we never really understood what was going on.

The day that we went into court to attempt to have the injunction quashed, one of the lead lawyers looked at us and said, "I'm going to lose today big-time because this judge hates my guts, but we'll win on appeal."

You want to light your hair on fire and run screaming from the building, but you cannot.

We spent almost six weeks living in the city, talking to lawyers. It could have been a stressful time, but we made our headquarters at the Metropolitan Hotel, where Wally was treated like a little prince.

The city was seized by the epidemic of severe acute respiratory syndrome (SARS), which spread from China, Hong Kong, and Singapore to twenty-nine countries worldwide, affecting 8,098 people and causing 774 deaths, including forty-four in Toronto—the SARS capital of North America. Tourists stayed away in droves, having fallen prey to RATS (reluctant American tourism syndrome).

Ultimately, fifteen hundred hotel workers lost their jobs that summer. The Metropolitan welcomed us with open arms and cheery smiles, providing a luxury suite and all amenities at a gracious discount. In return, Wally played entertainer.

The idea of living in a hotel is a commonplace fantasy. The reality is not commonplace at all. We took Wally out for his morning walk, picked up our lattes and fruit, and returned to find the room cleaned, sheets changed, bed made, and a fresh flower in a vase.

Wally worshipped Eduardo, the South American bellman who balanced soccer balls on the toes of his shoes and steered the ball with all kinds of fancy footwork. Stanley achieved an elevated position in his Asian family because he knew the famous arrested author. Stanley wanted to walk Wally desperately, but Wally would only go to his designated spot, do his business, and drag Stanley back to the hotel. Brian, who could get you anything you wanted any time of the day or night, sometimes came to the room just to kick a ball around with Wally and gossip about hotel goings-on. We missed Ronnie at the door and several of the check-in clerks, casualties of the SARS scare and RATS.

One of the maids, who was too shy to give her name, was afraid of Wally when we first occupied room 2007. Over the weeks, she grew to know him and us. Several of my books have been translated into Chinese, and I shared them with her. I think she enjoyed them, but I have no idea how good the translation was. During the process, I had cryptic requests from the translator asking things like, "If a person is two pickles short of a jar, where did the pickles go?" and "Where is your 'neck of the woods' and why is it in your neck?" I had written a story about a cow that kicked the "bejeebers" out of me and fear that readers in Taiwan may well believe that western farmers have a strange addition to their anatomy.

Gradually, the shy maid became Wally's friend. She kicked the ball for him and wasn't bothered when he would lie on the rug, rolling on his back like a flipped-over frog. When I showed her the spot behind Wally's ear where the fur is heavenly soft, she smiled, watching him cave into a mystic state.

"This is Wally Dog," she said in her careful English, introducing a new maid to him. "He is good dog. No bark. Plays ball with feet. He is all boy dog. No circumcised."

I had not even noticed her looking.

We cleared our heads of lawyers by discovering parks and neighborhoods and walking Wally through them. Leafy ravines, back alleys, and crowded market streets flooded our senses with something other than constitutional mumbo jumbo.

Back at the hotel, Wally played *Eloise at the Plaza*, sneaking out of the hotel room to hucklebutt the halls and sliding across the marble floor in the lobby. He had many admirers. Everyone who worked at the Metropolitan seemed to have a dog—everything from manager Jeremy's couch-potato Nova Scotia duck tolling retriever that would not retrieve to doorman Paul's black-and-tan rottweiler. They all had time for Wally and knew exactly where to rub him to get his back leg scratching.

Hotel guests were also friendly. I could always tell when Wally and Stephen ran into a KLM flight crew in the lobby because they both came back to the room smelling of French-milled soap and perfume.

Occasionally, we met a guest who was nervous of Wally.

"His name is Wally and he's quite friendly," I told them, giving him a pat. "If you look at his face, he looks like a bicycle seat with eyes." Who could be scared of that?

I do not remember what or how we ate during those long weeks. Friends were a constant source of barbecues. I slapped salads and sandwiches together in the room. Sometimes we met poets in the ethnic parts of town and ate fish with their heads on while arguing about existential questions. In midweek, we took a day or two at the farm, checking the animals and tending the garden. I mixed up large batches of Wally food and froze it for the days to come.

While we were in the city, a young man from a farm family watched over the livestock and the grounds. The sheep and horses were out on pasture with an automatic waterer, so they were pretty much on their own. Greg kept the lawn mowed and the chickens fed. He had been doing chores in the days before Stephen's arrest and the police had followed him and traced his license plate. That such an innocent and honest person had been "tailed" deeply offended me.

When we returned to the hotel, it was always the same thing. A grand greeting for Wally and a note in the room from the manager welcoming Wally back with carefully wrapped gourmet dog biscuits. We felt secure there, almost as if we were surrounded by a rich and caring family.

As the civil litigator predicted, the judge finally ruled against every learned argument presented to him, and the injunction stood. Stephen surrendered sealed bankers' boxes containing his archives, computer files, and whatever else seemed relevant to the court, and they were locked away in a room where wiretap evidence was stored. It was July, the best month of summer, and time to go home. We returned just in time to lock up the cats.

A stray family of kittens had shown up in the woodpile in early February. The gray mother and her seven kittens appeared and disappeared—one day scampering playfully along the cedar-rail fence and the next hidden from sight. Eventually, three calicos stayed in the barn to manage the mice population and eat spare chicken eggs. They were splashy females who kept to themselves but never minded a pat. They were also about to come into heat.

Stephen struck a cash deal with a local vet to spay the lot of them after hours. In the meantime, I kept the lovelies in a spare chicken pen bedded with shavings. Every time we drove around the circle in the lane we passed the cats, lounging like courtesans on the chicken perches.

There is always one week in July that captures summer's peak. The garden is alive with vegetables coming into their own. Fanning leaves of broccoli surround bright green heads, and green beans grow inches overnight. Sweet corn rises and sunflowers bloom, while radishes as big as babies' fists are pulled from the ground to grace salad bowls filled with leafy greens. Day lilies, phlox, pansies, and crazy daisies burst with color, and clematis, morning glories, and sweet peas climb trellises and fences. Wally runs crazy through the garden and comes up slightly scented with oregano.

We had that glorious week that summer of 2003. Then we were run out of not just our house, but out of the country as well.

33

A Raid at Dawn

Through a fog of sleep, I heard *ping, ping, ping* as many as six times. I thought the security scanner in the lane was picking up a herd of deer crossing. Then there was pounding on the front door, so hard that it rattled the upstairs window in the hall. I was standing there in my nightshirt looking down on a plethora of police cars, their rooftop lights spinning giddy at dawn. Stephen scrambled for his clothes. It was a raid.

Wally woke with a start when Stephen turned off the security system and opened the door before they got out the battering ram. I had jumped into some clothes and took Wally downstairs, using a belt as a leash, fearing he would be shot if he launched himself off the front porch like a stealth bomber, as he usually does in the morning.

It was all the yada yada you have seen in the movies. To me it felt like an instant replay of the arrest, but with a larger cast and crew. Two officers wearing suits presented the search warrant while oodles of others "secured the perimeter." Some were in full uniform; others wore incongruous Hawaiian golf shirts.

Eddie Greenspan had warned us they might try pulling this stunt, but after two and a half months the possibility seemed remote. He had advised us to maintain calm and cooperate, which is generally my plan when confronted by men with guns and a mandate to use them.

I took Wally outside on his leash and introduced him by name to each one of the nameless officers. Looking them straight in the eye, I told them Wally was a friendly dog. I then asked if they minded me taking his leash off in his yard, because I did not want him shot. Many grunts later, I let Wally go. He did not try to engage any one of them in play; he did not even piddle on their cruiser tires.

I did my chores, feeding the chickens and cats and calling the sheep in from the field for a head count. The scene in the lane was astonishing. Already, one "casual Friday"–clad officer was setting up a video camera, taking footage of the exterior of the house, while another snapped digital still photographs. Much later, a judge would ask them, "Why am I looking at all of these pictures of chickens?"

Stephen was trying to contact Eddie and wanted to speak to him on a secure line because it now seemed probable that our phones were being tapped. When I got back to the house I began packing a bag, since we were being evicted. Everything I put into it, including underwear, had to be inspected by the "soother," a silver-haired detective-sergeant who introduced himself as "call-me-Alec." The other suited officer followed Stephen around. Upstairs, I snuck on my computer and tried to send an e-mail message to my cancer support group to tell them to secure all personal files and photos on the site, because I feared my computer was no longer secure. It was to no avail. In the year and a half since my surgery, the group had doubled in size. Once you are part of that sisterhood, you become fiercely protective. Now I feared for their privacy, not to mention my own.

"Call-me-Alec" gave me his business card, complete with cell phone number, pager number, and e-mail address. He told me they would call when it was permissible for us to return to our home. Putting the card in my wallet, I smiled. Now the media would have a contact on-site.

We went to my mother's apartment in town, assuming that her phone line was secure. After explaining to her what was going on, she stung me by saying, "I'm just glad your father's not here to see this."

My parents had come to live near us a couple of years earlier. They had an independent-living apartment in a building that was connected to a retirement home, so they could take advantage of meal programs and entertainment activities if they wanted to. It was not ideal, but it worked in a circumstance that saw my mother sometimes calling me for a refresher course on making egg salad sandwiches.

My father had died almost a year to the day after the first police raid. After eighty-two years, his body just gave out. A recovered pill popper and alcoholic, he had spent part of his retirement founding a program called Dentists in Distress to serve the needs of that peculiar community of professionals who earn their living in other people's mouths.

On his computer, he wrote a memoir of his covert activities as an army dental corps officer who also served as a secret code translator during World War II. I do not think he ever got over knowing about the Normandy invasion before it happened and knowing the certain perils facing soldiers whose teeth he had worked on. Osteoporosis bent his spine, but he still played a mean steel guitar. My father had always been so proud of me. It was hurtful to think he would feel otherwise were he alive.

While mother and I grimly went for coffee, Stephen spoke with Eddie and tried to get some sense of what was happening. Eddie told us to return immediately and inform the police of the exact location of my office and computer. His position was that since I was not named in the warrant, my material should not be touched. Driving back to the farm, I started making media calls, and "call-me-Alec" soon began receiving more media attention than he had ever had in his career.

Cars and pickup trucks with curious bystanders lined the road at the end of the farm lane, which was blocked by a cruiser and a substantial policewoman. Dutiful notes were taken concerning Mr. Greenspan's opinion vis-à-vis my office and computer. Then we left the spectacle that had become our lives.

We were back at the hotel preparing to go for dinner when the call came saying the police were leaving the house. They had seized both of our computers and other items that would be identified at some point, including a rifle and a shotgun.

As writers, our tools were taken. As farmers, we could no longer protect our livestock. As people, we were inextricably changed.

34

When a House Is Not a Home

With more trepidation than I have felt in my life, we returned to the farm the following day. It felt like a foreign place. Furniture was rearranged. The kitchen table was stripped of its familiar books and clutter. Everything appeared to have been shifted and left somewhat ajar.

Of course we checked, and our computers had been taken, along with backup discs, files, and both Stephen's and my manuscripts. What else was hard to say? Stephen was missing the book *Creating Web Sites for Dummies*. Our handwritten trial notebooks had been rifled and many were missing. Later, we discovered that recipe cards had also been itemized and seized. I know that my lamb and artichoke stew is legendary but never imagined it would come to this.

Books and papers had been moved in my office. The firearms possession license that I kept in a kitchen cabinet was placed square in the center of my desk, perhaps to notify me that I was now in their crosshairs. I was also missing computer discs on which I had stored the family histories of everyone in the township for a local history book that I edited. What fun the police would have reading about who begat whom in Minto Township and the origins of the Women's Institute.

In the guest room, family photo albums that were normally stored in the drawer of an armoire were scattered across the bed, presumably to let us know that our privacy had been thoroughly invaded. I imagined police officers sprawled across the bed looking at pictures of Stephen and I standing beside bigger fish than they had ever dreamed of catching. Likewise a box of photographs in the exercise room had been plundered, and photographs several decades old of me in a fetching bathing suit had been laid on top. I wiped them to remove fingerprints.

My lingerie drawer had been rifled. Looking for what? Everything in the dresser drawers went into the laundry, and I embarked on a washing and drying marathon.

When we were robbed, we came home to a house that had been attacked. But we did not feel violated. Thievery is understandable. It was still our home, just without a bunch of stuff.

After the police search and seizure, we came home to a house that had been raped. For the first time in more than twenty years, I did not feel safe in my own home. We had to get away.

I prepared food for Wally, ordered refills of all our prescriptions, and packed everything I thought we could conceivably need wherever we went.

The sheep and horses ran in from the field when I whistled for them. It was heartbreakingly beautiful to watch—the palominos with white manes and tails flying and the sheep, some black and some white, like dominoes on the green pasture. They crowded around the feed troughs for a treat of grain, and I cried for the first time since the jingle-jangle morning raid.

We had no plans and no time frame, but whatever happened I could not impose on neighbors or farm-friendly Greg to feed caged cats every day. The spaying was off; the whore cats freed. Likewise, I flung open the chicken pen, and the hens eagerly dashed to the grass and bugs that they craved. Cat food and chicken scratch grain was set out in large self-feeders along with an automatically refilling water bucket for the hordes. We locked the doors and fled.

The impact of what had happened was beginning to sink in. What the police could not do directly, they had achieved with this seizure tactic. The contacts Stephen had sworn to protect would be laid bare in an examination of his computer files. Our financial records were gone. Electronic address books and years of collected contacts were no longer available. For me, and for the most supportive group of women I have ever known, there was no privacy—our most intimate fears and very private maladies were laid bare. And the work was gone—manuscripts, works in progress, speeches, farm records, bad poetry—even the eulogy I wrote for my father.

"What they have done to you is outrageous," Eddie Greenspan told Stephen. "But when they touched Marsha's stuff, they crossed a line. You'll see."

After three stock-still days in the city, a publishing friend threw a lifeline, an invitation to his cottage in northern Quebec. It was a classic family cottage, set on a hill overlooking a pristine lake and accessible only by boat. We could not have hoped for a finer hideout or a more genial host. Everything was perfect, from the cottage theme song, "Ghost Riders in the Sky," to the floor-to-ceiling walls lined with thousands of books and the mosquito-proof wraparound porch.

Wally had to be kept separate from an aged dachshund named Pandora, who was the grande dame of the place. Age had slowed her and her pointy muzzle was graying, but she knew her territory and was not about to brook any nonsense from some upstart. The old dear was all of the dachshunds of my childhood bundled into one.

Anything new and different appealed to Wally. He was up and down the steps to the lake like a yoyo, sniffing around the boathouse, chasing chipmunks up birch trees. The water off the end of the dock was deep and dark and perfect for swimming. Wally would not follow us in, but he barked at our heads, which must have seemed to him to float, detached, in the water.

Drifting, floating, and watching, the clouds melted coiled muscles into Slinky toys. We walked in the woods, and a plan began to form.

I had a former boyfriend who remained a friend long after we both met our current mates. Bruce was a Kansas City–born lawyer who devoted his life to jazz music and preserving its history. Along with producing his own films, he also attracted the attention of screen legend and jazz aficionado Clint Eastwood. It turned into a friendship and a professional relationship that benefited both and allowed Bruce to grow as an artist while doing something he loved.

A dyed-in-the-wool resident of the West Village in Manhattan for most of his life, Bruce now lived in Boston near the university where his wife was a professor. A bit of a curmudgeon when it came to the concept of raising children later in life, he found himself, like Clint, captivated by a baby, an adopted Chinese daughter. Still, I knew Bruce well enough to know that he had to keep one foot in New York City, and I wondered if the rent-controlled apartment he had occupied for almost three decades was empty. I left a message on his answering machine over the clunky old mobile phone that was the only link to the outside world at the cottage.

Bruce called me back from a mansion in Bel-Air, where he was working on music for a film and was continually interrupted by delivery people, leaf blowers, and pool cleaners. It almost seemed cruel and unusual to take a fast-talking, take-charge New Yorker and put him in the heart of La-La Land. The project was for Marty (Scorsese), and Jay (McShann) was coming in to play. They hoped to nab Dave (Brubeck) at Monterey (the jazz festival). Nobody drops names like a New Yorker in the film biz.

All Bruce needed to hear was that we were on the lam, and the keys to the apartment were ours. In fact, he had two apartments side by side, one that served as an office. He was in California for months. Enjoy.

35

The Fugitive Card

ife with Stephen had never been boring, but now it had ricocheted wilder than any Wally Ball. What better place to bounce into than the Big Apple?

The apartment—on a tree-lined side street off of Avenue of the Americas—was almost equidistant between the Hudson River, Washington Square Park, the gay bars of Christopher Street, and the vendors hawking knockoff Louis Vuitton handbags on Canal. A classically cramped one-room space about the size of my farm kitchen, it had a queen-size bed, cable TV, a kitchenette, and window views of the brick wall next door. We turned up the air-conditioning and tuned out the past.

The five-story building was also home to many dogs, from button-eyed bichon frises to steel gray Weimaraners. Long-legged, hollow-cheeked model/actress/waitress types carried teacup-size Yorkshire terriers in their pockets, and children were dragged around by "designer dogs" like puggles (pug/beagle hybrids). I had never seen so many bull-dogs outside of the show ring.

Gradually we explored the neighborhood on foot, afraid to move our truck from the free parking spot we found right across the street from the apartment. Having a free place to stay in New York is sublime; having a free parking space is heaven sent. Besides, New York is a city made for walking. As novelist Paul Auster's mystery-writer protagonist, Quinn, describes it in *The New York Trilogy*: "New York was an inexhaustible space, a labyrinth of endless steps, and no matter how far he walked, no matter how well he came to know its neighborhoods and streets, it always left him with the feeling of being lost."

Orienting ourselves to the neighborhood was an exercise in getting lost. Heading west, we walked Wally beside the river where the New York Trapeze School's soaring poles and cables allowed Average Janes and Joes a chance to fulfill big-top fantasies high above a safety net. South toward SoHo, we took turns standing on the sidewalk with Wally, while one of us slipped into antique shops selling original Biedermeier furniture and crystal chandeliers. It was only a few blocks' stroll up colorful MacDougal Street to Washington Square Park with its built-in chess tables and marble arch. Wally stared longingly at the fenced-off grass in the park; even the off-leash dog park was gravel and dirt.

Walking north was the hardest on Stephen because it meant passing his favorite hangout in New York, a trendy restaurant featuring the food of Tuscany that spilled into an expansive street-side patio. SUV limousines idled a few feet away from celebrity patrons while waiters in white shirts sidled among packed tables.

Bruce had introduced us to Da Silvano a decade earlier, when we were in New York after selling Stephen's first book. Not much had changed, except now there was a huge poster from one of Clint Eastwood's spaghetti westerns hanging near the six-seat bar.

We were on a strict budget, something that is near impossible to manage in Manhattan. Smart martinis, lush wines, and gnocchi with lobster at Da Silvano were not in the cards. Instead, we discovered Ottomanelli's butcher shop on Bleecker Street, where a few slices of superbly aged proscuitto was a treat and the ground chuck served Wally's needs, as well as ours.

The butcher brothers at Ottomanelli's loved Wally, who strained at his leash trying to follow the carcasses of lamb that were paraded through the shop via the front door. I asked for dog bones, and the boys tried outdoing each other, coming up with bigger and better bones every day. Sometimes they were so big I felt like a caveman hauling them home.

Providing Wally with bones to enjoy was the least I could do, since he could not play with balls in the apartment. The floors were wood, and the rolling and bouncing balls would have made the people in the apartment below feel as though they were living under a bowling alley. We also hid Bruce's daughter's large stuffed toys. Wally seemed to think Raggedy Ann and SpongeBob were bitches in heat.

Although he did plenty of walking with us, I felt badly that Wally had nothing to play with in the room. As a concession, I bought him a cheap foam-filled pillow with a sturdy corduroy cover and allowed him half an hour of supervised humping, which he relished, complete with sound effects that rivaled ferrets in rut. The look on his face when I hauled that pillow out of the closet was positively lascivious. Dogs enjoy such simple pleasures.

Just being itself, New York is constant entertainment. Walking through Times Square on a weekend is like being a red blood cell flushing through a heart valve, swept along in a roller coaster rush that is alive and moving and cannot stop. Even at stoplights, the crowd seems to bob and weave in anticipation. There is no stillness, and the air smells oddly of car exhaust and pretzels. The exhilaration of the place is intoxicating, suffocating, and surfeit with subatomic strangeness.

I expect that most of the people in that sort of crowd have never stood in a snow-encrusted forest and listened for the creak of branches and footfall of deer.

The great jazz pianist McCoy Tyner gave an outdoor concert at Lincoln Center. It was free. We were on to something. When I read that "saxophone colossus" Sonny Rollins was playing a free concert in Central Park we arrived early on a soft summer evening with our French bread sandwiches and smuggled wine. Our seats were scant yards from the stage. From the opening calypso to the final cadenza, it does not get any better than that Sonny Rollins live performance. Our troubles seemed far away.

Occasionally, I checked in on the farm. My mother visited it every few days with her friend Aileen. They fed the cats and collected tomatoes. Greg mowed the lawn and checked on the animals, content in their green pasture.

Before we left the farm, a benefactor gave us a computer to travel with. Stephen had it set up in the apartment, and I used Bruce's computer in the office apartment next door. The question was what to write; all our reference points were gone.

Stephen spent most of his time sending screeds to his publisher, who was taking advantage of the outrageous situation by absconding with all the proceeds from his book *Karla*—hundreds of thousands of dollars—not one penny of which ended up in the author's hands.

We scraped together whatever money we could. The radio program that I had supplied regular segments to for more than a dozen years had a "bank" of my pieces stored. I called and wrote them, looking for checks as well as ways to file columns from New York. No one answered.

As tight as money was, Stephen still managed to persuade me to go into Da Silvano for just one drink for "old time's sake." Owner Silvano Marchetto greeted us like old friends. In the space of a few minutes we caught up on everything that was happening in his life, including the absolute hell of having an apartment painted in the summer.

We perched at the bar just off the patio under a stream of cool air.

A new barkeep came on duty. She was a slender brunette with flawless skin and wide, flashing eyes. Actress Cameron Diaz was holding court on the other side of the restaurant, and models as tall as basketball players stretched their endless legs toward the street, but none of them were as stunning as the young woman behind the bar.

"So you like Tennessee Williams," she said, pointing to a four-inch-thick biography of the author that Stephen had appropriated from Bruce's library. "Did you know he died choking on the lid of one of his pill bottles in the Hotel Elysée up on Fifty-fourth Street?"

Her name was Jessica, and she had a graduate degree in English literature. A fisherman's daughter from Long Island, she grew up on beaches where millionaires now competed to build the largest mansion. Of course, she was also an actress and singer. She had written a comedy piece that had been showcased. Tending bar bored her mindless, but it paid the bills.

She was also a good listener. Prodded even slightly, Stephen could tell the story of what brought us to New York with dramatic tension worthy of the Williams name. He played the fugitive card on Jessica. She was captivated, outraged, and absolutely had to read his books. Every time we said we had to leave because we really intended to just have a quick drink and were not flush, as a consequence of being on the lam, she "tsk tsked," poured another round, and asked for more details. When we finally did leave, she presented us with a bill for twenty dollars, rolling her eyes and pursing her lips.

I started to stammer, tried to say something in protest. Jessica turned serene.

"I believe Mr. Willis more than covered that," she said, referring to another Bruce who was in the building.

Jessica tucked her bartending schedule and e-mail address into the Tennessee Williams bio and told us to bring Stephen's books the next time she was on duty. Ah, sweet bird of youth.

Eventually, Jessica and most of the waiters at Da Silvano read the dog-eared copies of Stephen's books that circulated through the restaurant. When Jessica was working during the day, we brought Wally, and he sat just outside the door with his own water bowl and the occasional meatball from the kitchen. We never did have the gnocchi with lobster (Jack Nicholson's favorite), but the waiters were always bringing us superb samples from the kitchen—grilled artichokes, carpaccio, Tuscan pecorino, and lemony pasta. The bill was always the same.

Some evenings Silvano came over and wrapped his arms around our shoulders and told Jessica, "A free drink for my friends," to which she responded with a generous smile.

Every celebrity featured on Page Six of the *New York Post* passed through the restaurant, and Jessica gave us the lowdown on each one. She hated the pretense but loved the talent, and cringed at egos so large they sucked the air out of a room. Jessica was writing a screenplay. One day they would answer to her. I believed it.

"Outside of my home and office, Da Silvano is my favorite spot anywhere," wrote Graydon Carter, the editor in Chief of *Vanity Fair*. Exactly.

36

Making It in New York

Stopping by Da Silvano was on our list of things to do the day the lights went out. We were in the apartment and assumed we had done something to blow a fuse. Then we heard neighbors in the corridor outside and learned that the entire building was without power. Gathering up Wally, we joined the stream of people and dogs going down the staircase, thanking our stars that we were not stuck in the tiny elevator.

Avenue of the Americas was filled with people all walking uptown amid the crawling traffic, cell phones glued to their heads. The first thing we learned was that it was not a terrorist attack—a cause for celebration. The second thing we heard was "Canada did it." The blackout was not confined to Manhattan. More than nine thousand square miles of northeastern North America were powerless, including our faraway farm.

Assessing our situation at the apartment, I came to the conclusion that Bruce had never anticipated a power outage. He did not even have a flashlight. Without air-conditioning, the room was already feeling the effect of the ninety-two-degree temperature outdoors. We needed water, ice, batteries, tinned goods, and candles. Pronto.

At the convenience store on the corner, people were being allowed in a few at a time. Manuel knew me and let me in right away while Stephen and Wally waited outside in the confusion. I knew the store well and quickly filled a handcart with supplies. Everyone was looking for candles. I found them on a bottom shelf with cleaning products. Like everything in a convenience store, they were priced inconveniently high, and I did not want to spend all of our cash on them. In a gesture of pure, selfish survival, I put two packages of candles in my basket and stuffed three more at the back of a shelf filled with boxes of pasta. If the blackout lasted, I had a stash of candles. I felt so guilty that I called out to a neighbor I recognized from the building (a schipperke owner) and showed her the remaining candles.

Other cashiers were marking up the price of batteries, but Manuel let me pay the regular price. We had always got along. Whenever I had tried speaking Spanish to him he had covered his ears and laughed, saying I had a terrible accent. Now I was glad to have made him smile.

"*Usted tienne hielo?*" I said brokenly, knowing everyone was after ice. He gestured with his eyes to the back door of the store.

"Meet me outside," he said.

Behind me a woman whose makeup was melting whined about the lack of orange juice. "So how am I supposed to make a screwdriver?"

I passed off gallon jugs of water to Stephen, along with a big bag of groceries and told him to get back to the apartment with Wally. I was on a mission. At the back door, Manuel met me with three bags of ice cubes wrapped in a garbage bag.

My *muchas gracias* was straight from the heart.

"Hey, keep the dog cool," he said with a grin. I dropped a bag off for an elderly couple in the building. They were doing fine and had a pantry worthy of Mormons.

We had dinner by candlelight and walked Wally around the block with our flashlight to guide us. Everywhere, people gathered on stoops and shared tidbits of things they had heard, happy that it was just a hydro *schlamozzle* and confident that it would be over soon. Some neighborhood restaurants and bars stayed open. COLD BEER AS LONG AS IT LASTS read the signs.

The next day we needed more ice, and the idea of a roasted chicken consumed us. A cabdriver at the end of the street told Stephen that New Jersey had power. The only problem with slipping across the Holland Tunnel for supplies was fear of losing the parking space.

We were parked right next to a construction Dumpster in what was a war zone for the people living on the street. Actress Sarah Jessica Parker (*Sex in the City*) and her husband, Mathew Broderick (*The Producers*), had purchased a brownstone that they were renovating, endlessly. Among other things, this involved removing tons of earth from the basement—a feat that was accomplished one five-gallon pail at a time by workers who did nothing except dig, haul, and dump all day long, while workers in the upper floor hammered away all day, a distinct distraction in an otherwise quiet neighborhood.

The construction mess in front of the house took up two free parking spaces—yet another irritant in a city where entire books have been devoted to finding parking spaces. Every Thursday morning between 9 A.M. and 11 A.M., anyone who had a car parked in the street had to be prepared to move it to allow access for the street cleaner. It was a bizarre fraternity of car owners that turned out each Thursday. Some people even hired drivers specifically to sit in their cars and wait for the street cleaner, maintaining their sacred parking spot. It had been many weeks and the street cleaner never arrived, but the protocol never changed.

One day Stephen moved the truck and was backing back into place when Sarah Jessica's contractor snuck up behind in his pickup truck and aimed for our space. I was on the sidewalk with Wally and went into "warrior" mode—occupying the space and throwing up my hands.

"Gid outta here," I bellowed, game face firmly affixed. "You'll hafta go through me to park here, fella."

I held my ground like a true New Yorker. Across the street, the lovely man who tended the street's flowers broke into applause. After that, the contractor greeted me as though I was a long-lost friend when we met on the street. Now the tools of his trade came in handy for us.

Stephen moved the truck into the street and I pulled a borrowed piece of plywood from the construction site, placing two orange road cones on top, to give the appearance of a hazard below. We came back to find our spot secure. I was beginning to think I could make it in New York.

And so we whiled away the summer, going to free concerts, exploring exquisite shops, eating and drinking at the top end of the game. Wally bully-walked everywhere with us, accepting the fact that there was no "green" for him to touch. He became a curb dog, able to share the sidewalk with other dogs and let them sniff him with impunity.

We had been a part of it. New York was a therapy that melted our little town blues. Now it was time to go home and fight.

The butchers at Ottomanelli's sent Wally off with a knucklebone bigger than his head, and we spent our last night in New York tearing up the town with darling Jessica.

37

Rattling Cages

When we got back to the farm there were twelve kittens rotating among the three calico cats. It was impossible to determine which kittens belonged to which mother. If a kitten wanted milk, it just bellied up to whichever mother was closest and latched on. We had a communal cattery.

The garden was overrun with weeds and zucchinis the size of canoes. Pumpkins popped up on vines that meandered through cornstalks. Sunflowers stretched more than eight feet tall. The sheep were mildly interested in my return, and the horses pranced and bucked for grain.

Wally went mad in the yard, chasing balls, chasing chipmunks, wearing pails on his head, and crashing into trees. He had to mark and remark his territory. The process of establishing the perimeters of Fortress Wally was so lengthy I thought he might be more bladder than dog.

I set my house in order as much as possible. Our computer supplier came through with a pay-when-you-can computer for me to use. A raft of kind letters awaited response. Fellow authors were appalled that the police could essentially steal a person's livelihood and not have to answer for it. I decided to address that issue at a public reading. It was time to let my inner bitch loose.

Literary festivals are gentile affairs. Every once in a while a poet cast as "a wild man" will roar a few rhymes or a self-styled "crazy lady" novelist will spew forth stream-of-conscious descriptives and collapse in the heap of her broom skirt. Overall, it is just writers smiling sweetly and reading their work with whatever passion can be brought to it. Then there is eating and drinking and camaraderie, which is all anyone usually remembers.

I was the middle of three readers with an audience of about 150 scattered on a hillside. I read some funny stories about the farm, and the crowd warmed to me. Then I started reading from my unfinished novel—just a few paragraphs describing the life of a child in a nineteenth-century Scottish Presbyterian cult. I stopped. Flipping through the few pages I had in hand, I told them that the police had confiscated the remainder of my book when they seized my computer. Explaining the circumstances, I made it clear that while I am proud of Stephen's work, it is not mine—and I did not know that writing about Presbyterians was a felony. I explained my feelings of loss and what I had lost—not just professionally, but also personally, for no reason I could adduce and with no resolution in sight.

The gauntlet was laid: "I feel invaded and raped and deprived of the ability to do what I love—which is writing. The legal battle to get my computer back may well cost me the farm, which has always been my magical haven. And why would I be so unjustly punished? It seems to me it boils down to the simple sin of loving and being in the proximity of a writer who has dared to blow the whistle and refused to name his sources."

I fully expected to hear Wally barking his approval on cue from his vantage point overlooking the scene with Stephen. Instead, I heard nervous clapping that grew, and both of my fellow authors gave me a hug.

Eddie Greenspan was right. In terms of the human tide, it was one thing for the police to shut down a writer whose critical speech examined crimes of depravity and police ineptitude, but it was quite another to destroy the career of a middle-aged humorist-shepherd with a bent for Presbyterians.

My comments ran in the Writers' Union newsletter, and a wire service carried a story in which I demanded the return of my material. Eddie characterized the seizure as "utterly and totally scandalous." We were rattling cages, and the troops rallied. Not only the Union, but now publishers, PEN, and the Journalists for Free Expression were seeing that something was radically amiss, something that could impact any writer if the authorities could sledgehammer me the way they had.

Then there was the unenviable detective-sergeant who had given me his business card the day of the raid, including his e-mail address. I passed it along to the two hundred or so women in my cancer support group who were concerned about the invasion of their privacy in the months the police had allegedly spent poring over every document, e-mail, and image on my computer.

"How would you feel if your wife was in the group and her private info was being passed around?" asked Carol in West Virginia.

Deb in Georgia echoed the sentiments of many when she accused the detective-sergeant of being a "pervert," and offered a prayer for me. "We pray for our sister, Marsha, that she is not only vindicated from her personal assault (as she is NOT the author, you idiots) but that God repays you folks for the injustice to her."

From Colorado, Laurie made a sensible comment and query to which she received no reply: "When I first heard of the confiscation, I assumed that the law enforcement officials would browse through and keep any information they felt was pertinent to the investigation and then return the rest intact to our group member. Would you be so kind to explain why this hasn't happened after these several months?"

Meanwhile, we were flailing. The Writers' Union offered us a grant to tide us over, and another benevolent writers' group that normally assists authors felled by illness or accident forwarded funds that staved off bankruptcy.

Although Stephen filed a lawsuit against his thieving publisher, the money owed him from his best-selling book was gone. Once again a defense fund was established, and the same good friends stood pat.

We were still leery about staying at the farm on weekends. Friends who were traveling often let us stay at their homes, and when the executive director of the Union saw how freaked-out we were, she offered us her private lakefront retreat.

Arriving at each new destination was an exercise with Wally. I had to check low tables for anything he could damage with one sweep of his tail or swallow whole just because it looked edible. One friend had a room filled with a collection of stuffed frogs—from Jim Henson's Kermit to Beatrix Potter's Jeremy Fisher. Wally only caught a glimpse of it, but when I heard a thumping sound upstairs that afternoon, I found him banging his nose against the closed door.

We also returned to the Metropolitan Hotel when media outlets were paying expenses. It was like old home week with all of the regulars vying to handle the luggage and play soccer with Wally. Management sent up a bottle of wine, chocolate-covered strawberries, and biscuits shaped like dog bones for "Prince Wally."

Infamy spawned invitations for dinner, and our first night back at the Met was spent in a ribald reunion with friends at Bistro 990. After a summer of Italian *amuse-bouche*, the unpretentious French fare was welcome. We skirted reality in favor of fun until closing time.

Back at the hotel, the lights were on, and the classic tape of Oscar Peterson's "Night Train" was playing, as we had left it for Wally's pleasure. Presuming he was asleep on the bed, I fetched his leash for a quick walk in the park. However, it was hard to find him under the feathers.

They were everywhere. Opening the door to the bedroom sent feathers and down drifting into the air. Wally sat up, suddenly awake, with plumage fringing his ears and protruding from his nose. He wagged his tail, sending a cloud of feathers wafting onto the carpet.

"Where's my Wally?" Stephen called, unaware of the catastrophe in the other room.

Wally crouched at the sound of his master's voice. His pink lips curled back in a wicked grin and ambient feathers stuck to his teeth. I tried to hold Stephen back, but he strode through.

"What the—!"

Wally launched straight into his arms, simultaneously emitting a fart that I suspect could be heard by the British tourists in the room across the hall.

We tried to confine the feathers to the bedroom, but Wally tracked them around and blew them out of his nose, et cetera. I did the best I could scraping them off of the duvet cover into a hotel laundry bag, but they seemed to embed themselves in the carpet, and they crept between the layers of curtains. I felt as though I was shrouded in feathers, from my eyebrows to between my toes. Never wear black velvet if you meet a duck that is molting.

We slept with our heads under the covers that night. Wally snorted, snored, and gacked when a feather got stuck in the back of his throat.

In the morning, I called housekeeping to confess. I did not mention Wally. I did not have to. So many hotel staff visited the room that I felt there should have been a yellow crime scene tape sealing it off. Even the concierge abandoned his post to bear witness to the excoriated feather pillow.

As for Wally, he bore no shame and took no blame. True to bull terrier tradition, he assumed that if he was allowed to hump a pillow in New York, all future pillows were fair game. I took note and blushingly paid the eighty dollars for Wally's sexual misadventure.

38

Overreach and Overkill

Any security *ping* in the lane at the farm signaling the trespass of a foreign object caused Stephen and me to rush to a window to see who was invading our space now. Usually it was the friendly FedEx courier or some innocent reader who wanted to have a book signed. However, on Monday, October 20, 2003, it was another police cruiser.

Just one, how odd, I thought, wondering when the cavalry would arrive. Damn it all to hell, what now?

The fresh-faced constable was delivering two summonses charging both of us with two criminal charges each of careless and improper storage of firearms. If convicted, the maximum sentence on both charges was four years in jail. I was so mad I could have spit, but Stephen put his arm around me and guided me back into the house.

The rifle and shotgun seized during the raid had never been returned, and we had just begun to miss them. Wally had taken down a fox in broad daylight a few weeks earlier. He shook it so hard that small blood vessels burst in his right ear resulting in spilled blood between the skin and the cartilage that forms the ear structure. As hematomas go, it

was small and did not require surgical intervention, eventually returning to normal with a slight ripple effect left in his ear.

Over the years, I have had a cow stricken with rabies. Coy dogs and
wolves have ravaged ewes and lambs. In the spring, foxes and raccoons
regularly pick off wild ducklings and geese at the pond. Such is nature,
however, and my farm has always seemed to have a larger share of predators than might otherwise be expected. A thirty-two-hole golf course,
campground, and residential development bordering the farm had
sprung up over the years, eliminating wildlife habitats and sending the
fugitives into my hills and glades.

After taking a gun safety and hunter education course, I had tried
my hand at goose hunting a few times. It was magical to sit at the edge
of a cornfield in the crisp autumn dawn and hear the geese honking in
the distance, drawing them closer with our goose calls until their beating wings were directly overhead. Nothing ever fell from the sky for
me. I learned that I had no stomach for killing, and just being at the
edge of the cornfield was my trophy. However, I will protect my own if
need be. It just happens that Stephen is a far better shot.

Now we were being arrested for being farmers and doing what
farmers must do sometimes. What bothered me most was that it was an
entirely bogus charge. It is written into the laws of the land that
firearms can be stored as we had them—unloaded but at the ready when
required "for the control of predators." Our guns were legally obtained, and we were licensed to possess them.

Eddie Greenspan immediately recognized the vexatious nature of
the charges and arranged for us to have our fingerprints and mug shots
taken locally, instead of waiting for them to haul us off in cuffs. Laying
gun charges against both of us would sully both of our names and cre-
ate even more stress in the relationship. It was a cheap shot by any measure but one meant to divide and conquer and sow further confusion in
an already confused public mind.

Eddie had also just been advised that the authorities were going to lay a few additional charges in Stephen's case at a court appearance later in the week.

"How many is 'a few'?" asked Stephen.

"I don't know," said Eddie. "A few, like in five or six."

At the appointed hour, we went into the local police station to be booked and processed. I tried not to glare while they took my mug shot. Each time the officer rolled one of my fingers across the inkpad and over to the fingerprint sheet my side bumped against his gun. To make the time pass, I imagined my dentist father as Dr. Christian "The White Angel" Szell, the way Laurence Olivier played him in the 1976 movie *Marathon Man*, using his drill to torture the people I knew to be responsible for this deliberate harassment.

Once released, I joined Stephen on the sun-filled porch of the station house. Before we could speak, his cell phone rang. It was a national television network calling to ask him for a response to the new charges.

"How in hell did you find out about the gun charges?" Stephen asked, since we had not told anyone.

"Gun charges? What gun charges?" the reporter replied. "I'm talking about the police press release we got early this morning, announcing the ninety-four new charges of breaching court orders against you."

"The wha——?" cried Stephen, as though a feather pillow had exploded over his head. By the time we got home half an hour later, there were two satellite trucks and television crews set up in the yard to film our arrival, while half a dozen tape-recorder-toting radio reporters milled around. The answering machine was crammed with media requests for interviews.

The sheep and horses congregated at the gate to watch the circus. Wally wove through the mazes of cables and light stands that film crews brought into the house for their interviews. He had a knack of almost—just almost—upending everything he came into contact with, including the interviewers themselves.

When I watched and listened to the coverage later in the day, I could hear the dull thuds that occurred when Stephen was giving stand-up interviews on the front lawn, and Wally brought his ball over to be kicked. When the TV crews finished filming Stephen, they often turned to Wally just for fun. Viewers seeing a loopy-nosed dog running around with a soccer ball in a pail were justifiably confused by the serious topic of the reportage.

"This is obviously an attempt to demonize me and to influence public opinion and any judge or jury who might become involved," Stephen told the press.

Eddie Greenspan was more like Wally, beside himself with glee. "A few" additional charges would have only registered on the public radar as additional evidence to confirm that Stephen was a low-life, scum-sucking, true-crime writer who should be hung and quartered like a stuck pig for writing such vile, nasty books. The announcement of almost a hundred additional charges put the scenario so far over the top that any thinking person read: vendetta.

"I have never acted for anybody with this many offenses in my life," crowed Eddie, likening the police action to charging a highway speeder for every tenth of a mile he drove over the speed limit.

"To put it mildly, it is overreach and overkill," he offered, adding that Stephen had better lie low or the charges could reach two hundred. "We're close to the Guinness record already."

While the police tried to get a word in edgewise to justify the charges, Eddie declared that it was all about persecuting an author who criticized and exposed the actions of politicians, police, and prosecutors. "Had he written a book favorable to the government, I don't think we would be here," he said, promising "a huge battle."

Try as they might, the police could not set their spin against the tide of what they had started. After solemnly advising the publisher of Stephen's first book that she was distributing material that was the subject of criminal charges, they refused to specify the allegations. In sheer frustration, the publisher told the press she thought the police would be better off spending their time investigating what happened to the child who had been missing for the past three days rather than laying charges against an author. Then she ordered a new print run.

Every organization associated with free speech and issues to do with writing was mobilized, and the attorney general was bombarded with demands for an inquiry.

When we attended Stephen's court appearance a few days later, the judge waived the reading of all of the charges in the interest of the court's time. There were twenty-eight charges alleging that names of victims protected under a court order had appeared on the Web site, however briefly. Fifty-eight charges referred to Stephen's first book, *Invisible Darkness*, a seven-year-old book that had already been the subject of a police investigation, culminating in Stephen's exoneration three years earlier. Eight of the charges pertained to the new *Karla* book. One charge was also laid against the company through which we handled our publishing business.

"What are they going to do? Put the company in jail?" Eddie wondered out loud as new bail conditions were set.

In the hallway, the silver-haired detective-sergeant who had been receiving missives from irate cancer survivors all over the world approached me with a stricken look and reached out.

"How are you feeling?" he asked. "Are you okay?"

I expect that I gave him the same look of hostile incredulity that appears in my mug shot. This was the guy who had supervised the raid on our farm and ignored Eddie Greenspan's admonition to leave my office and computer alone. He was also the ignoramus who had ordered the firearms at my farm seized, facilitating my arrest.

And now he wanted to know if I was "okay"?

As it turns out, I was doing much better than Wally.

39

Still in There

We thought of Wally as indestructible—a muscle on paws with a head hard as bedrock. Aside from his bout of "goofy guts," he had never been sick, just been banged up by his own misadventures. I have the same level heart murmur he does, and it has never interfered in my life.

He was not doing anything out of the ordinary when the pain first gripped him. He slid front-legged first off the sofa and gave a yelp. An awkward landing, perhaps, or a toenail caught in the rug.

A stoic fellow, Wally seldom yelped. One of the few times I ever heard him express pain was when the goat broadsided him.

Goats are not my thing, especially billy goats, which are almost as smelly as camels. I talked myself into taking one when a loyal reader cheerfully advised me that she had done what I did, moved from the city to the country to farm, but instead of sheep she decided to raise goats.

I told her the only kind of goat that interested me was the rare Tennessee fainting goat, a strange sort of creature whose legs stiffen when it is startled or overexcited. This stiffening causes it to fall over in what looks like a dead faint. After a few seconds the silly things resume whatever they were doing as though nothing had happened. The condition is called myotonia, and it has something to do with defects in the chloride channels in muscle membranes that cause interference with the transmission of electric impulses to the muscles. It does not hurt the goats. They just drop like flies.

As luck would have it, this person had received just such a goat in the first shipment of Boer goats she had bought out west. The seller had thrown it in "for fun." Offered a free goat, I could not resist. Mya the Myotonic Goat arrived just in time to give to birth to a doeling. Already, I had a herd start.

Mya was a gentle goat of many colors—brown, tan, black, and white. Her amber eyes carried a constant question, and her horns curved backward, like her black goatee. The spawn of her loins turned out to be the product of an accidental mating with a pygmy goat named Crazy Larry, and his daughter lived true to his name. While Mya was docile, little beige Toni hit the ground running, jumping, and climbing and never stopped. Mya never tried to bound over a fence, because just the thought of it excited her so much she stiffened and fell over. Toni, on the other hand, liked to climb walls and tap-dance on the roof of the barn.

The confrontation between goat and dog came one day when Toni took things too far. Amused by the pair and typically not seeing any dark clouds on the horizon, I let them out of their pen during the day. Occasionally they found their way to the front porch, which is Wally's domain. Toni delighted in standing on her hind legs, prancing like a weightless Lipizzaner stallion and nibbling on the leaves of a corkscrew hazel at the side of the walkway to the house.

Wally demurred. He appeared to be as amused as I was by these fanciful goat tricks. One morning, Wally was sitting in his place, leaning against the door like an old man watching a bocce ball match, when Toni leaped up on the porch and gave him a nudge. Mya got it into her she-goat mind that Wally needed to be taught a lesson. She ran at him and crushed him into the door before he had a chance to react.

Those horns have no flex. Wally collapsed and started to wail—sharp, pained yelps. Stephen carried him inside where he continued to whimper like a baby. He lay on his bed, shaking and moaning for half an hour, while I called the veterinarian.

After a thorough going-over, the vet could not find anything broken. Wally stopped complaining a few hours later. But he refused to go outside. For weeks, we had to leash him and cajole him outside to do his business. The very sight of the goat set him shaking.

He gradually overcame this extreme phobia. He went with me to plant seeds in the garden, hucklebutting my carefully planted rows of beans and carrots and peas and turning the whole thing into more of a Birds Eye garden than an orchestrated effort. All the while, he had a "third eye" trained on the goats.

One day, Wally and the wandering goats surprised each other in the lane. Toni ran away at the speed-of-goat, prancing along the top of the cedar rail fence and bounding into a field. Mya took three steps and fell over in a dead faint. In that moment, Wally saw a critical flaw in his attacker. The worm turned.

Three days later, Wally was in the front yard when Mya came around the corner. His prey sense tingling, he chased her down, latching onto her scraggly tail. Mya's goat screams were heard throughout the county. She fainted, and Stephen pulled Wally off. With farm animals, even barn cats, Wally had always been a "live and let live" kind of guy. But his behavior with Mya clearly demonstrated that he was one to hold a grudge. As far as Wally was concerned, she had attacked him for no reason, with malice and forethought, hurting him badly, and for that she was going to pay.

After the incident I had to keep the goats and the dog in strict isolation from each other or risk confrontation. Mya well understood the power of her horns, but Wally knew that he could make a running goat fall. Toni, who he could not catch, with the satanic sworl on her fore-head, acted as agent provocateur between them. Sheep may be sneaky, and goats have agendas, but pygmy goats are demonic rabble-rousers.

The painful yelps of his goat-butt past repeated themselves in Wally's cries the night he slipped off the sofa. He could not find a comfort zone in bed and cried all night.

We cried with him. At 8 A.M. we had him at the university emergency clinic. Naturally, it was a Sunday. Rudimentary X-rays showed no fracture. We were sent home with pain medications for him, but by the middle of Sunday night he was hideous with pain that the pills could not touch. Stephen was already exhausted with worry, so I took Wally to the guest room and held him through a night of cries and whimpers that jarred my being. His front legs were painful to the touch, and his blood was boiling. We had him back at the clinic as soon as we could raise someone to open the doors. He was admitted immediately. A short time later he was in the intensive care unit.

What followed was a rapid series of tests that Texas oil billionaires could only hope they could buy: complete blood work and biochemical panels, urinalysis, full-body ultrasound, echocardiogram, joint taps, and neurological consultations. There were eleven specialists trying to solve the mystery of Wally's excruciating pain. The diagnosis was inconclusive—speculation ranged from meningitis to invasive tumors—but in the end they had no idea. Somewhere in there a spot of possible trauma was seen on Wally's spleen—not life threatening, but the sort of injury that could have been caused by contact with a blunt object—a goat horn, for example.

By nightfall, Wally was stabilized, flushed with painkillers, but with no end in sight. Stephen's grief and frustration were beyond words. I had only seen him this way a decade before when brief contact was established with his long-lost daughter, then a grown woman and graduate student in medieval studies at Berkeley in California. She was calling because she had been diagnosed with a devastating cancer. Stephen wanted to go to her, but she said it would be too upsetting for her mother. Thankfully, she lived and prospered. Nothing was going to separate Stephen from Wally, as he had been from his only daughter.

I saw vets huddled together and knew they were considering just how much agony Wally should have to endure. His pain was in my bones, but he was still in there when we met eye to eye. We vowed not to give up.

I took the symptoms of my "diagnostic mystery" dog to my Internet community of bull terrier experts, regurgitating the results of tests I did not fully understand. The response was clear and firm—check for tick-borne diseases, such as Lyme and others, and put him on a specific antibiotic immediately.

Wally's attending vet was on duty in the intensive care unit that night. Watching Wally fade slowly, he felt helpless. Stephen talked to him on the telephone around 2 A.M. that morning. I had printed out information about the symptoms of tick-borne diseases and the antibiotic used to treat them. Although skeptical because such diseases were not prevalent in our area, the vet readily agreed that it was worth a try when Stephen reminded him that Wally was a traveling man.

Twelve hours later, Wally was wagging his tail for all it was worth and walking on unsteady legs. One more night in the ICU and he was dragging vet techs down the corridors.

We had the boy back, without any conclusive diagnosis. I owed his survival to people whom I had never met. I owed his bill to my mother, who paid the half I could not.

My father had always loved Wally.

40

A Terrierist in the Office

Thankfully, Wally was home resting on the December day when the truck blew up. It was our old Ford Bronco, which had been relegated to four-wheeling around the farm and hauling feed and firewood.

We were halfway home from a neighbor's barn with twelve bales of hay in the back when we smelled an acrid electrical odor and spotted a few sparks spitting out from under the steering column. Halfway up the lane, Stephen's sweatpants took an ember and started smoldering; we decided it was time to evacuate. Hurling snowballs had no effect. Soon flames were visible under the dashboard. I left Stephen to pull the bales out while I ran to call the fire department.

In short shrift, thick black smoke billowed from the truck. I stood with Stephen on the hill overlooking the lane. A wind either way could have spread the flames to a plot of sumac or the cedar-rail fence that rises heroically along the lane, but the calm held even as snow began to fall. Stephen arched his brow when he saw me holding the kitchen fire extinguisher. We were far beyond that now. In the distance, there were sirens, and neighbors were already doing drive-pasts in their pickup trucks.

The gas tank was half full. When it exploded it was like having a Scud missile land in the front yard.

'Twas the season to feel helpless. All that was left of the Bronco was a charred shell.

We did not have the energy or the will to cut a tree that Christmas. Our sole present—and all we really needed—was Wally with us. Christmas Day, we tied a ribbon on him. He gnawed on a bone worthy of Ottomanelli's, while my mother visited and took a bubble-filled Jacuzzi in the tub that had been Stephen's gift to me in better times.

"Good lord, we're washing your mother for Christmas," Stephen said with a laugh. We had to get back on track and in fighting form.

Early in the new year, the police began responding in earnest to Eddie Greenspan's requests for discovery materials. Volume upon volume of bound legal-size documents showed up at his office. Some were as long as three hundred pages. There were discs filled with photographs of the farm, and tapes of "witness" interviews, which had also been transcribed. Countless court orders were collected, along with every newspaper, radio, or television interview that Stephen had given in the past decade.

In terms of volume, this was way too much information for Eddie to examine in detail. Some of it might have relevance, but much was repetitive and had no bearing on the defense case. Banalities such as road conditions on any given day or where the officer ate lunch and what he billed the government for overtime are hardly germane to anything. Yet sometimes in those banalities there are revelations. Kirk Makin, an investigative journalist of our acquaintance, once pored over the discovery materials involving a convicted murderer, Guy Paul Morin, and found that officers had created duplicate notebooks, including fabricated information that helped wrongfully imprison the innocent man. Such anomalies make it prudent to examine everything submitted and then turn it around to see if it fits like a Rubik's Cube, or had something suspiciously askew.

We had to attend the offices of Greenspan Partners in order to review the mountain of material. By agreement with the prosecutor, a rather hysterical sort, the discovery materials could not leave the law office and could not be copied. In order for us to assist, we had to leave the farm for weeks on end in the dead of winter, relying on hired hands or neighbors to tend the flock.

Coincidentally, a friend was spending a month in Berlin. He allowed us to stay at his condo—a vast labyrinth filled with books and countless artifacts that a bull terrier could trip over, run into, or sneeze into oblivion. We could not leave Wally alone there while we worked at Eddie's. And Eddie was deathly afraid of dogs, having been bitten when he was a child by a dog he characterized as a "terrierist." In adulthood, he thought of the movie based on Stephen King's *Cujo* as a documentary.

Although capable of making clear and unequivocal arguments against breed-specific legislation personally, Eddie does not keep company with canines. Period.

When we broached the subject of bringing Wally in the back door and hiding him in the room where we worked, the office manager's eyes widened, as though held open by toothpicks, and her hands gyrated in front of her like an out-of-control mime. No dog was ever allowed in the office, and words associated with things canine were seldom uttered, except as pertaining to vile females. The prohibition was not limited to dogs; cats were held in equal disdain. In fact, if it was not human and could crawl, slither, or otherwise inhabit space, Eddie preferred it to be elsewhere. He kept a tank of freshwater fish in his office and stopped naming them after one died.

"There was a cat that lived in the basement for over a year," we were told on the QT. One of the lawyers who worked on the second floor of the historic bank building found a kitten freezing in the street and brought it into the office. It thrived in the basement, amid a catacomb of vaults where clients' files were stored in a climate-controlled environment. There was also a gymnasium down there for the employees, but the only time Eddie ever ventured to the basement was when his barber came to give him a trim in his own private chair.

The cat lived right underneath Eddie's office until, late one night, it wandered upstairs while Eddie was preparing a case. They crossed paths, causing pandemonium that Eddie could barely describe the following day. The cat left the building, and the lawyer who gave the cat haven may also have left. Eddie has an absolute focus on the law, but he is sometimes fuzzy about who people are. Many articling students found themselves passing the great man in the hall only to be asked, "Do you work here? Do I know you?"

These stories gave me faint hope that we could try bringing Wally into the office disguised as a small, stocky, junior lawyer.

Stephen begged like a cairn terrier after liver treats, and we were finally allowed to sneak Wally in while Eddie was having a nap. The *click, click, click* of his nails on the marble floor sounded like ice picks being driven into a glacier. He was in, and our job was before us.

The young lawyer whom Eddie had assigned to work with us, Vanessa Christie, told us what to look for and what to make note of to help them. A wisp of a woman, with blond hair trailing down her back Alice-in-Wonderland style, her oval, blue-gray eyes could stare discursively, or light up with laughter at the mention of anything to do with her favorite vintage television show, *Welcome Back, Kotter*. No one meeting Vanessa in the coliseum of the courtroom would ever suspect that she could crack up on a moment's notice at the line: "Up your nose with a rubber hose." She took to Wally instantly, and I expect if she thought she could have pulled it off, her own rottweiler would have had a bed under her desk, too.

41

"Trubbles on the Wane"

Wally had a dog bed in a vault off the room we worked in at Eddie Greenspan's office. Law bores dogs. They do not even know they need licenses.

We were no fun for Wally, sitting at a desk, reading and scratching notes. When he wanted to let us know that there was more to life, he lay on his back and rolled, slapping his head around and moaning in the back of his throat. We closed the vault door within a few inches and it was virtually soundproof, otherwise any lawyer passing the office might think we were their most frisky clients ever.

The reading material was frustrating but sometimes hilarious, particularly when homicide detectives were assigned to write reviews of Stephen's books.

Often we stayed at the office late into the night. I kept Wally's food in the refrigerator upstairs where there was a kitchen and dining area. No one ever asked who was eating meat loaf every day. In fact, I was warming Wally's food in the microwave one evening when one of the junior lawyers wistfully said the smell reminded him of home. Me, too.

Stress creeps up on you. For the first time in my life my cholesterol was high enough to warrant medication. Stephen was grinding his teeth. At night, we took Wally on long walks through the snowy streets of our friend's neighborhood where houses were being renovated and everything was moving upscale.

I stared into the windows of those houses and imagined the lives of the people who lived there. Why did they paint the living room that shade of chocolate brown? Was their bed underneath the Chinese paper-globe lantern in that room on the second floor? Yellowing leaves meant they were overwatering their *ficus benjamina*.

It was not voyeurism in the classic sense, only a way to get out of my own head and away from its thoughts. Like transcendental meditation, it took me to another place. Sometimes it made me want to sit down and write, but that discipline was far away.

In the normal course of winter, Wally would have been dive-bombing in pristine snowdrifts. In the city, he could barely find a pristine spot to yellow. He took it like a real dog and discovered that when he was in the office even the slightest whimper or threat of a bark got him a cookie in the vault.

Closing in on spring, we had analyzed thousands of pages of repetitious legal material, much of it blacked out with grease pencil. By one of those coincidences that seems almost predestined, I happened to watch a segment about stain removal on Martha Stewart's television show. Vinyl erasers that work on crayon marks also remove grease pencil. It was like cracking a code. I was able to reveal enough information for us to know that Stephen's case was eminently winnable. I felt terribly smart, like Nancy Drew, the girl-detective heroine of my childhood who solved mysteries with her roguish nuisance of a dog at her side—Togo, the bull terrier.

We returned to the farm for the summer, buoyed by a cash award from Human Rights Watch, an international organization that administers the estate of playwright Lillian Hellman. She established the annual awards in her name and that of her partner, Dashiell Hammett, to support persecuted writers, usually in totalitarian states such as Iran, Nigeria, and China. A black mark on a democratic government, the award announcement was national front-page news and a first for a Canadian writer.

Wally made the news that summer, too, at least in the local papers. After nine court appearances, the firearms charges against us were dropped. The prosecutor finally admitted the obvious—there was no prospect of conviction. Even though I knew we would be exonerated it felt as though a huge weight had been lifted. It had also been a worry to my law-abiding mother, and I called her with the good news as soon as we left court.

"Oh that's good," she said. "Now I can die and you'll be able to come to my funeral instead of being in jail."

Wally hucklebutted on the leash outside of the courthouse while Stephen gave an impromptu press conference. A newspaper photographer ended up sitting the three of us down on a grassy knoll for a portrait. His editor loved pictures with dogs in them. We smiled for the camera, but I appear slightly stunned.

That is because I was. Seconds before the picture was taken, Wally whacked me with his head, nailing my upper lip. It was just one of those "Hey, we're having fun" kind of whacks. Seconds after the picture was captured my lip began to bleed profusely. Ten minutes later, I looked like a thick-lipped mullet. Never mind, it was a day to celebrate. We took Wally to lunch—a quarter-pounder with cheese. No mustard, sauce, or pickles for the dog.

The corn was ripe when we got a call from Greenspan Partners to attend their offices for a special announcement.

Eddie fondled a suspender while he told us the tale. The senior prosecutor on the case called him out of the blue. She said she was in the neighborhood and asked if she could drop by. In poker terms, this breezy attitude was a "tell," since the woman seldom ventured from her office north of the city and she normally traveled in a pack with two or three young male prosecutors who accompanied her everywhere like Bene Gesserit acolytes.

The offer was to reduce the charges to one lowly count. Everything else was dropped. Millions of dollars had been spent, and for it the government would extract seventy-five hours of community service from Stephen. Ironically, he ended up writing educational film scripts on the topic of bullying.

While the deal was hammered out, we took Wally fishing on Manitoulin Island. Lake Manitou is the world's largest freshwater lake on an island. Manitoulin Island in Georgian Bay is so large that it has many substantial landlocked lakes. To me it has always been a heaven-on-earth kind of wilderness haven. We have gone there for years, staying at Wee Point Cottages in a handcrafted log cabin, where the kitchen wallpaper features sunken treasure ships in the Caribbean, and a tapestry of a deer hangs over the sofa. The place is authentic, and the people are at home with who they are.

You can never spend too much time messing around in boats with dogs. We strapped a life preserver on Wally and ventured forth on Lake Manitou, home of lake trout, pickerel, bass, and jumbo perch. If a person cannot catch a fish on Lake Manitou they are either cursed or they are fishing with Wally.

While Mingus and Diva had spent most of their fishing time sunning themselves on a towel between the tackle boxes in the standard-issue, aluminum fishing boats, Wally had to be in on the action. He sat at the prow, riding to our secret fishing spot with his ears pinned back to the wind and his pink tongue dragging from the side of his face.

We cut the engine and slid quietly into a clear-water bay, where there was a drop-off shoal that harbored bass whose fillets would not fit on dinner plates. Our lines were rigged with big rubbery jigs that apparently resemble food that fish eat, and we cast them out, singing across the water and sinking into the depths. With every cast Wally sang, too. "Aroo. Aroo, aroo"—so loud that it woke up a sleeping mud turtle that surfaced to take a look. I had to cover his head with a towel to shut him up, but that made him dance in place, dog nails tapping out a sort of Morse code to the fish, announcing we were there.

It did not matter. Fish or no fish, the "trubbles" were melting away.

42

Make That Day Last for All Time

When it finally came, I will not say it was a great day in court, but it was a great day to have over with. Stephen's case had finally ended. We were now supposed to get on with our lives. There were even signs that I might have my computer files returned.

The farm had morphed back to being our home, with winter nights snug in flannel sheets. The weather was uneven; some days temperatures were freezing and others were as mild as we had ever seen. Wally often went into couch-potato mode, snoozing beside the crackle of the woodstove.

Spring was so close that a few Canada geese had taken up their usual residence on the thawing pond when my old palomino mare, Lady, slipped into a snowbank and never left it. She was "cast," with her hind legs seemingly paralyzed. The neighbors came, and we tried everything to upright her, until there was nothing left to do.

I spent a long night with Lady as she lay wrapped in blankets. Like Farmer Hoggett in the movie *Babe*, I sang to her, those tender lyrics composed by John Hodge to the Symphony no. 3 in C-minor for organ by Camille Saint-Saëns, about making a loved one a special day with a morning "golden and true" and night washed in moonshine:

"I would make that day last for all time."

Wally sat with us for a time. He licked my salty tears and lay across my feet where I sat on a bale of straw. Still as a statue, he listened while I talked to Lady, resting my head on her warm neck, listening to the last of her breath. Early the next morning the vet came, and she slipped back to the Land of the Unicorns from which I always felt she had come. My dear old gal was thirty-three, the same age Roy Rogers's Trigger was when he died.

We buried Lady in the shade of a young maple on a rise overlooking the fields she had roamed all of her years on the farm. Life and death are the reality of farming, but nothing makes it easy. Soon I was into the lambing season, and the barn seethed with new life while lilac buds swelled and April showers washed winter away.

Just when the familiar rhythm of nature started kicking in, Wally sent us into crisis mode again with a virulent relapse of tick-borne disease. His collapse was total, and the nightmare of the screaming wails returned. An entirely insidious disease, whichever of the many strains Wally picked up in our travels, it never left his body—just went into hiding, waiting for an opportune moment to reappear. This time it also opened the door to an autoimmune reaction that presented itself as a form of crippling arthritis.

Again, the antibiotic worked its wonders. In a couple of days, Wally was waddling down the clinic corridors, his deliberate step becoming more and more akin to that of a bulldog on a mission. To relieve the arthritic swelling in his joints he was placed on a steroid called prednisone.

As is usual, the initial dosage of steroid was large. So was Wally's reaction. We were told to expect him to drink a lot more water and excrete in proportion. He would also have an increased appetite.

Increased does not begin to define what happened. Bull terriers naturally take things to extremes; put them on steroids, and they crank it even higher. Wally did not just drink water, he absorbed it bowlfuls at a time in gargantuan slosh-fests. He could not pass a puddle in the lane without attempting to drain it. The result became known as the "Two-Minute Pee." I was up and down with him throughout the night like a mother with a newborn. Carrying a bowl and a bottle of water in my purse became a habit, and schedules were adapted to Wally's needs. When we traveled we allowed an extra half an hour on the road due to the necessary pit stops, and he could not be left alone for any length of time without requiring a trip outdoors.

The type of steroid athletes are sometimes caught using causes the same urinary effect, and I wondered how they possibly get through long innings of baseball or bike rides through mountain passes without bursting. Testing be darned, look for the athlete who is always in the washroom.

Food demands were constant and unrelenting. Wally was already a big boy and needed no further bulking up. We bought him diet dog biscuits and doled out his daily food ration over three feedings. Every pocket I had either held a cookie or cookie crumbs. Aware of this, Wally could be counted on to chew the pockets out of any garment he had access to or could rip from a hanger.

He also became a laundry hound, specifically an embarrassing connoisseur of underwear. As vigilant as we were, he managed to unearth a pair from a travel bag after we spent a weekend at a dog show. Underwear is blameless, and once the deed is done there is no point in placing blame, but I will say it was a rather large pair of underwear that was missing its critical area.

I spent the next twenty-four hours hoping that Wally would pass the wad of cotton, but nothing moved through him, and he was sickly. We were off to the clinic, where Wally's file was now as thick as a family Bible. The veterinarian who examined him could actually feel the un-moving mass in his intestine. Wally was scheduled for surgery.

I know of many bull terriers who have blocked their guts and sur-vived the scalpel. However, with Wally it was not going to be easy. The vet explained the high dose of prednisone he was on could cause the in-ternal sutures to fail and make healing more difficult. There were no guarantees. Visiting him in the intensive care unit was all too much like saying our good-byes.

We drove home and waited interminable hours for word. I knew ex-actly the space Stephen was in, because I was there myself. I thought of how close we had become, so much so that words were not needed. When Wally was in the house it sometimes seemed we had our own se-cret language.

"Wally with you?" Stephen would ask over the intercom between our offices.

"He's bocce ball at his place," I might respond.

Translation: "Wally is in my office, sitting with his paws between legs on his dog bed."

Experts have studied dog language skills intensively, finally stating with authority that dogs can learn the meaning of up to two hundred words. Any dog owner could have told them that. Wally even under-stands words that are spelled, such as *c-o-o-k-i-e*, *b-a-l-l*, and *o-u-t*.

We were also trained to understand Wally's language. When ste-roids turned him into a cookie monster, his rule was that anytime a per-son opened the door to the truck, a cookie tithe had to be paid to the fur pal in the backseat. He knew the driving route to town so well that he made certain landmarks into his private cookie tollbooths. At the stop sign on O'Dwyer's Lane, he demanded a cookie. The sign at Andrews Berry Farm was an automatic cookie requisition point. At home, he sat and stared at the cookie jar, rocking on his hindquarters and mumbling to himself, as though willing the jar to slip from the shelf and render its booty.

He was Wallman and Walnuts, Wallmeister, Wallaroo, and Walla-walla-ding-dong. At Christmas, he got more cards than we did from bull terrier friends around the globe, some of them simply addressed to "Wally the Wonder Dog." The mail lady got a big kick out of the paw prints on his mail.

As Winkie Mackay-Smith prognosticated, he became "indistinguishable from a three-year-old in a dog suit." And he was ours.

43

Always Trust Your Cape

The surgeon had Wally sliced open on the table, where she contemplated the bulging intestine. The easy thing, the thing she was trained to do, was to snip it open, liberate the offending garment fragment, and stitch the pieces back together. Instead, she thought outside the box.

The blockage was in the area between the small and large intestines. Dog Anatomy 101 indicated that the largest battle had been fought, since the underwear had moved through the twists and turns of the small intestine, which is said to be anywhere from two to three and a half times as long as the animal itself.

The surgeon decided to give massage a try, patiently kneading the cloth into the large intestine, where it would have room to move on down, eventually passing into the outside world. The intern who explained the process closed her fingers to her thumb repeatedly, describing it as "like working sausage meat in a casing."

When we picked Wally up a day later, she asked us if we wanted the blockage. They kept it in a jar. We just wanted Wally.

He left the clinic like a rock star. Vets and technicians popped out of examination rooms to pet him and wish him well. Wally knew where every cookie jar in the joint was and made his rounds, including a visit to the unfortunate cookie jar in the accounting department.

With the slit down his gullet closed by metal staples, his stomach looked something like a xylophone. I caught him dragging himself across the grass a few days into his recovery, but the staples held. A new rule in the house sends underwear directly into the washing machine.

Wally's health has been closely monitored since then. He takes more herbal supplements than I do, plus a low dose of aspirin to control a blood clot that is floating around his goat-butted spleen, and blood pressure pills to make life easier on his kidneys. That gristly muzzle of his might be graying, but his coat is shiny and his eyes are bright. Watching him do figure eights with his ball in his pail, you might take him to be half his age.

Five years is a milestone for cancer survivors, and I made it without a cigarette.

I let the sheep go, after determining that my ewe-wrestling years were numbered. Lady's palomino daughter, Karma, and Mya the Tennessee fainting goat have the run of the fields. More beasts will find sanctuary here, I have no doubt. If it eats, I do not seem to be able to turn it away.

After two years in captivity, a selection of the files on my computer was finally returned to me on a single disc. It seemed so small in my hand, considering that it was a remnant of a lifetime of writing.

For the first time in two years, I looked at the novel I had been working on. I liked what I read, but I wondered who the author was; she seemed to be a person different from me. I tried to connect to it, to get back in the saddle again, as everyone was urging me to do. None of the words that came felt right.

In the past, I averaged almost a book a year, and I was never self-conscious about tossing an idea around and shaping it into a story. Now it seemed to me that when I tried to write it came out in code. Writing is not only about fearlessness but also about momentum and pacing. When the police took all my files and my computer I was abruptly and irrevocably interrupted. Somehow I had to find my way back to that place I was starting to believe was lost to me. It would take a coincidence.

A friend had lost her companion of seventeen years, a lovable mutt named Daisy that she got at the pound. All of her dogs had been strays that she allowed to choose her and then embraced wholeheartedly. But meeting Wally, she fell into the same thrall about bull terriers as had novelist John Steinbeck. She had to have "one of him." Steinbeck waited two years to get his puppy, Angel, from a breeder in 1965. I did not want my friend to go through the same wait and offered to help her find a puppy from a reputable breeder through my connections in the bull terrier world. Soon the drums were beating and a puppy of impeccable breeding and temperament was found.

You do not just get a bull terrier, you get a whole experience. I envied my friend the adventure she was about to embark on, knowing it would change her life so much for the better. When she met her white puppy, Obie, they bonded for life.

We took Wally to play with the young whippersnapper and he turned into an overgrown puppy himself, trying to snare puppy toys and sending Obie scurrying behind the sofa. That day it was hard to believe Wally had been with us for almost a decade.

On the way home, snapshots in my mind quick-flashed through the Wally years. How could I have managed through them without having that mug to smile at every morning? When the worst things happened, he never wavered. When the funniest things happened, he was at the heart of them.

Flipping through my life, I realized I had never been alone at the farm, had never been without a dog. It was dogs, always dogs that had been a constant.

Lady the boxer opened a world of stories in my head. Ah, yes, I remembered her well. I sat down at my computer. My legs were jiggling, and I bounced in my chair. I remembered a time when I worked at a magazine and my friend Ernest came by my desk, pausing to ask, "Do you always dance when you write?" Yes, I suppose I do, when Wally is not sleeping on my feet.

I typed the title to a first chapter, "There Were Always Dogs," and I started writing. Whatever pall had been cast across me before— intimidation, depression, fear—left me from the core out. I had the optimism of the eight-year-old in the Guy Clark song "The Cape" who thinks he can fly and keeps trying to prove it by flapping his arms and jumping off a garage into his adulthood. In the end, it is all a leap of faith, and as the song says:

"Always trust your cape."

My trusted cape of words came back to me. One final step remained. As usual, I took it with Wally.

Our book had to find its way to readers. It had to be introduced to booksellers and librarians, and the venue for that was BookExpo, a huge convention where publishers push their wares and flaunt their authors. We would be there.

I buffed Wally's "ball-nose" and donned my author's uniform. My purse bulged with cookies, balls, a bowl, and bottled water.

Snarled in traffic and running late, Stephen dropped us off. We hurried across the lobby, my high heels and Wally's nails clicking sharply. I have been to these things before, but never with my heart pounding.

Then I saw the escalator. It rose diagonally, spanning the light-filled atrium toward a wall of windows three stories above, where the convention was in full swing.

Wally had never been on a staircase that moved. He had never seen people move toward the sky without walking. Security cleared us, and we were headed for that first unfolding step when he grasped the situation. He plunked down at the base of the escalator, refusing to move while people began piling up behind us. I knelt down and stared into those varminty triangles he has for eyes.

"Hey, Wally," I implored. "Please. It's showtime!"

He gave me his best "gotcha" grin, taking the next step that came up. He had a clear path ahead and wasted no time. Tearing up the escalator, with me clinging to the extended leash, he ran right up the skirt of a librarian. Her startled cry and his surprised bark alerted everyone to the fact that "Wally was in the building."

We collected ourselves at the top of the escalator and I took a great gulp of air as we headed for the booth. Bully-walking in front of me like a forceful Winston Churchill, Wally looked as though he knew exactly where he was going and what he had to do.

At the booth, a line awaited us under a huge poster of Wally's visage, with the black, raggedy heart circling his nostrils and a look in his eyes that defies you to imagine what goes on inside that egg-shaped head.

They called Wally's name and clapped when he bounced tennis balls off his nose for them. One ball bounced into the crowd, and he chased after it, tangling his leash among legs in the lineup. Sorting it out led to some intimate moments with conventioneers.

While I signed books, Wally either sat at my side demanding cookies or tried to upend the book-signing table in pursuit of ankles to lick. He was true to himself, an authentic bull terrier whose mission is to have fun.

44

Here's to Life

Brothers and Sisters, I bid you beware
Of giving your heart to a dog to tear.

—Rudyard Kipling, "The Power of the Dog"

ally and I made a lot of new friends through "his" book. We all had dogs of one kind or another in common, but I was surprised to learn how many people out there broke a limb through a childhood fantasy trying to fly. I also met a legion of Roy Rogers fans who used to dress up in cowboy outfits to watch the television show and still know all the words to "Happy Trails." Mostly, we met people who had a story to share about a dog, a cat, a parrot, a ferret, even potbellied pigs. Wally always got credit for being the dog that saved our lives, just by being himself and refusing to let us go one day without a smile.

We made appearances at all sorts of dog festivals, from Woofstock to Slobberfest. When you write a book about a dog you are subject to attend venues that are unconventional for most authors. For instance, there is the annual Blessing of the Animals that takes place in October to commemorate the feast of St. Francis of Assisi. It is hard to turn down an invitation that celebrates an ecologically friendly friar who allowed himself to be displaced from a hovel because a donkey needed shelter. Once blessed, Wally stretched full length on the lawn of the church and watched the cats wince when they were sprinkled with holy tap water. More than one dog mistook a goldfish bowl for a watering hole.

I was asked to attend a book signing at a dog show held near Niagara Falls and participate in an honorary parade of bull terriers that had been rescued after being abandoned, abused, or orphaned from their original family by unfortunate circumstance. How anyone could ever deliberately give up a bull terrier (or any other faithful Fido) I do not know, but their sad stories ranged from being found half-starved with signs of having been used as bait for dog fighters or turfed when it was discovered they were deaf. Rescue parades of any breed never fail to see men, women, and children smiling through their tears. These are dogs that made it back to a place of hope and found their happy ending, sometimes after months of rehabilitation and patient, tender care.

Before we went to the show, I reflected on Wally's brief time in the show ring, recalling how perfectly groomed and pampered those high-performance dogs are. They live in a rarefied world that made me think about the opposite side of that picture: the dogs that have no homes and end up in shelters where a death sentence could be just days away through no fault of their own. Maybe we could do something to help those dogs.

I looked up the animal shelters in the area and made a few calls. Operating as they do on shoestring budgets with wish lists for everything from paper clips to cat litter, the shelters were more than happy for any bone tossed their way. I came up with an idea called "Wally's Week." Simple enough, during Wally's Week anyone adopting a dog at a specific shelter gets a copy of *Wally's World* in a goody bag filled with all sorts of useful supplies to help adopter and adoptee adapt to their new lives together—everything from dog shampoo to chew toys. Quicker than I thought possible, I had sponsors ranging from pet supply stores to pet friendly hotels, and Wally's favorite cookie company.

Whenever we showed up at a shelter toting a ton of goody bags there was a photo opportunity that ended up on the front page of the newspapers. No editor could resist Wally's mug. Wherever we went, we met big-hearted volunteers, mascot cats, and dogs that desperately wanted someone they could love.

The pathos of shelter life is as palpable as some of the aromas, not just animal odors either. There is also a scent that can only be described as "fear." Some shelters were bare-bones, with barred cages like little jail cells. Others were state-of-the-art with heated floors, Plexiglas doors, skylights, and individual outdoor runs. Some of the open-space catteries featured climbing elements and stacked cat beds where felines curled up together and purred. More than one manager told me that it was sometimes hard to adopt out cats because prospective owners thought they looked so comfortable. In other crowded shelters there might be as many as 125 cats in conditions so crowded that closets were converted into nurseries for kittens unceremoniously dropped off in boxes or retrieved from Dumpsters, or worse. Stress was never far away. One dog barks, and it sets off the whole kennel.

We toured all over with Wally's Weeks. The boy wonder got used to traveling like an aged rock star, sprawled on his blue blanket in the back of the truck, snoring or resting his head on Stephen's shoulder as they both drove the vehicle. When I hoisted the bandanna with his name embroidered in gold thread over his head, Wally knew it was showtime, and he trundled off to sniff butts with a homeless dog or give a TV crew a demonstration in the art of soccer. He knew he was a star, and he knew he was special.

Still, sometimes gawkers backed away from Wally, insisting, "Pit bulls like that shouldn't be allowed." That attitude of fear grew out of increasingly overblown media coverage resulting from devastating dog attacks that would never have occurred if a responsible owner was four feet away at the other end of a leash. The truth is that all dogs can bite, but politicians like to seize on specific breeds and restrict them as some sort of easy panacea for the masses, instead of focusing on the real societal problems that lead to animal cruelty and careless disregard for compliance with local regulations.

In a world gone doggone mad, any breed or look-alike is a potential target for discrimination. Italy has banned more than ninety breeds, including the Pembroke Welsh corgi, the collie, and the Saint Bernard. Breed-specific legislation has stigmatized every breed, from rottweilers to chow chows, dobermans to German shepherds and Irish wolfhounds to Scottish deerhounds. Most particularly, every variation of bull-and-terrier-type dog—whether purebred or crossbred—has been targeted as a "ticking time bomb." What a load of hogswallop. Yet in the province of Ontario, Canada, where I live, purebred American Staffordshire terriers, Staffordshire bull terriers, and so-called pit bulls, or any dog that a person in authority believes resembles one, are compelled to be muzzled, confined, and neutered, or they can be seized and euthanized or sold to research labs. The politicians who passed the law claimed it was the most popular piece of legislation they had introduced. They were proud of killing thousands of dogs and puppies that were summarily surrendered or seized.

Wally never had to wear a muzzle or fear being plucked from the front porch, but the only reason that bull terriers have not been subject to the ban is the terrible fear that Canadian politicians have that they will come under fire by hockey commentator and former Boston Bruins coach Don Cherry, whose bull terrier Blue was one of my inspirations to seek out the breed. Mr. Cherry holds sway, having been voted the seventh "Greatest Canadian" in a massive public television polling, ahead of multitasking inventor Alexander Graham Bell and hockey legend Wayne Gretzky. It is a pity that they do not have hockey commentators in Italy.

So it came to pass that Wally the Wonder Dog became an ambassador in the crusade against BSL. How could anyone who met him imagine needing to put a muzzle over that graying and ball-battered Roman nose? You would not be able to appreciate that irrepressible grin through a bucket of leather worthy of Hannibal Lecter, and tennis balls just would not bounce back properly.

We reached a pinnacle when Wally was sent on a goodwill meet-and-greet with British royalty. I warmed immediately to the tweedy Duke and Duchess of Hamilton, when they asked to be called Kay and Angus and wanted to spend more time playing with Wally than talking with me. In their native Scotland, the be-castled couple was involved in the rescue of Staffordshire bull terriers, the duchess's breed of choice. In fact, she had been detained for hours on one occasion when authorities suspected that she and her duke had broken into a facility to remove an impounded dog.

"I didn't tell them a thing," the pixyish matron told me with a smile, sipping her tea and brushing cake crumbs from the sleeve of her peach-colored sweater. "I just demanded to have my lawyer present. Isn't that what they say you should do on *Law & Order?*"

Angus proudly showed me the Swiss Army knife he used to pick locks when they were breaking into dog pounds holding Staffies or other "pit bulls" sentenced to death for nothing more than their appearance. I had found role models who could trace their antidisestablishmentarianism back to Robert the Bruce. Wally promptly licked the royal hands that fed him cookies under the table. I worried that he might try grooming Her Grace's ankles, but I think Kay might have enjoyed that.

A few weeks after his brush with the royals, we noticed Wally favoring his right leg. His stride appeared more bully and bowed than before. It was a slight thing, nothing anyone who did not spend a great deal of time watching him would have noticed. I massaged his back, feeling for tension, and then I found a walnut-size lump under his shoulder. It was hard and immovable, unlike fatty tags I had seen on older dogs that only cause cosmetic grief. A cold chill ran through me.

At the university vet clinic we lucked out because the resident who had cared for Wally through a bout of arthritis was still on duty and she took over his case with a full knowledge of his lengthy history. On X-ray, a cloudy mass appeared to be attached to the femur bone at the joint, where there was a ragged edge on the normally smooth ball-socket bone. Then the words tumbled out of the accumulated special-ists: *tumor*, *aggressive*, *bone cancer*, and, as always, *more tests*. No one who had ever carried Wally's Bible-thick file wanted to look us in the eye, and ours were already brimming with tears.

The things dogs do not know is one of their blessings. Wally walked over to Stephen and whacked him on the calf with his nose, a none-too-subtle cookie request. Any cookie he wanted was his for the taking. A biopsy was scheduled. Someone said something about ampu-tation, and my mind shut down.

At home, Wally played "pounce" on the squeaky toy he borrowed from his young friend Obie's vast collection on their last visit. It was a lime green ball outfitted with stubby legs that made it bounce weirdly. I rarely allowed him to play with it, fearing he would remove the voice box, as was his wont when he was a puppy. Watching him play, I won-dered to myself, What is the matter with me? If it gives him pleasure to make a toy squeak I should let him do it 24/7 and take joy in having the opportunity to watch him.

Stephen and I spent the weekend imagining Wally with three legs and projecting our own fears. All of my research said most dogs just accept their new condition and get on with their lives as dogs will do. Sunday afternoon, Wally chased a soccer ball down an empty road and head-butted it into a trickle of a creek that manages to flow even in frigid temperatures. Then he stood at the edge of the snowbank— wagging his tail, with his pink tongue lolling out of the side of his face while I struggled to retrieve the ball, using a stick to fish it toward me. Wally revered me as though I were an action hero. I tried to imagine him as a tripod and wondered how he would ever get out of a snowdrift or ride a big round bale of hay.

The next day we sat through six hours of testing. His ultrasound was clear, and his X-rays showed no problems in the lungs. Then the surgeon began the biopsy of the "tumor," and as he made the incision what came to be technically described as "a Jell-O-like goop" exuded. It was rushed to pathology, where no trace of cancer cells was found. The damage to the joint was put down to natural degeneration of the bone in a dog with arthritis who still liked to play in the fast lane. The goop was just leaked joint fluid. There was no explanation. Wally the Makes-Them-Wonder Dog had done it again.

The coincidence of this was not lost on me. I took the vet aside and showed her a lump on the back of my knee about the size of half of a boiled egg. It is firm but not painful to the touch and does not interfere with my movement, so I have just ignored it. Diagnosticians call it a popliteal cyst, although the term "baker's knee" is often used colloquially, which I find grossly unfair, since I have never mastered the art of flaky pie crust.

I remembered the words of the last dog show judge Wally and I met in the ring: "Looking more and more like your dog, Miss."

Wally snored all the way home, lying on his back, exposing the once-again shaved belly where ultrasound paddles had mapped their own glide path over the years. We listened to a favorite recording by Joe Williams of the ballad "Here's to Life" and took to heart the hopes it offers "for dreamers and their dreams" that all their storms be weathered:

"And all that's good get better."

I cannot overestimate the good that Wally brought into our lives and the lives of those he touched. Whether he was lying in wait outside of Stephen's shower to lick his master's knees dry, or leaping into the flow of the garden hose to suck back its demons, he engaged life. And though he did not like lightning or thunder, he helped us weather our storms, always with a generous heart and a happy grin above the black dot so perfectly centered on his chin.

We lost our boy all too soon and all too suddenly a few months after his tenth birthday. Our friends Sandra and Harvey were visiting us for a robbery-free Thanksgiving weekend, complete with televisions in every room and high-thread-count sheets on the beds. We had everything to be thankful for. Wally's book had sold in America, and offers were coming in from around the world. I had pictures all over my office of shelter dogs that had found homes because we had reminded people of their need. Stephen and I were writing, and the harvest was good.

Wally was bright-eyed and playful, interrupting conversation with long sloshing slurps from his water bowl followed by burps that belonged in a barroom. We walked in the forest along sun-dappled paths lined with pine needles where Wally chased after his orange and yellow balls. It was all "Look at me. Look at me do this. Throw it again. Don't ever stop."

Sated and rested, Sandra and Harvey left us on an afternoon crisp with autumn. Something about Wally's demeanor changed. We knew every nuance of his step and turn of head. Heck, I knew his normal temperature range but had no idea of my own. Always delicate when it came to his stomach, Wally vomited some forest browse surrounding a wood chip and we thought he had purged himself of whatever was troubling him. But that was not to be.

Just before dawn, Wally got me up and went downstairs to go out. As always, the Oracle-of-What-Comes-Out followed with a flashlight. This time I found blood in his stool, a crisis I had never seen. Wally hauled himself back upstairs and nudged Stephen to let him under the covers. He never complained, but I knew something big was wrong.

We rushed him to the animal clinic where our friend Dr. John Reeve-Newson had determined Wally should be treated on a basis that allowed a continuity of treatment that would serve an aging dog best. Dr. John also likes bull terriers and is qualified to judge them, as is his partner, psychiatrist Richard Meen. They are the first gay "dog show couple" to have been outed at the Westminster Dog Show. It happened on national television when Dr. John was judging Best in Show. Some people thought it was part of a sequel to the movie *Best in Show*.

"Wally, you've been on more drugs than Judy Garland," Dr. John joked after his first review of the file. When he saw Wally that morning, there was no joking. We hoped what we were seeing in the lethargic, pained dog on the examining table was a case of "dietary indiscretion" that could be resolved with electrolyte fluids, antibiotics, and analgesics for pain. Duly kissed on the nose, we entrusted Wally to Dr. John's blanketed arms.

By late afternoon, the hoped-for improvement had not occurred. We visited and Wally smiled at us, but through the haze of medication he did not recognize his ball. He needed all-night supervision, so we took him to Dr. John's twenty-four-hour emergency clinic, where a team was waiting for him. Wally tugged on the leash to get away from the cage where he had been lying all afternoon. He stood impatiently, waiting to get into his truck. What he wanted, I knew, was to get to his hotel, where Paul would open the door to the truck and welcome Prince

Wally, and he would cruise up to the twentieth floor in the little room that moved. When we pulled up in front of another vet clinic, I felt I had betrayed him.

No one takes a beloved pet to an all-night emergency clinic without knowing that things are not as they should be and maybe never will be again. I held Wally's face and looked in his eyes. He was there, but not happy. We watched him trudge off with his new vet. Then I saw him look up at the open-faced new fellow at his side, and the old Wally kick came into his step as he realized that he had a new captive audience and new cookie jars to discover.

If I slept that night, I do not remember it. Just after dawn, the phone rang and it was the clinic advising us that they were scheduling an ultrasound because Wally was not improving. Dr. John had been in to see him during the night. I wished I had been there, too.

There was nothing conclusive after a series of tests. Nothing to do but operate. We rushed to his side.

Wally had been given a curtained-off private space in intensive care. The beeping of monitors and the sound of stainless-steel tables rolling across linoleum reminded me of my own surgery.

"How are you doing, son?" Stephen asked.

That great head rose, and Wally looked at us. The "there you are" light came on in his eyes and then his nose sank into the blanket, next to his paw with the IV-unit connection. I lay on the floor, his head next to mine. His muzzle quivered, and I wondered if there might still be a shard of porcupine quill trying to surface through his leathery lips. It had happened before. While Stephen talked to the vet, I patted him, comforted him, and hummed the "Wally Boy Wally" song that had come out of nowhere when he was a puppy.

Stephen came down to mind-meld, rubbing his dog behind the ears in that spot where the fur is so heavenly soft.

"You be good and we'll be waiting for you," he said in a steadier voice than I could have managed. Wally had dodged so many bullets, surely he could pull this one off, too.

Before we left I gave one last glance through the curtain, and my eye caught on the splash of white fur against the orange-brown stripes along his back. I thought my heart would fall out of my chest.

No hours ever passed more slowly. No wait was ever longer.

When the vet's phone call came I heard every word of it as a surreal dream. Wally was on the operating table and inside of him there was a catastrophe. They had removed his gall bladder because it was blocked with bile. Then further revelations began. His stomach had torqued, flipping over on itself somehow. This is something that occurs in deep-chested breeds such as Great Danes, bloodhounds, and even Labrador retrievers, without any definitive reason or defect. Although Wally's stomach had corrected itself, in the process the blood flow had been restricted, and fully two-thirds of his stomach was irreparably damaged.

Veterinary medicine and the best after care might have prevailed, but Wally's pancreas was also shot, a mess of calcification. It was no solace to be told that it was amazing Wally had even been able to walk down the hall. There was only a 15 percent chance that he would make it out of surgery and no guarantees after that, except that he would have to be tube-fed and confined for weeks with the prospect of long-term pain and torsion recurrence.

I wanted to be with him. I wanted to stuff his guts inside him and have him come home with me—away from the scalpels and the lights and the beeping. But I knew it was time to let Wally go. It was the hardest thing for Stephen to make that final decision; the one that you second-guess yourself on for the rest of your life. There is no mind of winter. There is not. Not for me.

We buried our darling with his pails and his balls across from the soccer pitch on the farm where he played out his days to our never-ending delight.

W. H. Auden captured the feeling so eloquently in the elegiac poem "Stop All the Clocks":

He was my North, my South, my East and West,
My working week and my Sunday rest,
My noon, my midnight, my talk, my song;
I thought that love would last for ever: I was wrong.

A friend ended a biography of his childhood saying: "Memory is, finally, all we own." That may be, but I got so much more from life with Wally the Wonder Dog. I do not know where I would be had Wally not been in my life. Stephen has always had the courage of his convictions to keep him going, but we both missed having a family. With Wally, we became one. For me, he lives in everything I do and every dog I touch. He taught me to appreciate the politics of dogs and to challenge ignorance and ignominy. He taught me to look for something good to happen in every day, and to make it happen if I could not see it. I will never hear another burp without smiling.

There will never be another "one of him," but I cannot live my life without a dog. Someday, sooner rather than later, I expect that another miniature rhinoceros will appear in my dreams and become a reality, a responsibility, and a third musketeer to laugh with us through the rest of this remarkable adventure.

Here's to life.